CONNECT TO YOUR CAREER

Strategies for Success in the Workplace

Fourth Edition

Suzann Thibodeaux, MEd, PhD
Corporate Consultant
Former Faculty at Azusa Pacific University

Julie Jaehne, MS
Workplace Initiatives Consultant
Former Faculty at University of Houston

Publisher
The Goodheart-Willcox Company, Inc.
Tinley Park, IL
www.g-w.com

Copyright © 2025
by
The Goodheart-Willcox Company, Inc.

Previous editions copyright 2022, 2019, 2015

All rights reserved. No part of this work may be reproduced, stored,
or transmitted in any form or by any electronic or mechanical means,
including information storage and retrieval systems, except as permitted
by U.S. copyright law, without the prior written permission of
The Goodheart-Willcox Company, Inc.

Library of Congress Control Number: 2023934405

ISBN 979-8-88817-181-3

1 2 3 4 5 6 7 8 9 – 25 – 28 27 26 25 24 23

The Goodheart-Willcox Company, Inc. Brand Disclaimer: Brand names, company names, and illustrations for products and services included in this text are provided for educational purposes only and do not represent or imply endorsement or recommendation by the author or the publisher.

The Goodheart-Willcox Company, Inc. Safety Notice: The reader is expressly advised to carefully read, understand, and apply all safety precautions and warnings described in this book or that might also be indicated in undertaking the activities and exercises described herein to minimize risk of personal injury or injury to others. Common sense and good judgment should also be exercised and applied to help avoid all potential hazards. The reader should always refer to the appropriate manufacturer's technical information, directions, and recommendations; then proceed with care to follow specific equipment operating instructions. The reader should understand these notices and cautions are not exhaustive.

The publisher makes no warranty or representation whatsoever, either expressed or implied, including but not limited to equipment, procedures, and applications described or referred to herein, their quality, performance, merchantability, or fitness for a particular purpose. The publisher assumes no responsibility for any changes, errors, or omissions in this book. The publisher specifically disclaims any liability whatsoever, including any direct, indirect, incidental, consequential, special, or exemplary damages resulting, in whole or in part, from the reader's use or reliance upon the information, instructions, procedures, warnings, cautions, applications, or other matter contained in this book. The publisher assumes no responsibility for the activities of the reader.

The Goodheart-Willcox Company, Inc. Internet Disclaimer: The Internet resources and listings in this Goodheart-Willcox Publisher product are provided solely as a convenience to you. These resources and listings were reviewed at the time of publication to provide you with accurate, safe, and appropriate information. Goodheart-Willcox Publisher has no control over the referenced websites and, due to the dynamic nature of the Internet, is not responsible or liable for the content, products, or performance of links to other websites or resources. Goodheart-Willcox Publisher makes no representation, either expressed or implied, regarding the content of these websites, and such references do not constitute an endorsement or recommendation of the information or content presented. It is your responsibility to take all protective measures to guard against inappropriate content, viruses, or other destructive elements.

Image Credits. Viktoria Kurpas/Shutterstock.com

Preface

Connect to Your Career is more than a text about how to get a job; it is a technology-driven 21st century reflection of how adults find and cultivate careers. Finding a job you enjoy is a long process, one that is outlined in this text.

The job-search process begins with writing a plan that will build a foundation on which your professional reputation will rest. Next, you will draft employment documents that will attract attention from employers and position you as an outstanding candidate. Then, you will sort through numerous job postings to weed out scams and occupations for which you are not qualified. Finally, after some effort, you will be prepared to apply for jobs that you will enjoy, make you feel fulfilled, and are in line with your career plans.

To facilitate your understanding of the job-search process, *Connect to Your Career* was designed with one overriding goal in mind: to help you understand how to use technology, such as social media, job-search websites, and digital devices, to connect to a career. Technology will be an essential part of your career search, so it is important to know how to leverage it to help you find the career of your dreams.

Upon completing this text, you will able to
- identify your skills, talents, and career strengths to develop a career plan;
- practice job-specific and soft skills required by employers;
- learn how to brand yourself as a professional in the workplace;
- build, protect, and maintain a professional online presence that will lead to employment;
- develop professional networks to assist you in the job-search process;
- learn how to protect your identity and personal information while searching and applying for jobs online;
- create résumés that highlight your strengths and present you as a qualified job applicant;
- create cover letters that convince employers to grant you interviews;
- apply for jobs online and in-person and manage the job-search process;
- prepare for various types of job interviews, including virtual interviews;
- understand how to behave professionally while participating in a job interview;
- use post-interview techniques to help keep the job-search process in perspective;
- develop an understanding of what employers expect so you can be successful at your new job; and
- learn what it means to be a professional and connect to your career.

Your new career will come first from planning and then acting. Appreciate the time that it takes to secure your future employment and enjoy the journey of creating new professional connections, sharing your insights on social media, and gathering professional followers. It is time for you to *Connect to Your Career!*

About the Authors

Suzann Thibodeaux is an accomplished author and career expert who has dedicated her career to helping individuals achieve their professional goals. With over 20 years of experience working for top-tier universities and consulting for Fortune 500 companies, Dr. Thibodeaux has become a trusted voice in the field of career development. Her career began in academia, where she earned a PhD. After teaching at several universities, she transitioned to consulting. Over the years, she has provided guidance to thousands of professionals, from entry-level employees to top executives. Dr. Thibodeaux's approach to career development is grounded in research and practical experience. She helps individuals identify their strengths, clarify their goals, and develop a roadmap to achieve them.

Julie Jaehne has been an adjunct faculty member for 21 years at the University of Houston in the College of Education. Via distance learning, she has taught instructional technology courses and teacher certification courses. Ms. Jaehne also has extensive experience with the use of technology in kindergarten through 12th grade instruction. She is a published author of multiple computer application textbooks and tutorials. In addition, she is a Career Education consultant and adviser for community workplace initiatives. Ms. Jaehne holds a bachelor's degree in business administration from Baylor University and a master's degree in education with a concentration in occupational education from the University of Houston.

Reviewers

The authors and publisher wish to thank the following industry and teaching professionals for their valuable input into the development of *Connect to Your Career*.

Laura Alfano
Vista College
Richardson, Texas

Dorothy Anderson
College of the Desert
Palm Desert, California

Arin Baynard
Seminole State College
Sanford, Florida

April Bledsoe
Ivy Tech Community College
Bloomington, Indiana

Dr. Larry A. Connatser
Virginia State University
Petersburg, Virginia

Christy S. Dunston
University of North Carolina at Chapel Hill
Chapel Hill, North Carolina

Jeffrey A. Evans
Ivy Tech Community College
Indianapolis, Indiana

James Freygang
Ivy Tech Community College
South Bend, Indiana

Nicole A. Graves
South Dakota State University
Brookings, South Dakota

Mindi Heitland
Waukee Schools
Waukee, Iowa

Diane Klemme
University of Wisconsin–Stout
Menomonie, Wisconsin

Anne Landon
Lycoming College
Williamsport, Pennsylvania

Shauna Maher
Chattahoochee Technical College
Marietta, Georgia

Amelia Maness-Gilliland
Colorado Technical University
Schaumburg, Illinois

Michael Glenn McBride
Virginia Highlands Community College
Damascus, Virginia

Kevin G. Mess
College of Southern Nevada
Las Vegas, Nevada

Crystal Neville
McLennan Community College
Waco, Texas

Dr. Sandra Poirier
Middle Tennessee State University
Murfreesboro, Tennessee

Marci Reiter
Cleveland State Community College
Cleveland, Tennessee

Dr. José R. Ruiz
Southern Illinois University
Murphysboro, Illinois

Paul D. Shuler
Texas Higher Education Coordinating Board
Austin, Texas

Ken Starkman
Fullerton College
Fullerton, California

Marci Stone
Fortis College
Salt Lake City, Utah

Catharine Weiss
Lasell College
Newton, Massachusetts

Julie A. Willits
Pennsylvania State University
University Park, Pennsylvania

Amy Wolfgang
Wolfgang Career Coaching and
    Coaching 4 Good
Austin, Texas

TOOLS FOR STUDENT AND INSTRUCTOR SUCCESS

Student Tools

Student Text

Connect to Your Career is a technology-driven 21st century reflection of how adults find and launch a new career. It reflects a seamless integration of technology and real-world application to guide students as they self-assess and discover who they are as future employees.

G-W Digital Companion

- For digital users, e-flash cards and vocabulary exercises allow interaction with content to create opportunities to increase achievement.
- The digital companion provides students with practical skills and knowledge that will help them succeed academically and in their personal lives.
- The digital companion features interactive modules that cover a range of financial topics, making it easy for students to learn and apply practical skills to manage their money. They will learn how to create a budget, track expenses, save for the future, invest wisely, and manage debt responsibly.
- The digital companion is accessible from any device, which means students can access it anytime, anywhere. Whether they are on campus or on the go, they can learn at their own pace and convenience.

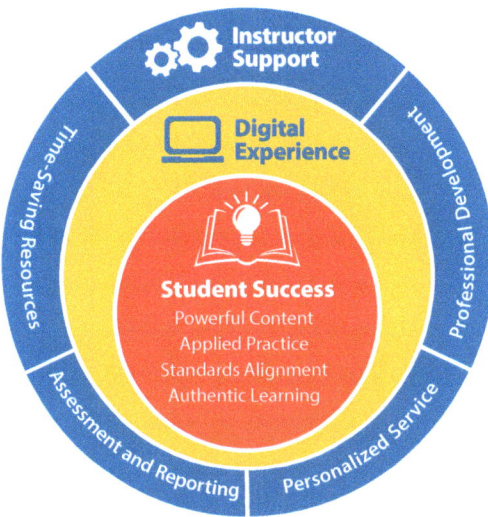

Instructor Tools

LMS Integration

Integrate Goodheart-Willcox content within your Learning Management System for a seamless user experience for both you and your students. EduHub LMS–ready content in Common Cartridge® format facilitates single sign-on integration and gives you control of student enrollment and data. With a Common Cartridge integration, you can access the LMS features and tools you are accustomed to using and G-W course resources in one convenient location—your LMS.

G-W Common Cartridge provides a complete learning package for you and your students. The included digital resources help your students remain engaged and learn effectively:

- **Digital Textbook**
- **Drill and Practice** vocabulary activities

When you incorporate G-W content into your courses via Common Cartridge, you have the flexibility to customize and structure the content to meet the educational needs of your students. You may also choose to add your own content to the course.

For instructors, the Common Cartridge includes the Online Instructor Resources. QTI® question banks are available within the Online Instructor Resources for import into your LMS. These prebuilt assessments help you measure student knowledge and track results in your LMS gradebook. Questions and tests can be customized to meet your assessment needs.

Online Instructor Resources

- The **Instructor Resources** provide instructors with time-saving preparation tools such as answer keys, editable lesson plans, and other teaching aids.
- **Instructor's Presentations for PowerPoint®** are fully customizable, richly illustrated slides that help you teach and visually reinforce the key concepts from each chapter.
- Administer and manage assessments to meet your classroom needs using **Assessment Software with Question Banks**, which include hundreds of matching, completion, multiple choice, and short answer questions to assess student knowledge of the content in each chapter.

See www.g-w.com/connect-to-your-career-2025 for a list of all available resources.

Professional Development

- Expert content specialists
- Research-based pedagogy and instructional practices
- Options for virtual and in-person Professional Development

Focus on Your Career

The instructional design of this textbook includes student-focused learning tools to help you succeed. This visual guide highlights these features.

Chapter Opening Materials

Each chapter opener contains a chapter overview, a list of learning outcomes, and a list of Workplace Connection activities. The **Overview** summarizes the topics that will be covered in the chapter. **Learning Outcomes** clearly identify the knowledge and skills to be gained when the chapter is completed. A list of end-of-chapter **Workplace Connection** activities provides a preview of the assignments that appear at the end of each chapter.

Workplace Skills

The Workplace Skills feature explores essential skills needed in today's workplace. Workplace skills are employability skills that help you find a job, perform in that job, and gain success in your career.

Time Management

Time Management features provide advice and tips for planning and controlling how you spend your time. Time-management skills will help you throughout your education and career search.

The Best App for That

These helpful hints recommend smartphone apps that will make connecting to a career a more efficient process. Downloading apps can save time and make employment documents available when access to a computer is not convenient.

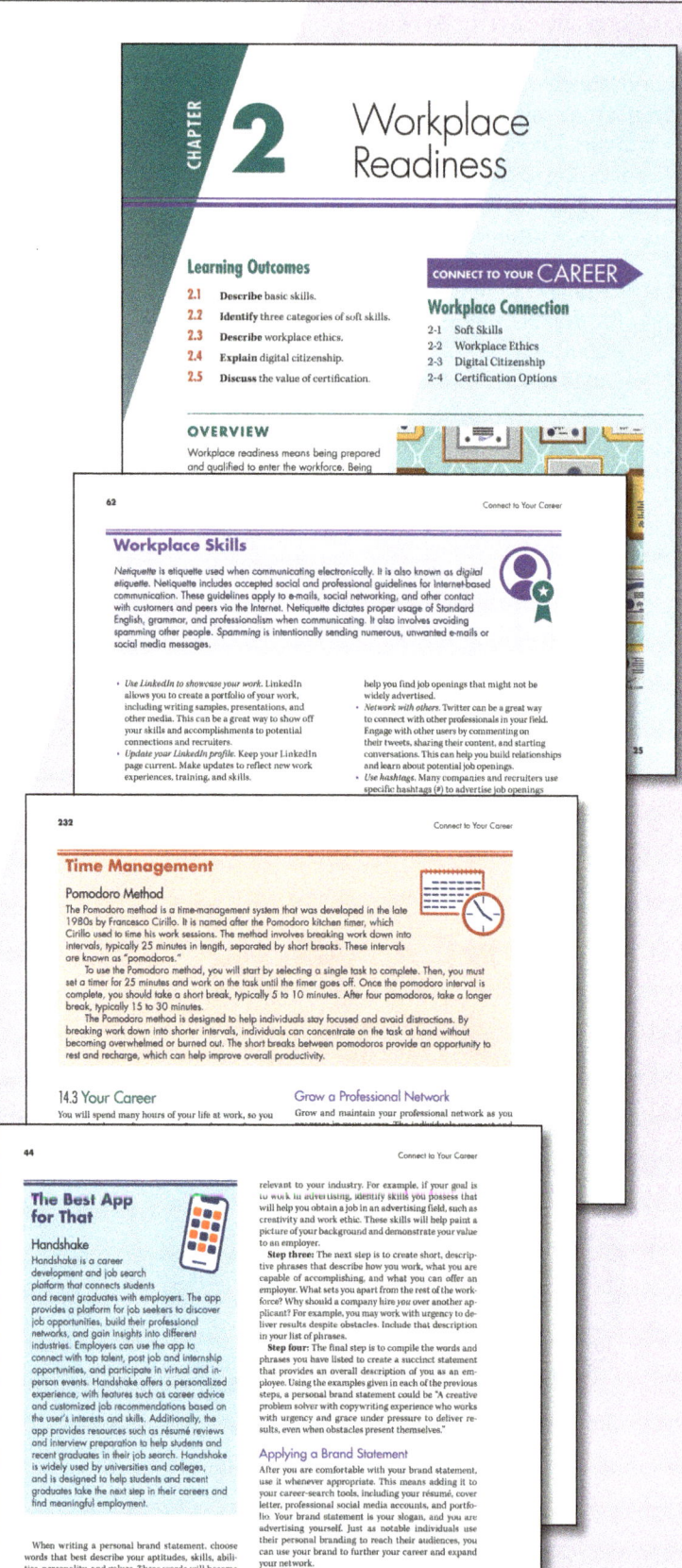

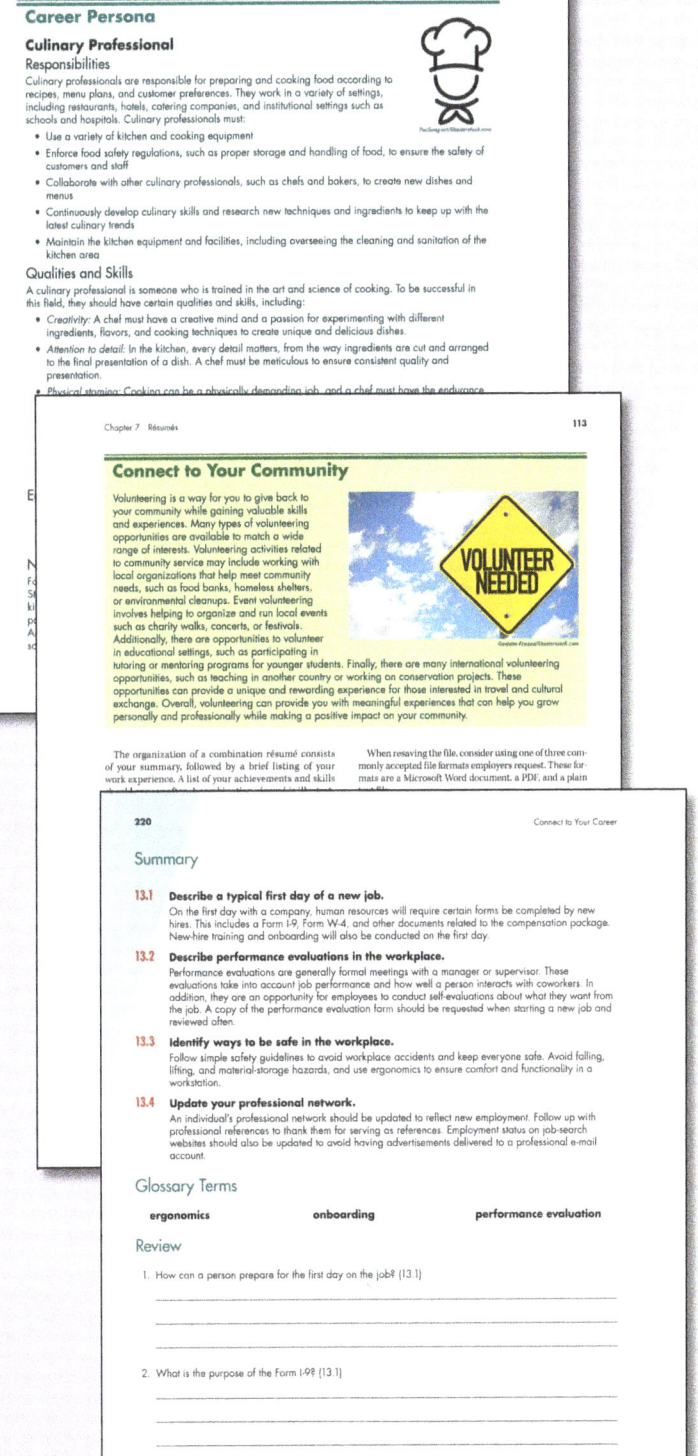

Career Persona

Career Persona features highlight the responsibilities, qualities and skills, and educational requirements for various careers. Each feature ends with suggestions for the next steps you can take if you are interested in pursuing a career in that field.

Connect to Your Community

Being a part of your community and having a positive impact on it can help you grow personally and professionally. The Connect to Your Community features provide examples of how to become involved in your community.

End-of-Chapter Content

End-of-chapter material provides an opportunity for review and application of concepts.

- A concise **Summary** reiterates the chapter outcomes and provides a brief review of the content for student reference.
- **Glossary Terms** identify vocabulary presented in the chapter to reinforce the importance of career-ready terms that are needed in the job search.
- **Review** questions highlight basic concepts presented in the chapter so students can evaluate their understanding of the material.
- **Application** activities challenge students to self-reflect on who they are as potential job candidates.
- **Workplace Connection** activities provide opportunities for self-assessment as content is presented. Numerous activities invite students to record their personal reactions, research, and responses to scenarios encountered during the job-application process. These activity files can be downloaded from the G-W Learning digital companion.

vii

How to Use This Text

The *Connect to Your Career* text and accompanying digital resources will help you begin a successful career-search process. The text presents proven strategies that use technology as a tool to find the career that is the correct fit for you. You will be guided through the steps of planning your career, establishing your online presence, protecting your online identity, and networking in the 21st century. Integrated in this technology-centric approach are traditional résumés, as well as nontraditional résumés, that are sure to capture the eye of an employer.

As you make your way through the chapters, try to relate each topic to how it applies to you. By following these suggestions, you can make the most of your career preparation experience.

- Read the Learning Outcomes listed in the chapter openers. Each Learning Outcome is tied directly to the headings within the content. In addition, they are repeated in the chapter summary and applied in the end-of-chapter activities. The connection of Learning Outcomes throughout the content helps you focus and apply important information as you read each chapter.
- Learn how to brand yourself as a professional in the workplace. Develop a personal brand statement, as well as a 30-second elevator pitch. By doing so, you will succinctly create a snapshot of who you are as a job candidate. This exercise will help you prepare as you interview, as well as network, with individuals who can help you land a job.
- Write your résumé. Your résumé is one of the most important documents you will create in your job-search journey. You will have opportunities to begin the process as you progress through the second half of the text. Ongoing revisions will lead to a document suitable for submission with a job application on completion of the course.
- Note the Connect to Your Career boxes placed strategically at the end of major sections of content. Numerous activities provide practical, realistic, and interactive exercises that enable you to apply the concepts that you learn to your own job-search experience. Digital versions of these activity files are available on the G-W Learning digital companion.
- Complete the end-of-chapter activities. By doing so, you will be able to self-assess your learning. This self-reflection is important to helping you determine who you are as a potential employee.

Organization

The text is divided into 5 units and 14 chapters to accommodate classes that are presented online or face-to-face. The units may be covered in any order that meets the requirements of the class. However, it is suggested that Unit 1 be the first unit introduced.

There are five conceptual units that follow a sequential progression of preparing for a career. Topics covered in these units include Career Planning, Online Presence, Job-Application Process, Landing a Job, and Your Career.

- Unit 1 focuses on career planning and the starting line in a person's job search. The content aligns with the real-world experience of conducting a self-assessment, writing a career plan, and creating a personal brand.
- Unit 2 explains the integration of the Internet and social media as tools for the job search. The creation of a positive online presence in the networking process, while learning to protect personal identity, is covered in detail.
- Unit 3 provides coverage of some of the most important aspects of a job search—résumés, cover letters, and job applications. The chapters also reflect approaches and methods for creating and tracking employment documents.
- Unit 4 guides job seekers through interview preparation, execution, and reflection. This allows students to experience every aspect of a job interview, from scheduling and participating in an interview to assessing what was learned.
- Unit 5 emphasizes what to expect when a job offer is made. Additionally, information is provided about how to make the most of the first job in a new career.

New to This Edition

The fourth edition of *Connect to Your Career* has been updated to make it more relevant in today's workplace. Some of the major changes to the text include the following:

- Added new features, including Career Persona, Connect to Your Community, and Time Management
- Updated tables and figures as needed throughout chapters to better illustrate topics
- Added new figures to help reinforce chapter concepts, including Self-Talk Tips (Chapter 4), Job-Search Process (Chapter 9); Mock Interview Tips (Chapter 10); Virtual Interview Tips (Chapter 11); Onboarding Topics (Chapter 13); Common Elements of a Successful Career (Chapter 14)
- Added new content on cloud computing
- Added tips on recognizing employment scams
- Discussed the latest trends in creating résumés and provided several sample résumés from various career areas
- Provided new samples of cover letters
- Distinguished between in-person and virtual interview practices
- Discussed the first day on the job from the perspective of an on-site worker and a remote worker
- Provided updated information and figures related to Form I-9 and Form W-4
- Added new content on multicultural workforce
- Outlined common elements that help define a successful career
- Added a teamwork or group component to several end-of-chapter activities

Brief Contents

UNIT 1 Career Planning

Chapter 1	Preparing for Your Career	2
Chapter 2	Workplace Readiness	25
Chapter 3	Personal Brand	42

UNIT 2 Online Presence

Chapter 4	Managing Your Online Presence	56
Chapter 5	Networking for Your Career	74
Chapter 6	Protecting Your Identity	87

UNIT 3 Job-Application Process

Chapter 7	Résumés	104
Chapter 8	Cover Letters	127
Chapter 9	Applying for Jobs	144

UNIT 4 Landing a Job

Chapter 10	Preparing for the Interview	160
Chapter 11	The Interview	180
Chapter 12	Evaluating the Interview	192

UNIT 5 Your Career

| Chapter 13 | Your First Day on the Job | 210 |
| Chapter 14 | Starting Your Career | 229 |

Contents

UNIT 1 Career Planning

Chapter 1 Preparing for Your Career.....2
- 1.1 Career Preparation 3
- 1.2 Career Plan 3
- 1.3 Self-Assessment.................6
  - Aptitudes 6
  - Abilities 7
  - Personality 7
  - Values 8
- 1.4 Skills Assessment 8
  - Soft Skills 8
  - Hard Skills 8
- 1.5 SMART Goals 10
  - Specific 10
  - Measurable....................10
  - Attainable.....................10
  - Realistic 10
  - Timely 10
- 1.6 Career Pathing 10
  - Career Ladder..................11
  - Career Lattice 12
- 1.7 Career Portfolio................12

Chapter 2 Workplace Readiness 25
- 2.1 Basic Skills 26
- 2.2 Soft Skills 26
  - Thinking Skills 26
  - People Skills 27
  - Personal Qualities 27
- 2.3 Workplace Ethics 29
- 2.4 Digital Citizenship..............29
  - Cloud Computing 29
  - Software and File Downloads 30
  - Intellectual Property 30
  - Netiquette.....................30
- 2.5 Certification 30
  - Benefits of Certification.........31
  - How to Earn Certification 32

Chapter 3 Personal Brand 42
- 3.1 Your Personal Brand.............43
- 3.2 Personal Brand Statement........43
  - Creating a Brand Statement 43
  - Applying a Brand Statement 44
- 3.3 Personal Commercial 44
  - Developing a Personal Commercial 46
  - Rehearsing a Personal Commercial 47

UNIT 2 Online Presence

Chapter 4 Managing Your Online Presence...................56
- 4.1 Creating Your Online Presence 57
- 4.2 Professional E-mail Account 58
- 4.3 LinkedIn Account 59
  - Create an Account and a Profile 59
  - Connections 61
  - LinkedIn Tips 61
- 4.4 Twitter Account................62
  - Create an Account and a Profile 62
  - Followers 63
  - Posting to Twitter 63
- 4.5 Instagram Account..............64
  - Create an Account and a Profile 64
  - Posting to Instagram 64
- 4.6 Positive Thinking 64

Chapter 5 Networking for Your Career 74
- 5.1 Professional Networking..........75
  - Face-to-Face Networking 75
  - Online Networking 76
- 5.2 Networking Etiquette 76
  - In-Person Etiquette 77
  - Online Etiquette................79
- 5.3 Professional References 79

Chapter 6 Protecting Your Identity......87
- 6.1 Identity Theft..................88
- 6.2 Employment Scams.............88
  - Recognizing Employment Scams 89
  - Reporting Employment Scams ..89
- 6.3 Internet Usage.................90
  - Cookies 90
  - Session Hijacking 90
  - Phishing 91
- 6.4 Malware 91
  - Software Viruses 91
  - Adware 91
  - Spyware......................91
  - Ransomware 91
- 6.5 Create and Maintain a Security Plan 91
  - Antivirus Software 92
  - Mobile Security 92
  - Secure Passwords 92
  - Multifactor Authentication 93
  - Security Settings 93
  - Cloud-Based Backups..........93

UNIT 3 Job-Application Process

Chapter 7 Résumés................104
- 7.1 Résumé......................105
- 7.2 Keywords 105
  - Trending 106
  - Applicant Tracking System Software.......106
- 7.3 Sections of a Résumé 107
  - Heading 107
  - Summary 108
  - Experience 108
  - Education 108
  - Special Skills..................108

xi

7.4 Résumé Formats 110
  Timeline Résumé 110
  Skills Résumé 110
  Combination Résumé 110
7.5 Saving a Résumé 113
  Microsoft Word Document 113
  PDF 113
  Plain Text 115
7.6 Nontraditional Résumé 115
  Web-Based Résumé 115
  Visual Résumé 115

Chapter 8 Cover Letters 127
8.1 Cover Letter 128
8.2 Parts of a Cover Letter 130
  Heading and Date 130
  Greeting 130
  Introduction 130
  Body 132
  Complimentary Close 132
8.3 Cover Letter Submission 132
  Submit by E-mail 132
  Upload to an Online Job Board . . . 136
  Submit a Hard Copy 136

Chapter 9 Applying for Jobs 144
9.1 Job Applications 145
9.2 Applying for Jobs in Person 145
9.3 Searching and Applying for
    Jobs Online 145
  Searching for Jobs Online 145
  Applying for Jobs Online 149
9.4 Sunday Evening Plan 149
9.5 Managing the Application Process . . . 149
  Time Management 150
  Stay Current 150
  Keep in Touch with Your Network . . . 150
  Set Job Alerts 150
  Download Apps 150
9.6 Tracking Applications 150
  Applications 150
  Leads 151
  Interviews 151
  Staying Persistent 152

UNIT 4 Landing a Job

Chapter 10 Preparing for the
Interview 160
  10.1 Invitation to Interview 161
  10.2 Company Research 161
  10.3 Job Interview 162
    In-Person Interview 162
    Virtual Interview 162
  10.4 Interviewer Questions 164
    General Information Questions 164
    Behavioral Questions 165
    Stress Questions 165
  10.5 Questions to Ask 166
  10.6 Interview Preparation 168
    Mock Interview 168
    Night Before the Interview 169

Chapter 11 The Interview 180
  11.1 First Impressions 181
  11.2 The Interview 183
    In-Person Interviews 183
    Virtual Interviews 184
    Pre-Employment Tests 184
    Lying in an Interview 185
  11.3 Second Interview 185

Chapter 12 Evaluating the Interview 192
  12.1 Post-Interview Techniques 193
    Evaluate the Interview 193
    Send a Thank-You Message 193
    Manage Emotions 197
    Continue the Job Search 197
  12.2 The Employment Process 197
    Evaluate the Job Offer 197
    Negotiate 198
    Respond to the Job Offer 198
    Employment Verification Process 200

UNIT 5 Your Career

Chapter 13 Your First Day on the Job . . . 210
  13.1 Day One 211
    If You Are Hired as an On-Site Worker . . . 211
    If You Are Hired as a Remote Worker . . . 211
    Employment Forms 211
    New-Hire Training 213
    Flextime 216
    Overtime 216
    Personal Cell Phone Use 216
    Workspace Etiquette 216
  13.2 Performance Evaluations 217
  13.3 Workplace Safety 218
    Accident Prevention 218
    Ergonomics 218
  13.4 Update Your Professional Network . . . 219

Chapter 14 Starting Your Career 229
  14.1 Professionalism 230
    Punctuality 230
    Dependability 230
    Time Management 230
    Emotional Regulation 230
  14.2 Multigenerational and Multicultural
       Workplace 230
  14.3 Your Career 232
    Become a Good Employee 232
    Respect Money 232
    Grow a Professional Network 232
    Stay Current 232
    Have Realistic Expectations 232

Appendix A Punctuation 243

Appendix B Capitalization 247

Appendix C Number Usage 249

Glossary 251

Index 255

UNIT 1
Career Planning

Chapter 1 Preparing for Your Career
Chapter 2 Workplace Readiness
Chapter 3 Personal Brand

Dzmitry Abrazhevich/Shutterstock.com

Why It Matters

Success in the workplace requires early and diligent planning. Understanding the job-search process can help you pursue the career path that you have set out to follow. However, a lack of direction and focus will hinder your ability to search for, locate, and apply for jobs that will lead to a fulfilling career.

The job-search process requires that you assess your aptitudes, abilities, personality, and values as you apply for positions. Evaluating your skills will help you market yourself and become a successful candidate for employment. In addition, establishing your personal brand will help identify who you are as a job candidate. After your evaluation is complete, you will be ready to create a career plan that can take you one step closer to your goals. Each of these activities can help you market yourself and become a successful candidate for employment.

1 Preparing for Your Career

Learning Outcomes

1.1 **Explain** the concept of career preparation.

1.2 **State** the purpose of a career plan.

1.3 **Discuss** the importance of self-assessment as a career planning step.

1.4 **Identify** two types of personal skills that should be a part of a skills assessment.

1.5 **Explain** the purpose of setting SMART goals.

1.6 **Discuss** career pathing options.

1.7 **Define** a career portfolio.

CONNECT TO YOUR CAREER

Workplace Connection

1-1 Emerging Occupations
1-2 Career Plan
1-3 Aptitudes Inventory
1-4 Abilities Assessment
1-5 Values Assessment
1-6 Skills Inventory

OVERVIEW

Think about it. On average, people spend at least 30 percent of their time each day at work. Finding a career that will satisfy you in your work life is probably high on your list of priorities. The first step in the career-search process starts with career planning.

Career planning begins with conducting a self-assessment to evaluate your aptitudes, skills, abilities, and values. Through this assessment, you can focus your energy on what is necessary for you to accomplish in order to become a successful candidate for employment. Once your assessment is complete, you will be ready to set goals and create a plan that can move you closer to your chosen career.

Profit_Image/Shutterstock.com

1.1 Career Preparation

Finding a satisfying, fulfilling career that balances your work life with your home life is a goal that most people seek to accomplish. Like other goals we strive to achieve, preparation is the key to success. In order to find a satisfying career, you must adequately prepare for it. *Career preparation* is a journey that differs from person to person. However, most successful job candidates have certain similarities in common, including learning to define the difference between a job and career and understanding how to create a well-developed career plan.

A **job** is short-term employment for compensation. At different times in a person's life, jobs help to pay bills, offset school costs, and meet other financial obligations. These jobs can often serve as stepping stones toward future employment goals. However, in college, it becomes time to make plans for long-term employment.

A **career** is a long-term progression in one particular field with opportunities for growth and advancement. It is a lifetime endeavor that utilizes particular skills and expertise. A career generally requires more education than a job, and during your working years, it may change multiple times. Evaluating career opportunities that are right for you can be an overwhelming task that requires long-term planning. You spend most of your waking hours at work, so decisions made regarding employment should not be taken lightly.

In your educational experience, you may have been introduced to career pathways that categorize various jobs common in the workplace. As shown in **Figure 1-1**, *career pathways* are broad categories that focus on specific skills and competencies for various types of jobs. These pathways are a part of the 16 career clusters that are centered on related career fields. Within each pathway, specific industries are referenced. Selecting a career involves choosing the career pathway that is best suited to your aptitudes, skills, abilities, and values, and then selecting an industry within it.

With each passing decade, employment trends evolve. It is your task to try to predict future employment options in the career field of your choice. One of the ways to analyze the future employment outlook is to compare yesterday's job trends with current market advertisements. The federal government, as well as many individual states, compile and publish data for emerging occupations. **Emerging occupations** are new occupations that have developed or changed due to technological or other advancements. For example, in the past, an office clerk filed hard-copy papers in file cabinets. That job has changed to an emerging occupation for IT professionals who can prepare and manage the complex, multistage process of data cleansing, analysis, and visualization. A list of emerging occupations is listed in **Figure 1-2**.

The **Occupational Information Network (O*NET)** is an occupational resource that provides descriptions of in-demand industry areas in emerging occupations. O*NET OnLine is a tool that job seekers can use for career exploration and job analysis.

The US Department of Labor is another resource for job seekers. Through the Department of Labor, users can view job information, hourly standards for jobs, wage information, and occupational safety information. According to the Department of Labor, in-demand occupations are vital to our economy's health.

CONNECT TO YOUR CAREER

Complete 1-1 Emerging Occupations, pg. 19

1.2 Career Plan

A **career plan** is documentation of where a person is today in the job-search process and would like to be over the course of a career. The benefits of creating this plan include self-reflection, goal-setting, and a commitment to completing ongoing tasks.

The Best App for That

Glassdoor
The Glassdoor app is a job-search and recruiting app that includes a database of company reviews, salary information, and more. Job seekers can search the database to find anonymous reviews from former employees of companies. Former employees often share information about salaries paid at those companies, what it is like to work there, and other inside information that only employees can provide. Employers can post job openings, a company profile, and other information to use for recruiting new employees. From this information, job candidates can apply for a position directly through the app.

FIGURE 1-1

Career pathways are broad categories that focus on specific skills and competencies for various types of jobs.

Career Pathways

Agriculture, Food & Natural Resources
- Food Products & Processing Systems
- Plant Systems
- Animal Systems
- Power, Structural & Technical Systems
- Natural Resources Systems
- Environmental Service Systems
- Agribusiness Systems

Architecture & Construction
- Design/Pre-Construction
- Construction
- Maintenance/Operations

Arts, A/V Technology & Communications
- A/V Technology & Film
- Printing Technology
- Visual Arts
- Performing Arts
- Journalism & Broadcasting
- Telecommunications

Business Management & Administration
- General Management
- Business Information Management
- Human Resources Management
- Operations Management
- Administrative Support

Education & Training
- Administration & Administrative Support
- Professional Support Services
- Teaching/Training

Finance
- Securities & Investments
- Business Finance
- Banking Services
- Insurance
- Accounting

Government & Public Administration
- National Security
- Foreign Service
- Planning
- Revenue and Taxation
- Regulation
- Public Management & Administration
- Governance

Health Sciences
- Therapeutic Services
- Diagnostic Services
- Health Informatics
- Support Services
- Biotechnology Research & Development

Hospitality & Tourism
- Restaurants & Food/Beverage Services
- Lodging
- Travel & Tourism
- Recreation, Amusements & Attractions

Human Services
- Early Childhood Development & Services
- Counseling & Mental Health Services
- Family & Community Services
- Personal Care Services
- Consumer Services

Information Technology
- Network Systems
- Information Support & Services
- Web & Digital Communications
- Programming & Software Development

Law, Public Safety, Corrections & Security
- Correction Services
- Emergency & Fire Management Services
- Security & Protective Services
- Law Enforcement Services
- Legal Services

Manufacturing
- Production
- Manufacturing Production Process Development
- Maintenance, Installation & Repair
- Quality Assurance
- Logistics & Inventory Control
- Health, Safety, & Environmental Assurance

Marketing
- Marketing Management
- Professional Sales
- Merchandising
- Marketing Communications
- Marketing Research

Science, Technology, Engineering & Mathematics
- Engineering & Technology
- Science & Mathematics

Transportation, Distribution & Logistics
- Transportation Operations
- Logistics Planning & Management Services
- Warehousing & Distribution Center Operations
- Facility & Mobile Equipment Maintenance
- Transportation Systems/Infrastructure Planning, Management, & Regulation
- Health, Safety, & Environmental Management
- Sales & Service

Goodheart-Willcox Publisher; Information source: www.careertech.org

FIGURE 1-2

Emerging occupations are new occupations that have developed or changed due to technological or other advancements.

Emerging Occupations		
• 3D printing technician • Augmented reality developer • Bioinformatics analyst • Blockchain developer • Customer success manager • Data scientist • Dental hygienist	• Electric vehicle technician • Environmental technician • Geospatial technician • Information security analyst • Internet of things (IoT) developer • Medical laboratory technician • Mobile app developer	• Nurse practitioner • Occupational therapy assistant • Online marketing specialist • Physical therapist assistant • Robotics technician • Solar energy technician

Goodheart-Willcox Publisher

A career plan enables you to reflect on your progress, practice setting goals, and create a roadmap to accomplish those goals. It is not a static document and should be reviewed and updated at least twice a year.

A well-developed career plan contains all goals and milestones a person hopes to achieve within a given time period. These goals can range from the creation of a résumé or portfolio to establishing a retirement plan. Items listed in a career plan are called *action items*, as they all require some type of action on the part of the person who created it.

Common action items in a typical career plan are shown in **Figure 1-3**. Notice these items fall into general categories, such as academic, job-search, and career-research goals. An individual will decide which categories are more important and the point they are in their career search. For some, making money to purchase items like a car and house may be a category.

Once you have drafted action items that are important for your future, you can start writing your actual career plan. There is no right or wrong way to format this document. **Figure 1-4** shows an example of a template you could use to get started.

Before creating a career plan, it is helpful to first conduct a self-assessment and skills assessment, and then

FIGURE 1-3

Items listed in a career plan are called action items and are typically categorized as academic, job-search, or career-research goals.

Action Items for Career Plan	
Step 1 • Monitor and maintain a strong grade point average (GPA) • Evaluate skills, abilities, and aptitudes • Establish short-term job goals and long-term career goals • Determine which courses are required to meet career goals • Create a résumé • Create online career profiles • Visit online resources such as O*NET OnLine • Target a specific job to obtain • Use social media for professional networking **Step 2** • Continue to update online career profiles • Update résumé to reflect current career position • Recruit current coworkers for professional references • Expand knowledge of technology and learn new software • Set goals for position titles and salary increases	**Step 3** • Evaluate satisfaction with current job • Update career portfolio • Investigate corporations to gain long-term employment • Attend employee workshops • Review existing and potential employee benefits including 401(k) plans • Map out future career goals **Step 4** • Write a career plan that spans the next 10 years • Set a goal for financial independence • Determine which long-term assets to acquire, such as housing • Evaluate professional life in comparison with your personal goals • Network as a professional in field of expertise • Determine if additional academic training or certification is necessary

Goodheart-Willcox Publisher

FIGURE 1-4

A career plan template can be used to gain a head start on the development of a career plan.

Career Plan		
Career Item	Specific Action to Take	Target Completion Date

Goodheart-Willcox Publisher

set SMART goals. You will continue revising the career plan as you achieve your goals and set new ones.

CONNECT TO YOUR CAREER

Complete 1-2 Career Plan, pg. 20

1.3 Self-Assessment

One of the first tasks in the creation of a career plan is to complete a self-assessment. A *self-assessment* is a measurement of an individual's actions or attitudes as they relate to student and career performance.

Conducting a self-assessment enables a person to focus on career direction and provides information about natural aptitudes, abilities, personality, and values. Discovering this information can help identify job opportunities that result in successful and gainful employment.

Aptitudes

An **aptitude** is a characteristic that an individual has developed naturally. A person who has an aptitude for something can learn it easily and perform it well. Some aptitudes are *cognitive*, or mental. Other aptitudes are *physical*. For example, some college students have an aptitude for math, while others have an aptitude for ballet. Within both the cognitive and physical categories, aptitudes manifest themselves in familiar areas, such as art, computers, logic, mechanics, music, socialization, or writing. Different jobs require different aptitudes.

Read the job posting in **Figure 1-5**. In this job posting, the employer is looking for a candidate with an aptitude for empathy and compassion. At times, employers ask for a specific aptitude as opposed to formal training.

One key to job success is to find work in an area that matches your aptitudes. Understanding your aptitudes can provide clues regarding how to begin the job-search process. In order to plan a career, experts suggest selecting opportunities that match your strongest characteristics. Natural interests often match career goals. For example, aptitudes for one or more of the following are common:

- drawing
- mathematics
- repairing machines
- sports
- writing

Successful professionals who are experts in their fields likely found work that matched their natural tendencies or aptitudes.

Various tests can help identify your aptitudes and natural interests. An *informal aptitude test* helps distinguish your personality and skill set. These tests are usually available online through a simple Internet search. The results of these tests, while informal, can often point individuals in the direction in which they will likely find interesting and rewarding work. They can also be excellent practice for formal aptitude tests.

Formal aptitude placement tests, such as the SAT or ACT college placement exams, are used to measure overall achievement and compare performance to others. The ASVAB (Armed Services Vocational Aptitude Battery) is another example of an aptitude test. In this situation, the United States military administers the exam to students who are enlisting. They use the results to classify enlistees for training opportunities.

Experiences from the past can indicate direction for the future. People who started new jobs but quit soon after their hiring dates were likely working in a position that did not match their aptitudes. Some people begin a job or career and then realize that it is not as they had imagined. To effectively plan for a career, consider your interests. Working in a field that interests you will increase your chances for a happier, more fulfilling work experience. For example, students are likely to get better grades in the classes with subjects they find interesting than in the classes they find boring. The subjects you find interesting can lead to possible career directions. Finding enjoyable work begins with finding interesting work.

FIGURE 1-5

An aptitude is a characteristic that an individual has developed naturally. At times, employers ask for a specific aptitude as opposed to formal training.

Health Services Worker

Job Summary:
We are seeking a compassionate and dedicated Health Services Worker to join our team. In this role, you will be responsible for providing high-quality healthcare services to patients in a variety of settings.

Responsibilities:
- Assisting with patient care, including bathing, dressing, and hygiene
- Taking vital signs and recording medical history
- Administering medications and injections
- Assisting with rehabilitation exercises
- Providing emotional support and guidance to patients
- Collaborating with healthcare professionals to develop and implement treatment plans
- Maintaining patient confidentiality

Qualifications:
- Valid healthcare certification (e.g., CNA, HHA)
- Previous experience as a health services worker or in a related field
- Strong communication and interpersonal skills
- Aptitude for empathy and compassion toward others
- Ability to work well under pressure and in a team environment
- Commitment to providing excellent patient care

Goodheart-Willcox Publisher

CONNECT TO YOUR CAREER

Complete 1-3 Aptitudes Inventory, pg. 21

Abilities

Your aptitudes and skills are just the beginning of what employers seek. An employer will list a variety of abilities as part of a job posting. An **ability** is a mastery of a skill or the capacity to do something. Having aptitudes and skills is supported or limited by your abilities. For instance, a college student who has a musical aptitude and skills to reinforce it might not have the ability to perform under pressure in musical concerts. An ideal job placement is one in which a person's aptitudes, skills, and abilities align with one another. Examples of must-have abilities in job postings may include the following:

- assist others with little or no direction
- effectively handle multiple projects
- implement visual designs
- speak multiple languages
- think logically
- work long hours without tiring

It is important to determine your abilities when it comes to performing all the requirements of a job before applying. Even if all of the qualifications match on paper, a missing ability may mean it is necessary to continue looking for other opportunities.

CONNECT TO YOUR CAREER

Complete 1-4 Abilities Assessment, pg. 22

Personality

Personality is the unique blend of qualities that predict attitudes, values, and work habits, such as dependability, loyalty, and natural motivation. Your personality is tied to how you think and relate to others around you. In order to gain insight to your personality type for the purpose of career exploration, consider taking a personality assessment. Personality assessments can guide you as you explore potential career areas of interest.

There are multiple personality assessments on the market. One of the most popular assessments is called the Myers-Briggs Type Indicator (MBTI). The *Myers-Briggs Type Indicator® (MBTI®)* measures psychological preferences in how an individual makes decisions and views the world. The assessment measures a person's preferences toward extroversion versus introversion; sensing versus intuition; thinking versus feeling; and judging versus perceiving.

Understanding personality preferences is a good way for individuals to explore the type of career for which they are best suited. For example, someone who is introverted with a preference toward logical, step-by-step instructions is probably not well suited for a career in broadcasting, but rather engineering or computer programming. Taking a personality test can help determine these preferences.

Employers often rely on personality tests in order to predict job success for potential candidates. Although these tests are not always perfect indicators of workplace success, employers use them to select candidates who fit the position best. Before you start your career, it is wise to begin your own personality assessment so that you can investigate the type of career that works best for you.

Values

Values are principles and beliefs that a person considers important. They are the things that matter most to an individual. Values affect every part of life, including relationships and work decisions. Some values change with time, and others remain constant. Values that are not likely to change can be used as guideposts or directional markers toward a great career match.

Examples of values include the belief in working hard or the importance of caring for others. Other examples of values include:
- accountability
- commitment
- growth
- inner harmony
- trust
- work-life balance

All people have values, but many have not taken the time to identify them. Values are important principles in work relationships and environments. It is essential to identify your values in order to focus on finding a career that aligns with them.

CONNECT TO YOUR CAREER

Complete 1-5 Values Assessment, pg. 22

1.4 Skills Assessment

A skills assessment is another step in creating a career plan. A **skill** is something an individual does well. Unlike aptitudes, which come naturally, skills develop over time. However, skills fluctuate in their level of intensity. For example, skills can be gained by repetition or lost when not used. People are not born with skills. Instead, skills must be practiced and require consistent work. For example, a person who performs computer programming every day and then stops for an entire year will likely lose at least *some* technical skills. A skills assessment should take into consideration both *soft skills* and *hard skills*.

Soft Skills

Soft skills are applicable skills used to help an individual find a job, perform in the workplace, and gain success in any job or career. They involve behaviors that a person uses to relate to others, and they are not easy to measure. Soft skills are also called *employability skills*, *foundational skills*, or *workplace skills*. These skills often transfer from job to job. Examples of these skills include leadership, charisma, tact, personal and professional time management, conflict resolution, and professionalism.

Employers include skills as part of specific job requirements. They select words that best describe the skills required for the position they are looking to fill. These words are known as keywords. **Keywords** are words that specifically relate to the functions of the position for which the employer is hiring. For example, an employer might post an advertisement including keywords that describe someone who has developed time-management skills. Another employer might post an ad for someone with social skills. *Social skills* are skills that enable a person to work well with others.

Hard Skills

Hard skills are measurable, observable, and critical skills necessary to perform the required, work-related tasks of a given position. They are *job-specific skills* that a person is required to perform as an employee. Some hard skills include software and technology skills, speaking or writing in a foreign language, keyboarding, programming, and graphic design. All of your skills are marketable commodities. **Figure 1-6** lists examples of soft skills and hard skills that employers look for in today's job market.

Technology skills are of special importance in today's workplace. It is almost guaranteed that you use a great deal more technology than your parents did when they were your age. You might not realize that the technology you use to communicate with friends, such as texting, taking photos, conducting research, and accessing social media, can translate into proficient and employable skills. In addition to a host of technology tools at your disposal, you probably rely on apps to navigate directions, check the weather, or even purchase movie tickets.

FIGURE 1-6

Soft skills are applicable, transferable skills; hard skills are critical skills necessary to perform work-related tasks.

Types of Skills			
Soft Skills		**Hard Skills**	
• active listening • effective communication • flexibility • initiative • integrity • motivation • patience • problem solving • self-confidence	• teamwork • time management • trustworthiness	• accounting • carpentry • computer programming • data analysis • graphic design • machine operation • manufacturing • marketing • nursing	• project management • welding • writing

limeart/Shutterstock.com; Sergey Cherednichenko/Shutterstock.com
Goodheart-Willcox Publisher

Do not take your technology skills for granted. Completing a technology skills assessment can help you as you create a career plan. A *technology skills assessment* is a process in which an individual documents software and other technology skills possessed. It begins with identifying specific technology and then determining your level of skill with it. The assessment reveals the technology you use on a daily basis and the knowledge you possess about it. You will use this information with your current proficiencies as part of the data you gather to organize your job search. It also helps identify gaps that you need to fill during the next two to four years. This gives you an opportunity to research what is needed in your career so that you may identify new skills necessary for you to be successful. This assessment will also be of importance when the résumé-writing process begins. A sample technology assessment is illustrated in **Figure 1-7**.

FIGURE 1-7

A technology skills assessment is a process in which an individual documents software and other technology skills possessed.

Technology Skills Assessment					
	Current Proficiency Level			Desired Level of Accomplishment	
Technology	**Novice**	**Experienced User**	**Expert**	**Experienced User**	**Expert**
Adobe Photoshop		X			X
Google Docs	X			X	
Instagram	X				X
LinkedIn	X			X	
Microsoft Office	X			X	
Twitter		X			X
WordPress	X			X	
XML and HTML	X				X

DStarky/Shutterstock.com; Goodheart-Willcox Publisher

CONNECT TO YOUR CAREER

Complete 1-6 Skills Inventory, pg. 23

1.5 SMART Goals

Another step toward career planning is to create SMART goals. A **SMART goal** is a goal that is specific, measurable, attainable, realistic, and timely. SMART goals, as shown in **Figure 1-8,** help students ground themselves in the reality of earning an income after college graduation.

Specific

Goals should be specific and easily understood. For example, "I want to get a job" is not a specific goal. Stating "I want to have a job in finance" is a more specific goal. Specificity makes it easier to track progress and understand what you need to do in order to achieve your goals.

Measurable

Goals should be measurable. Otherwise, you may never be able to determine if you have actually achieved them. For example, a goal stated as "I want to determine if I'm capable of scoring above average on the MCAT" is difficult to measure. How can you determine your capability to pass a test? Restating your goal as "I want to score between 490 and 510 on the MCAT" is easier to measure; you will know if you achieved your goal when you complete the test.

Attainable

Goals should be attainable. For example, a goal for a college graduate should not be "I want to get a job as a partner at an established law firm." That goal is not attainable until practicing law for several years. Setting unattainable goals can have negative effects on a person's self-worth and self-esteem. Focus on what you are able to accomplish now and build your goals around it.

Realistic

Goals should be realistic. It is not realistic to expect high-level careers right out of college, nor is it realistic to expect career advancement after only a few months on the job. Setting realistic goals goes hand in hand with setting attainable goals. For example, working and living in Manhattan as an entry-level accountant clerk and making $30,000 annually may be attainable, but it is probably not realistic given the cost of living in Manhattan. Try to keep in mind what you have the ability to achieve and what you can realistically achieve, and then develop your career goals based on that realization.

Timely

Goals should have beginning and ending points. Establishing a time frame is a vital element of goal-setting. It allows you to keep track of where you are in achieving your goals, and it allows you to prioritize tasks. For example, if your goal is to gain acceptance to graduate school in the next three years, you may not have to start applying to schools for two years. Instead, you can focus on preliminary tasks, like taking preliminary exams and researching programs.

1.6 Career Pathing

Career pathing, not to be confused with career pathways, is a strategy an employee can use to determine personal career development. Through career pathing, an individual may be able to

- work toward promotions and move up within a company;

FIGURE 1-8

A SMART goal is one that is specific, measurable, attainable, realistic, and timely.

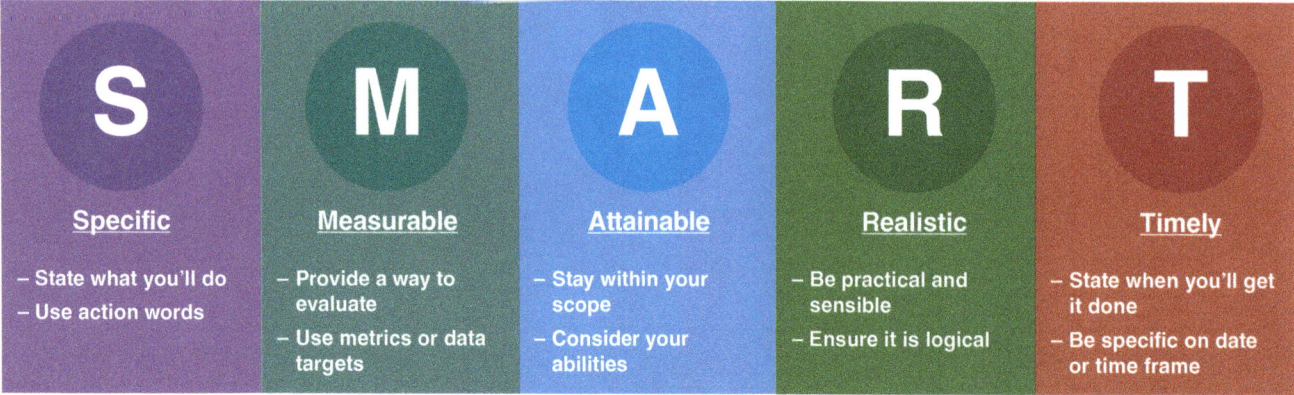

Goodheart-Willcox Publisher

Workplace Skills

Self-confidence is being certain and secure about one's own abilities and judgment. Self-confident people believe in their abilities to perform in a given situation. They know what they are good at, and they trust their instincts. Self-confidence is affected by self-talk, which is the practice of talking to one's self. Positive self-talk includes reinforcement of one's appearance and abilities and boosts a person's self-confidence. Negative self-talk disparages a person and reduces self-confidence.

- make a lateral move within a company to learn new skills and talents;
- change employers; or
- change careers.

Navigating a career is much like following directions on a GPS. Your career preparation, planning, and responses to employers' requirements will take many turns each year. Today's workforce is one that changes regularly. No matter which career you target, you will find shifts in how to prepare for it. The good news is that there is an unlimited array of job possibilities in many career fields and unlimited ways to gain skills to reach them. Learning about career ladders and career lattices can help you as you progress in your career.

Career Ladder

Many who find a career decide to stay with one company and climb something referred to as a career ladder. A **career ladder** is a sequence of jobs in one career field, from entry to advanced levels. Each career level is typically categorized by skill or education level, as shown in **Figure 1-9**.

FIGURE 1-9
A career ladder is a sequence of jobs in one career field, from entry to advanced levels.

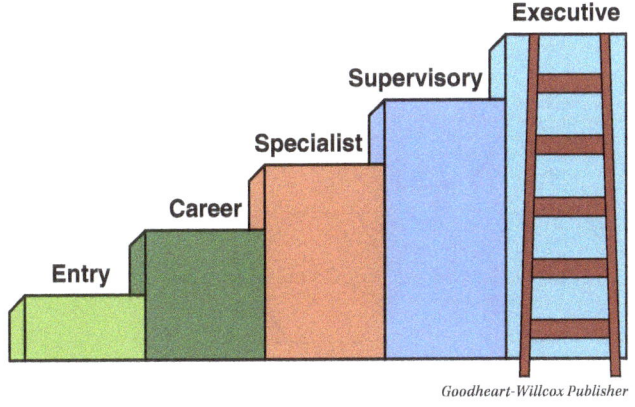

Goodheart-Willcox Publisher

Entry-Level Position

An *entry-level position* is the first career step for those seeking on-the-job experience. This is the best place to start for those who have little to no experience or prior training in a desired career field. Positions at this level are often introductory, with a lower salary than the other career levels.

Career-Level Position

A *career-level position* requires preparation and skills as listed by the employer for a particular job or position. This may be where you are as a college student. Many students may qualify for career-level positions after they serve as interns, volunteers, or apply for a position as college graduates.

Specialist-Level Position

A *specialist-level position* means that an employee has worked in a specific career field for at least a few years. This person may be able to apply for a better position in a company or navigate to a different corporation in order to provide expertise. A specialist-level position is task-centered. In other words, this position does not require managing or supervising other employees.

Supervisory-Level Position

A *supervisory-level position* is typically reserved when specialists have the requisite people skills and specific work knowledge to manage other employees well. These are typically employees who have a wealth of knowledge and experience or have been with the company for an extended period of time. This level of employment carries significantly increased responsibility and, for many jobs, presents a ceiling above which an employee may never climb.

Executive-Level Position

An *executive-level position* is the highest level in a career ladder or lattice. Executive-level duties include all of the above as career experience and also the ability to plan, organize, and manage a company. This level is reserved for presidents, vice presidents, and officers of the company.

Career Lattice

For some people, climbing a career ladder may not be the path to their ultimate career. Many individuals prefer lateral moves along with vertical moves. These moves can be seen in a career lattice. A **career lattice** is a series of lateral and vertical moves in one career field. The biggest distinction between a career ladder and a career lattice is that while a ladder refers only to the upward mobility of an employment field, a lattice also accounts for lateral transitions.

Imagine you are employed as a mechanic for an independently owned automotive repair shop. If you accepted a job with the same title working in the repair shop of a nationwide automotive dealer, you would not be moving up to a higher level of employment, but laterally to the same job in the same industry, but with a different company. There are many reasons to consider a move like this. For example, companies with larger employment totals may have more opportunities for advancement or higher wages. Additionally, the new job may not require any additional skills, but may yield new knowledge and experience that can be valuable in the future. By using a career lattice strategy, employees can achieve continued growth and career development throughout a lifetime. A visual representation of a career lattice is shown in **Figure 1-10**.

1.7 Career Portfolio

A **portfolio** is a compilation of materials that provide evidence of a person's qualifications, skills, and talents. As you begin planning your career, it is a good idea to start creating a portfolio. When you apply for a job, you will need to demonstrate to others how you are qualified for the position.

Showcasing examples of work you have completed or awards you have received is one way to communicate your qualifications. As a part of the portfolio-creation process, collect and save all documentation that demonstrates your accomplishments. Include copies of certificates, recommendation letters, and diplomas. If you have published articles or written other materials that are exemplary of your writing, include those also. In addition, gather evidence of academic or work projects you have completed. These items are testimonials that strengthen your position as a potential employee.

It will be helpful to select documents that position you as a great candidate for a potential job. Examples of information to consider adding to your portfolio include the following:
- causes where you have active involvement
- certifications and diplomas
- courses related to your desired job or career
- honors and awards
- internships
- leadership positions in organizations or jobs
- letters of recommendation

FIGURE 1-10

A career lattice is a series of lateral and vertical moves in one career field.

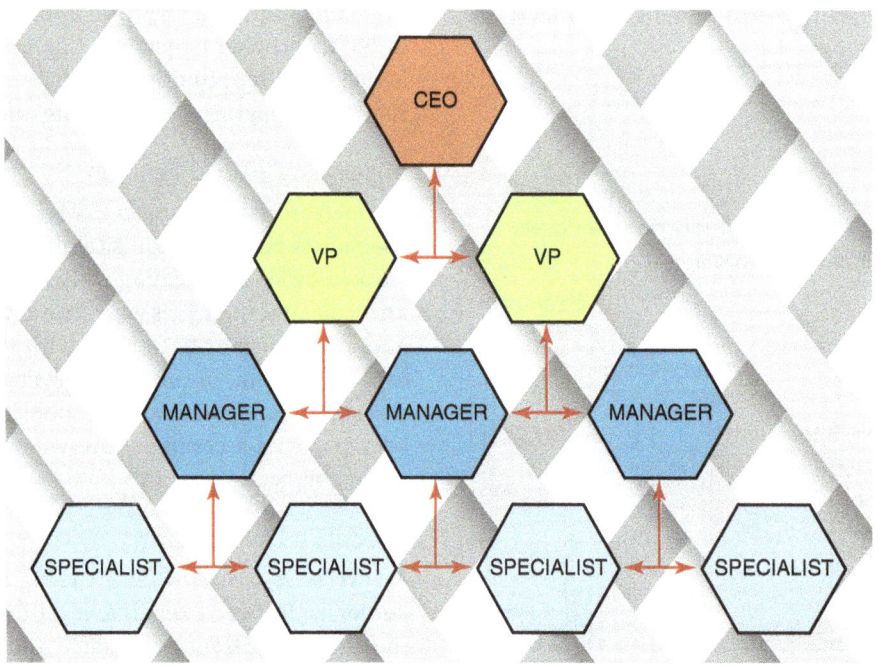

Goodheart-Willcox Publisher

- outstanding test scores
- patents
- references
- résumé
- volunteer work

Organization and presentation of a portfolio is important. Two common types of portfolio formats are print and electronic. For print portfolios, the creator hand carries the portfolio to job interviews to provide potential employers a chance to review pertinent work samples. Print portfolios are effective for original certificates, achievement awards, grade transcripts, and résumés.

An *electronic portfolio* contains content in digital form. Some common tools used to create an electronic portfolio are Microsoft Word, Microsoft PowerPoint, YouTube, Prezi, or WordPress. It is a best practice to develop your portfolio using familiar software, rather than spend time learning a new program. You can upload an electronic portfolio to a cloud service or blogging site that the employer can access. Some websites offer online portfolio-hosting services, some of which are free and others for which there is a charge. Alternatively, you may choose to create your own web page to post your portfolio. Through just one link, a potential employer has the opportunity to review your portfolio contents as desired.

An electronic portfolio has several advantages over a print portfolio. Electronic portfolios:

- provide virtually unlimited space for documentation
- can be viewed anytime
- can be updated or edited quickly and efficiently
- demonstrate technology skills

Developing a portfolio is an ongoing process, so do not be concerned if you are uncertain about what to add. In most cases, people have more information and documentation than they realize. The goal is to keep it simple and relevant. Portfolios that are cluttered with too much data are often ignored.

Types of professional portfolios vary, as shown in **Figure 1-11**. For example, if you are interested in pursuing work as a photographer, you will want a portfolio to display your photography skills. If your potential career involves writing, then much of your portfolio will highlight your written work. Select the type of portfolio that matches your career goals.

As you develop your portfolio, you may begin to uncover your career persona. A **career persona** is a unique blend of characteristics that defines who an individual is as a professional. It is the way that others perceive you in the context of your work, and it can be influenced by a variety of factors, including your skills, knowledge, and personal characteristics. Your career persona can be a powerful tool for building relationships, advancing your career, and achieving success. As you gain experience and grow in your profession, your career persona will evolve to reflect your professional identity and reputation.

FIGURE 1-11

A portfolio is a selection of related materials an individual collects and organizes to showcase qualifications, skills, and talents.

Types of Portfolios	
Portfolio Type	**Potential Uses**
Showcase	Document high grades, awards, achievements, and milestones, as well as photography and video captures of musical performances and public speaking
Process	Display progressive growth in academic skills highlighted with reflection pieces, such as original blogs, articles, or commentaries
Documentation	Demonstrate sustained academic success or work performance accomplishments
Hybrid	Display a combination of showcase, process, and documentation portfolios and include feedback from professional third parties
Professional	Display specific work-related accomplishments, company workshops, or training programs completed successfully, along with valuable skills used on the job

Goodheart-Willcox Publisher

Career Persona

Physical Therapist

Responsibilities

Motorama/Shutterstock.com

Physical and occupational therapists promote, maintain, and restore health by improving patient function and movement. Physical therapists usually work in private offices, clinics, patients' homes, and nursing homes. They spend much of their time on their feet actively working in partnership with patients. To improve patients' health, they may use:

- Exercises
- Stretching
- Electrical stimulation
- Ultrasound
- Ice
- Heat
- Gym equipment

Qualities and Skills

There are many personal characteristics that can be helpful for someone who is considering a career as a physical therapist or another job in the health services field. Some common characteristics include:

- *Compassion:* Healthcare professionals often work with people who are suffering from physical or emotional problems, so it is important to be able to show empathy and compassion toward others.
- *Attention to detail:* Healthcare professionals need to pay close attention to details in order to accurately diagnose and treat patients.
- *Good communication skills:* Healthcare professionals need to be able to communicate effectively with patients, as well as with other healthcare professionals.
- *Physical stamina:* Some healthcare professionals, such as nurses and paramedics, may need to work long hours on their feet and be able to lift and move patients.
- *Adaptability:* The healthcare field is constantly evolving, so it is important for professionals to be able to adapt to new technologies and techniques.
- *Interpersonal skills:* Healthcare professionals need to be able to work well in a team, as they often work closely with other professionals to provide care to patients.
- *Problem-solving skills:* Healthcare professionals need to be able to think critically and solve problems to diagnose and treat patients effectively.
- *Emotional stability:* Healthcare professionals may encounter difficult or emotional situations on the job, so it is important to be able to maintain emotional stability.

Education

- Bachelor's degree in recreation and fitness or healthcare related fields; some positions may require master's or doctoral degree.
- Doctor of Physical Therapy (DPT) degree
- Clinical work
- Passage of the National Physical Therapy Examination

Next Steps

If you are interested in becoming a physical or occupational therapist, you may want to conduct an informational interview with someone working in the field to learn more about this occupation. Consider joining professional organizations such as HOSA – Future Health Professionals. HOSA is a global, student-led organization empowering future health professionals through collaboration, education, and experience. In addition, you can begin taking prerequisite courses, such as anatomy, chemistry, and physics.

Summary

1.1 Explain the concept of career preparation.
Career preparation is a journey that differs from person to person. It includes learning to define the difference between a job and career and understanding how to create a well-developed career plan. Selecting a career involves choosing which career pathway is best suited to a person's aptitudes, skills, abilities, and values, and then selecting an industry within it.

1.2 State the purpose of a career plan.
A career plan is documentation of where a person is today in the job-search process and would like to be over the course of a career. It is a road map to accomplish those goals and should be reviewed and updated at least twice a year.

1.3 Discuss the importance of self-assessment as a career planning step.
Self-assessment is an important aspect of career planning because it allows individuals to focus a career search in industries that match their aptitudes, abilities, personality, and values. Conducting a self-assessment enables a person to focus on career direction and provides information about natural aptitudes, abilities, personality, and values.

1.4 Identify two types of personal skills that should be a part of a skills assessment.
Two types of personal skills that should be evaluated as a part of a skills assessment are soft skills and hard skills. Soft skills are applicable skills used to help an individual find a job, perform in the workplace, and gain success in any job or career. Hard skills are measurable, observable, and critical skills necessary to perform required, work-related tasks of a position.

1.5 Explain the purpose of setting SMART goals.
The purpose of setting SMART goals is so a person can set achievable goals. Generic, vague goals are difficult to measure, but SMART goals are specific, measurable, attainable, realistic, and timely. By setting SMART goals, individuals ground themselves in the reality of making an income after college graduation.

1.6 Discuss career pathing options.
Career pathing, not to be confused with career pathways, is a strategy an employee can use to determine personal career development. Career pathing options include earning a promotion, making a lateral move within the company, changing employers, or changing careers.

1.7 Define a career portfolio.
A portfolio is a compilation of materials that provide evidence of a person's qualifications, skills, and talents. Showcasing examples of completed work or awards received is an effective way to communicate one's qualifications when searching for a job.

Glossary Terms

- ability
- aptitude
- career
- career ladder
- career lattice
- career persona
- career plan
- emerging occupations
- hard skills
- job
- keywords
- Occupational Information Network (O*NET)
- personality
- portfolio
- SMART goal
- skill
- soft skills
- values

Review

1. Differentiate between a job and a career. (1.1)

2. What is the purpose of a career plan? (1.2)

3. Summarize the development of a career plan. (1.2)

4. Why is self-assessment important in career planning? (1.3)

5. What is an aptitude? How can aptitudes lead to job success? (1.3)

6. What is an ability? How does it differ from an aptitude or skill? (1.3)

7. Explain two types of personal skills that should be a part of a skills assessment. (1.4)

_____

_____

_____

8. How can setting SMART goals help you achieve success in your career? (1.5)

_____

_____

_____

9. What is career pathing? How can it aid in personal career development? (1.6)

_____

_____

_____

10. Define a career portfolio. (1.7)

_____

_____

_____

Application

1. What steps do you plan to take to prepare for your career? (1.1)

_____

_____

_____

2. How can a career plan help you achieve your long-term career goals? (1.2)

_____

_____

_____

3. Explain how jobs you have had up to this point will help you reach your career goal. (1.2)

4. How can self-assessment help you align your career goals with your personality in order to pursue a career path that is fulfilling and meaningful? (1.3)

5. What new abilities must you develop to work in your desired occupation? (1.3)

6. Name a hard skill that is required for your career of choice. How do you plan to develop this skill? (1.4)

7. Keywords are words that specifically relate to the functions of a position for which an employer is hiring. List five soft skills you think commonly appear as keywords in job advertisements. (1.4)

8. Think about a career that interests you. Write a SMART goal that will help you pursue your career. (1.5)

9. What does a typical career ladder for your chosen career look like? What types of skills and experience will you need to move up the career ladder? (1.6)

10. List information you would include in your portfolio. (1.7)

CONNECT TO YOUR CAREER

Workplace Connection

1-1 Emerging Occupations

1. Working with a partner or as part of a team, select and list two emerging occupations. Use O*NET and other online resources to research the items in the table, and record your notes.

   Occupation 1: _____

   Occupation 2: _____

	Occupation 1	Occupation 2
Job duties and responsibilities		
Skills and qualifications		
Educational requirements		
Employment outlook		
Relevant trends and developments		
Average salary		

2. Why is there a growing need for the occupations you researched?

   _____

   _____

   _____

3. Select one of the occupations. What are some of the benefits and challenges of working in this occupation?

   _____

   _____

   _____

1-2 Career Plan

Refer to Figure 1-3 to brainstorm ideas for action items you may include in your career plan. Consider actions you will need to take to progress along your desired career path. These items will serve as a foundation as you begin developing your plan.

Use the table that follows, or create your own, and list items that will be encompassed by your career plan. This plan should be revisited and may evolve as you progress through this text. Keep in mind there is more than one way to write a career plan. Create and maintain a document that works best for you. An example career plan entry is provided.

Career Plan		
Career Item	**Specific Action to Take**	**Target Completion Date**
Example: Obtain an entry-level position in healthcare.	Research entry-level careers in healthcare using apps such as Indeed.	1/15/--

1-3 Aptitudes Inventory

1. Create a list of your top five aptitudes. Examples include athleticism, photography, science, sociability, and creativity. Rank them 1 to 5, with the number 1 aptitude as the strongest.

   Aptitude #1:
   _____

   Aptitude #2:
   _____

   Aptitude #3:
   _____

   Aptitude #4:
   _____

   Aptitude #5:
   _____

2. Which one of your top five aptitudes would you most want to demonstrate to an employer? To what type of occupation does it align? Why do you think this is important for career success?

   _____
   _____
   _____
   _____
   _____

3. Conduct an Internet search using the phrase *career aptitude tests*. For example, the website 123Test offers a free career assessment at www.123test.com/career-test/. After completing the test, take a screen capture of the results or record the results below. What did you find out about yourself?

   _____
   _____
   _____
   _____
   _____
   _____

1-4 Abilities Assessment

Recall your top five aptitudes from Activity 1-3. How do these translate into your abilities? For example, you may have an aptitude for math, which may translate to an ability to analyze and interpret numerical data.

1. List your top five aptitudes and an ability that you have developed for each.

   _____
   _____
   _____

2. What other aptitudes do you have that could be developed into new abilities?

   _____
   _____
   _____

3. Consider other abilities you have. Which of these would be desired qualities an employer might look for in a candidate?

   _____
   _____
   _____

1-5 Values Assessment

1. There are many examples of recognized values, such as ambition, family, and integrity. Make a list of 10 values that are important to you. Rank each value in your list with the most important one marked as number 1. After listing your values, share them with the class.

   Value #1:
   _____

   Value #2:
   _____

   Value #3:
   _____

   Value #4:
   _____

   Value #5:
   _____

Value #6:
___

Value #7:
___

Value #8:
___

Value #9:
___

Value #10:
___

2. As a class, select three commonly held values among your classmates.
___
___
___

3. Collaborate to determine how each of the three values selected in the previous question might affect someone's job search and future career.
___
___
___
___
___

1-6 Skills Inventory

1. The following are examples of soft skills: attitude, ethics, time management, innovation, loyalty, and reliability. List and rank your strongest soft skills 1 to 5, with the number 1 skill as the strongest.

   Soft Skill #1:
   ___

   Soft Skill #2:
   ___

   Soft Skill #3:
   ___

Soft Skill #4:

_____

Soft Skill #5:

_____

2. The following words are examples of recognized hard skills: computer literacy, graphic design, accounting, and carpentry. List and rank your strongest hard skills 1 to 5, with the number 1 skill as the strongest.

   Hard Skill #1:

   _____

   Hard Skill #2:

   _____

   Hard Skill #3:

   _____

   Hard Skill #4:

   _____

   Hard Skill #5:

   _____

3. Describe why your top-ranked soft skill will be valuable in the workplace.

   _____

   _____

   _____

   _____

   _____

4. Describe how your top-ranked hard skill will benefit you in your job search.

   _____

   _____

   _____

   _____

   _____

CHAPTER 2
Workplace Readiness

Learning Outcomes

2.1 **Describe** basic skills.
2.2 **Identify** three categories of soft skills.
2.3 **Describe** workplace ethics.
2.4 **Explain** digital citizenship.
2.5 **Discuss** the value of certification.

CONNECT TO YOUR CAREER

Workplace Connection

2-1 Soft Skills
2-2 Workplace Ethics
2-3 Digital Citizenship
2-4 Certification Options

OVERVIEW

Workplace readiness means being prepared and qualified to enter the workforce. Being workplace-ready equates to success. Having the right set of skills and knowledge can help you succeed. Workplace success is, in a sense, determined by the employee, not the employer. For the most part, an employee can be successful simply by having the appropriate skills and following company policy. Additionally, employees can ensure a successful working experience by incorporating good digital citizenship.

In some industries, certification is essential to qualify for employment or to stay employed. Certification confirms that an individual has acquired knowledge and mastered skills for a specified area. Earning certification not only ensures workplace success, but also possibly projects a career forward.

TopVectorStudio/Shutterstock.com

Copyright Goodheart-Willcox Co., Inc.

2.1 Basic Skills

Employers look for potential employees who can help make their companies successful. There are many criteria used to sort through the hundreds of résumés submitted for open positions. Employers often initially look for a potential employee who is workplace-ready, or one who has the required skills, educational background, and experience. For example, an employer looking to fill an HVAC position will confirm a candidate is educated and trained.

Although different jobs and careers require different skills, all employees are expected to have basic skills. **Basic skills** are fundamental skills necessary to function effectively in society. They are also essential to functioning successfully on the job. These skills include reading, writing, speaking, listening, mathematics, and technology. They also include understanding how to apply these skills in a given situation.

- *Reading* involves acquiring meaning from written words and symbols to evaluate their accuracy and validity. Reading skills allow you to locate information from various sources, including books, images, and the Internet. Reading also helps you comprehend and evaluate material to ensure understanding and form judgments.
- *Writing* is using written words to express ideas and opinions. Writing skills enable you to communicate effectively on paper or while using a computer. Writing also requires you to edit and revise written communication for accuracy, emphasis, and intended audience.
- *Speaking* is communicating ideas verbally. Speaking skills enable you to present information clearly, maximize word choices, control tone, and adjust your message for your audience.
- *Listening* is hearing what others say and evaluating their messages for information. When you use listening skills, you pay attention to what other people are saying and understand the points being made.
- *Mathematics* is the study of numbers and their relationships. Mathematical skills enable you to use numbers to evaluate information and detect patterns so decisions can be made.
- *Technology skills* are skills that enable a person to operate a computer, mobile device, or other electronic component. They include the ability to use software and computer systems.

2.2 Soft Skills

Employers must ensure that applicants have the right education and work experience to meet the needs of the job. Additionally, the applicant's education and work experience will be reviewed to confirm that the individual has applicable *soft skills*, also known as *employability skills*, *foundational skills*, and *workplace skills*. Soft skills are used when talking to or communicating with others, which makes these skills important to have developed for both social and professional interactions. While not explicitly taught in school, relevant and common soft skills, such as positivity, self-confidence, and problem solving, are expected by employers.

When it comes to your career, employers often look for intangible qualities, such as determination and perseverance. Important soft skills for your career include professionalism, a strong sense of ethics, and the ability to work independently and as part of a team. In addition, communication skills, both verbal and written, are essential for career success.

You have likely already acquired many of these skills in school. However, some of these skills are gained through life experience, such as working at a job or interacting with others in social situations. These skills are not specific to one career, but rather transferable to any job a person may have. Thus, soft skills are also *transferable skills*. Soft skills can be categorized as thinking skills, people skills, and personal qualities.

Thinking Skills

Thinking skills are skills that enable a person to solve problems. Even if a person is unable to find a solution, thinking skills are helpful in assessing a situation and identifying options. Examples of thinking skills include decision making, creative thinking, problem solving, visualization, and reasoning.

- *Decision making* is the process of analyzing a situation and evaluating possible outcomes to choose the best solution. Decision-making skills enable you to weigh pros and cons in order to solve problems.
- *Creative thinking* involves developing or designing unusual or clever ideas about a given topic or situation. When you use creative-thinking skills, you develop unique or different ways to solve a problem.
- *Problem solving* is implementing a solution in the most efficient manner. Problem-solving skills help you carry out a plan or implement new processes to achieve a desired outcome.
- *Visualization* is the ability to form mental images. Visualization skills allow you to imagine how something will function or appear prior to an actual process.
- *Reasoning* is the ability to combine pieces of information or apply general rules to specific problems. Reasoning skills enable you to reach conclusions based on what you already know.

Time Management

Track Your Time

What is time management? Time management is your ability to plan and control how you will spend your time to achieve your personal and professional goals. You will benefit if you manage your time effectively. What is the best way to manage time? The first step is to analyze the time spent productively versus the time spent inefficiently on time wasters. Wasted time may include talking or texting on the phone, surfing the Internet, watching television, or procrastinating. The way that you spend your time reveals your values and goals. For at least one week, recount all of your time at the end of each day. It is helpful to categorize your activities. For example, categories might include e-mail, texting, personal Internet use, homework, reading, exercise, mealtime, breaks, and socialization. At the end of the week, total the time for each of your categories and analyze how you spend your time.

Once you have a better understanding of how you spend your time, the next step is to prioritize it. Rank your activities by importance to your personal and professional life. After you set your priorities, create goals to help you stick to them. Clear expectations will keep you on track and help you make good use of your time.

Lastly, schedule your time using a planner or calendar. Block out time for your priorities, just as you would for an appointment. Many time-management tools are available to help you make the most effective use of your time.

People Skills

People skills, also called *interpersonal skills*, are skills that enable people to develop and maintain working relationships with others. They help people communicate and work well with each other. These skills are necessary to complete job duties and ensure a positive working environment. In general, people skills have a significant impact on relationships with coworkers. Examples of people skills include social perception, negotiation, leadership, teamwork, collaboration, respect, and diversity.

- *Social perception* is the awareness of others' feelings and an understanding of why others may act a certain way. Socially perceptive people exhibit kindness and understanding. However, it is important to balance social perception with the ability to assert yourself politely and professionally when appropriate.
- *Negotiation* is discussing various positions of an issue and reconciling any differences of opinion. The key to negotiating is being able to pinpoint common goals among each position. This prepares everyone to argue facts from their point of view and reach an agreement.
- *Leadership* is the ability to influence or inspire other people. In the workplace, leaders encourage others and coordinate activities to reach goals.
- *Teamwork* is the cooperative efforts by individual team members to achieve a common or shared goal. Being a team member of a work group is similar to playing on a sports team. Success is measured in terms of the team's achievement, not the achievements of the individual team members.
- **Collaboration** is the act of working together with another person to accomplish a goal. To collaborate effectively, individuals must be willing to compromise. To **compromise** is to come to a mutually agreed-upon decision.
- **Respect** is the feeling or belief that someone or something is good, valuable, and important. It is important to respect diversity. **Diversity** is the representation of different backgrounds, cultures, or demographics in a group. This includes age, race, nationality, gender, mental ability, physical ability, and other qualities that make an individual unique. Work environments are usually diverse, and employers expect their employees to respect and appreciate the diversity within their organization.

Personal Qualities

Personal qualities are the characteristics that make up an individual's personality. Employers look for employees who are flexible and can adjust in a positive manner to work situations as they change. This includes being professional, having a positive attitude, and, above all, being ethical.

Career Persona

HVAC Technician

Responsibilities

Heating, ventilation, and air conditioning (HVAC) technicians install and repair heating and cooling systems in residential and commercial structures. HVAC technicians must be able to troubleshoot problems with the equipment and determine the best solution. They also perform a variety of other tasks, including the following:

- Perform math and measurement calculations
- Read blueprints, schemas, and work orders
- Test electrical circuits
- Determine compliance with regulations
- Communicate with customers to assess problems

Kilroy79/Shutterstock.com

Qualities and Skills

An HVAC professional should possess the following qualities and skills:

- *Electrical and mechanical skills:* An HVAC professional should have knowledge of electrical wiring and mechanical systems that are crucial to HVAC system installation, maintenance, and repair.
- *Technical knowledge and skills:* Many HVAC systems contain digital components and controls that an HVAC professional must know how to program.
- *Problem solving:* An HVAC professional should be able to identify, diagnose, and resolve problems with HVAC systems.
- *Attention to detail:* An HVAC professional must be thorough in completing all work tasks to ensure HVAC systems function properly.
- *Customer-service skills:* An HVAC professional should be able to communicate effectively with customers, answer their questions, and address their concerns.
- *Safety-conscious:* Awareness of and adherence to safety protocols and regulations is important.
- *Willingness to learn:* Technology and industry standards change quickly in the field of HVAC. An HVAC professional must continue learning to keep up to date on new developments in the field.

Education

- High school diploma or completion of vocational training program
- Apprenticeships under a licensed HVAC professional
- Licenses and certification, as required by states. National certifications are also available, such as from the US Environmental Protection Agency (EPA)

Next Steps

For those interested in becoming an HVAC technician, one of the best ways to enter the field is to pursue on-site experiences, such as through cooperative education programs, internships, and early employment or part-time employment while taking classes. Taking courses to gain a basic understanding of electronics is also helpful.

Examples of personal qualities include self-esteem, self-management, and responsibility.
- *Self-esteem* is the level of confidence in one's own abilities.
- *Self-management* is the ability to work independently without supervision.
- *Responsibility* is being trusted to complete duties or tasks.

CONNECT TO YOUR CAREER

Complete 2-1 Soft Skills, pg. 38

2.3 Workplace Ethics

Employers set many expectations for their employees. Perhaps one of the highest expectations is that employees will be ethical. **Ethics** are the moral principles or beliefs that direct a person's behavior. Ethics often conform to accepted standards of right and wrong. *Workplace ethics* are principles that help define appropriate behavior in a business setting.

Ethical behavior calls for honesty, fairness, reliability, respect, courage, tolerance, civility, and compassion. These and other qualities make our lives with each other peaceful and safe. Unethical behavior is considered wrong and is sometimes illegal. It includes actions such as cheating on an exam, stealing office supplies from an employer, surfing the Internet on company time, or returning merchandise to a store for a refund after using it.

Many companies have documents in place that outline ethical behavior. A *code of conduct* is a document that dictates how employees are to behave while at work or when representing the company. For example, some businesses do not allow their employees to wear clothing that has derogative comments that could be offensive to those with whom they work. A *code of ethics* is a document that dictates how business should be conducted. Its goal is to institute a value system for the company that will enable employees to make sound ethical decisions. For example, some businesses do not allow their employees to accept gifts from clients.

Unethical and illegal behavior includes discrimination and harassment. **Discrimination** is the unfair treatment of an individual based on race, gender, religion, national origin, disability, or age. **Harassment** is any unsolicited conduct toward another person based on race, gender, national origin, age, or disability. Harassment can take many forms, including inappropriate jokes, teasing, physical interactions, threats, insults, and intimidation. It can also include the displaying of offensive images, gestures, or objects.

CONNECT TO YOUR CAREER

Complete 2-2 Workplace Ethics, pg. 39

2.4 Digital Citizenship

Digital citizenship refers to the responsible use of technology and the Internet. It involves understanding how to use technology safely and ethically, and recognizing the impact that technology has on society and individuals. Some key elements of digital citizenship include:
- protecting personal information and privacy
- respecting the work and intellectual property of others
- being aware of online safety and security
- using technology for positive communication and collaboration

Being a good digital citizen also involves being aware of and responsible for one's online reputation and digital footprint. A **digital footprint** is a data record of an individual's online activities. A digital footprint, also known as an online footprint, is the record of an individual's actions and interactions on the Internet. This can include the websites you visit, the content you share, the comments you post, and the personal information you provide online. A digital footprint can be created by anyone who uses the Internet, including social media sites, search engines, e-mail, and mobile devices.

Digital citizenship is an important concept because technology and the Internet have become such integral parts of everyone's daily lives. Technology must be used in a way that is responsible and respectful of others.

Cloud Computing

Cloud computing is a type of Internet-based computing that allows users to access and use shared computing resources, such as servers, storage, and software applications. It is a way for individuals and organizations to use applications and store data remotely rather than on a local computer or server.

There are a number of ways in which digital citizenship and cloud computing intersect. For example, when using cloud computing services, it is important to be aware of privacy and security issues and follow best practices for protecting personal information and data. Digital citizenship also involves understanding the potential impacts of cloud computing on employment, the economy, and the environment.

Cloud computing allows for more flexible and remote working opportunities in the workplace, making it simpler for companies to hire and retain talent from anywhere in the world. This makes it easier for small- and medium-sized businesses to compete with larger organizations. In addition, companies that use cloud computing can reduce their IT costs and improve overall efficiency, which helps to fuel the economy. Running business applications on the cloud instead of operating data centers that house hardware and servers also helps reduce a company's carbon footprint. Cloud computing allows companies to practice digital citizenship by using technology more responsibly.

Software and File Downloads

It is unethical and illegal for an employee to use company equipment to download software that has not been purchased and registered by the employer. A *license* is the legal permission to use a software program and must be on file with the employer. Software *piracy* is the unethical and illegal copying or downloading of software, files, and other protected material.

In addition, digital security is an issue when downloading files. Employees should avoid opening files or e-mail attachments from unknown sources because they may contain computer viruses or trigger malware. If the file is malicious, it can exploit security vulnerabilities in the company's operating system and allow access to sensitive information, such as login credentials or financial data.

Intellectual Property

Intellectual property is something that comes from a person's mind, such as an idea, invention, or process. Intellectual property laws protect a person's or a company's inventions, artistic works, processes, and other original material. Any use of intellectual property without permission is called **infringement**.

A **copyright** acknowledges ownership of a work and specifies that only the owner has the right to sell the work, use it, or give permission for someone else to sell or use it. The laws cover all original work, whether it is in print, on the Internet, or in any other form or media. You cannot claim work as your own or use it without permission. **Plagiarism** is claiming another person's material as your own, which is both unethical and illegal.

Proprietary information is any work created by company employees on the job that is owned by that company. Proprietary information may be referred to as a *trade secret* because it is confidential information a company needs to keep private and protect from theft. Proprietary information can include many things, such as product formulas, customer lists, or manufacturing processes. All employees must understand the importance of keeping company information confidential. The code of conduct may explain that company information can only be shared with permission from human resources. Sharing proprietary information with people outside the company is unethical and, possibly, illegal.

Netiquette

Netiquette is etiquette used when communicating electronically. Netiquette includes accepted social and professional guidelines for Internet communication. It applies to e-mails, social media networking, blogs, texting, and chatting. In a business environment, it is generally considered unprofessional to use informal language and text abbreviations, as well as emoticons and emojis, when communicating with colleagues and clients through e-mail or other digital platforms. Always proofread and spell-check e-mails before sending them. When communicating electronically, it is important to follow the same common courtesy used in face-to-face discussions.

CONNECT TO YOUR CAREER

Complete 2-3 Digital Citizenship, pg. 40

2.5 Certification

The workplace is more competitive today than in recent history. Some jobs require a candidate to have a professional certification in order to be workplace-ready. **Certification** is a professional status earned by an individual after passing an exam focused on a specific body of knowledge. The individual generally prepares for the exam by taking classes and studying content that will be tested. Certification programs are usually sponsored by associations or vendors. There are many types of certifications in most industries and trades, as shown in **Figure 2-1**.

For example, a financial planning agency might require a financial planner to be certified as a qualification for the job. Other employers may prefer, but not require, certification. An individual may have a degree in accounting and be employable with that degree alone. However, some accounting firms may favor hiring accountants who are certified public accountants (CPAs).

There are certifications that must be renewed on a regular basis. For example, if you earned one of the many certifications sponsored by Microsoft, the certification is only valid for one specific version of software. When the next version is released, you must take another exam to be certified for the update.

FIGURE 2-1

Certification is a professional status earned by an individual after passing an exam focused on a specific body of knowledge.

Certifications by Industry

Administrative
Certified Administrative Professional (CAP)
Personal Assistant Certification

Automotive
ASE Certified Medium/Heavy Truck Technician
ASE Master Certified Automobile Technician

Financial Planning
Certified Financial Planner (CFP)

Health Support
Certified EKG/ECG Technician (CET)
Certified Nurse Technician (CNT)

Hospitality
Certified Hospitality Accountant Executive (CHAE)
Certified Hospitality Supervisor (CHS)

Human Resources
Professional in Human Resources (PHR)
Senior Professional in Human Resources (SPHR)

Information Technology
Cisco Certified Network Professional
Microsoft Certified Systems Administrator (MCSA)
Oracle Certified Java Programmer

Internal Auditing
Certified Internal Auditor (CIA)
Certification in Control Self-Assessment (CCSA)

Manufacturing
Certified Manufacturing Technologist (CMfgT)
Certified Professional in Engineering Management (CPEM)

Project Management
Project Management Professional (PMP)
Certified Associate in Project Management (CAPM)

Real Estate
Certified Commercial Real Estate Appraiser (CCRA)
Certified Residential Specialist (CRS)

Workplace Safety
Certified Environmental Health and Safety Management Specialist (EHS)
Certified Safety Auditor (SAC)

Workplace Skills
National Career Readiness Certificate (NCRC)

Goodheart-Willcox Publisher

Other certifications require regular continuing education classes to ensure individuals are current with up-to-date information in the profession. These classes are known as *continuing education* for which *continuing education units* (CEUs) are earned. If you are a teacher, your school system may require that you earn a specified number of CEUs every year to keep your teaching certification up to date.

Some certifications are not subject-specific but attest that the individual has employability skills. These certifications confirm that the person who earned the certificate possesses the skills to be a contributing employee. The focus of these certifications is on workplace skills. Individuals who earn this type of certification have demonstrated they possess the qualities necessary to become an effective employee.

CONNECT TO YOUR CAREER

Complete 2-4 Certification Options, pg. 41

Benefits of Certification

Hundreds of applications are submitted to employers each day for a limited number of open positions. Many criteria are used to screen these submissions, and certification has become one of them. For employers, certification takes the guesswork out of determining whether a candidate is qualified for a position. Anyone can claim to have a skill, but a certification confirms it. The certificate earned proves the holder met the required qualifications. Employers do not have to rely on a candidate's personal evaluation of skills possessed. Certification enhances a candidate's credibility and reputation.

For the employee, certification offers many of the following advantages:
- Certification is often voluntary. Those who seek it demonstrate ambition and dedication to a career.
- Certification provides personal achievement and accomplishment. Working to be recognized in your career area results in a sense of pride.

The Best App for That

CareerShift

CareerShift is a career management and job-search platform designed to help job seekers find their ideal job and advance their careers. The app provides a comprehensive set of tools and resources that help users research and identify potential employers, find job openings, and apply for positions. CareerShift features a proprietary database of millions of job listings and includes detailed information on companies, contacts, and hiring managers, enabling users to conduct informed job searches and increase their chances of success. The app also includes a résumé builder, cover letter generator, and interview preparation tools to help users create strong job applications and ace their interviews. Additionally, CareerShift provides salary comparisons and negotiations tools to help users understand what they are worth in order to negotiate the best compensation packages. Whether you are just starting your career or looking for a change, CareerShift is a valuable tool that can help you achieve your career goals.

- Certification may give you priority when interviewing for jobs as well as when being promoted on the job.
- Certification may increase your salary. Some companies offer higher salaries for those who are certified.

Becoming certified in your career area can allow your résumé to stand out from others. Hundreds of job seekers applying for the same position may all have similar work experience and education. However, certification proves that you have the skills needed on the job, and this distinction can put you at the top of the list of acceptable candidates. Research certification options in your chosen career field or areas of interest to decide if a certification is right for you. There might be many available in your career field. Conducting research can help you decide which is best for you and your career plans.

Certifications look great on a résumé, and earning certifications can help an individual gain valuable skills that can transfer to a career. The table in **Figure 2-2** depicts how academic skills can be transferred to a career.

How to Earn Certification

To earn certification in a specified area, it is important to prepare for the exam you select. There are several ways to accomplish this goal. One way is to take formal test-prep classes that cover important topics tested on the exam. These classes are usually offered at local colleges, universities, and businesses. Some classes are offered online. Be prepared to pay a fee for attending these classes.

The materials used in these classes are specifically developed to prepare individuals for the exam. The organization offering the certification may also publish training materials used for exam preparation. Alternatively, companies working with the certification organization may prepare study materials.

Another way to prepare for the exam is to purchase exam-preparation materials from a bookstore or online. There are many books available for those who wish to study without taking a formal class.

In addition to training materials, practice tests are often available as preparation tools. For each type of certification area, the test will usually have a specific format. Typical test formats include matching, multiple choice, or short answer. Before you take an exam, be aware of the test format so that you are not surprised on exam day. Practice exams are an effective way to prepare. Many of these practice tests are available online. If you are taking a formal class, practice tests will more than likely be a part of the curriculum.

A certification exam is usually administered by an official testing organization. These testing organizations have been approved by the certification sponsor. Do not take a certification exam at a location that is not an official test center. It will be necessary to pre-register for the exam, and in most cases, there will be an exam fee. Be prepared to show identification, such as a driver's license, when you arrive for the test.

FIGURE 2-2

Skills developed through earning a certification can be transferred to a person's career.

Transferable Skills		
Skill	**Application in School**	**Application at Work**
Accepting constructive criticism	Accepting instructor feedback on work	Accepting employer's feedback on work
Clarification	Asking instructor to explain assignments	Asking employer to explain assignments
Communication	Talking to instructors, advisers, counselors, etc.	Discussing career-related changes with human resources or employer
Networking	Working on group projects or finding help from peer tutors	Building professional relationships
Positive thinking	Avoiding negativity toward assignments and instructors	Avoiding negativity in a job search and career development
Reading	Reading and understanding class texts	Reading and understanding employee handbook
Research	Finding academic articles for research papers	Finding industry-related standards
Social interaction	Socializing with friends	Socializing with coworkers
Teamwork	Joining clubs and working in groups	Joining company-sponsored teams and collaborating with coworkers
Time management	Completing and submitting assignments on time	Meeting deadlines
Tolerance	Engaging in a diverse learning environment	Working in a multicultural company
Writing	Completing written assignments or essays	Writing work-related documentation such as procedures

davooda/Shutterstock.com; Goodheart-Willcox Publisher

Summary

2.1 Describe basic skills.
All employees are expected to have basic skills. Basic skills are fundamental skills necessary to function effectively in society. They are also essential to functioning successfully on the job. These skills include reading, writing, speaking, listening, mathematics, and technology.

2.2 Identify three categories of soft skills.
Soft skills are used when talking or communicating with others, which makes these skills important to have developed for both social and professional interactions. Employers often look for intangible qualities, such as determination and perseverance, as well as important soft skills for a career, including professionalism, a strong sense of ethics, and the ability to work independently and as part of a team. Soft skills can be categorized as thinking skills, people skills, and personal qualities.

2.3 Describe workplace ethics.
Workplace ethics are principles that help define appropriate behavior in a business setting. Specific information regarding how employees are to behave and how business is to be conducted is typically outlined in the company's codes of conduct and ethics.

2.4 Explain digital citizenship.
Digital citizenship is the standard of appropriate behavior when using technology to communicate, whether using cloud computing, downloading and using software and files, handling intellectual property, or practicing netiquette.

2.5 Discuss the value of certification.
Certification attests to workplace skills that an individual possesses. For the employer, certification helps identify qualified employees. For the employee, it confirms that the individual can perform in a given position.

Glossary Terms

basic skills	digital footprint	people skills
certification	discrimination	personal qualities
cloud computing	diversity	plagiarism
collaboration	ethics	proprietary information
compromise	harassment	respect
copyright	infringement	thinking skills
digital citizenship	intellectual property	

Review

1. What are *basic skills*? List some examples of basic skills. (2.1)

_____

_____

_____

2. What are *soft skills*? Where are you likely to have gained soft skills? (2.2)

3. How are soft skills categorized? (2.2)

4. List and describe examples of personal qualities. (2.2)

5. Describe *workplace ethics*. (2.3)

6. Differentiate between a code of conduct and a code of ethics. (2.3)

7. Explain *digital citizenship*. (2.4)

8. What is *netiquette*? (2.4)

9. Why is it important to an employer that an employee be certified? (2.5)

10. How can certification help an individual compete for a position? (2.5)

Application

1. Basic skills are necessary to perform nearly any job. Basic skills include reading, writing, speaking, listening, mathematics, and technology skills. Write two or three sentences describing how each of these skills is important in your chosen career field. (2.1)

2. List examples of soft skills you anticipate needing for your chosen profession. (2.2)

3. How do you communicate effectively with peers and team members? How can you use these skills in your future career? (2.2)

4. Decision-making skills are important in the workplace. How can you ensure that the decisions you make are fair and unbiased? (2.2, 2.3)

Chapter 2   Workplace Readiness

5. Transferable skills are skills that you have acquired in school or working in another career field. Consider the skills you have gained throughout your life. Describe how the skills you learned in one situation, such as in school or at a part-time job, can transfer to your chosen career field. (2.2)

_____
_____
_____

6. People skills enable a person to work with others successfully. Select one or two people skills from the bulleted list on page 27 that you feel you need to improve. Describe how you can improve the skills you selected as you progress through your job search. (2.2)

_____
_____
_____

7. How can you ensure that your own actions align with your future workplace's ethical values and policies? (2.3)

_____
_____
_____

8. All employees are expected to work in an ethical manner while representing their given companies. Describe the types of ethical decisions you may encounter in your profession. (2.3)

_____
_____
_____

9. Why do you think netiquette is an important part of workplace success? (2.4)

_____
_____
_____

10. List potential certifications required for your chosen career. Include the agency or company that issues the certification as well as any other pertinent information you need to know. If your occupation does not require certification, list certifications that can help make you more marketable as a job candidate in your field. (2.5)

_____
_____
_____

Copyright Goodheart-Willcox Co., Inc.

CONNECT TO YOUR CAREER
Workplace Connection

2-1 Soft Skills

Divide into small groups. Each group member should share a personal or professional experience involving a problem that had to be solved. The speaker should describe the problem and the solution (if resolved) while the rest of the group practices active listening. This may involve asking insightful or clarifying questions or giving feedback after the speaker is done. Then answer the questions that follow.

1. What did you learn about active listening from participating in this activity?

   _____
   _____
   _____

2. How would you rate your listening skills? What can you do to improve them?

   _____
   _____
   _____

Continue working as a group to practice your teamwork and collaboration skills. Brainstorm issues that you think need to be addressed either at your school or in the community. As a group, select one issue and work together to come up with a solution to the problem. Answer the questions to describe your team experience.

3. Briefly state the problem your team identified and your recommended solution.

   _____
   _____
   _____

4. Did someone on your team take on the role of leader? How was the leader selected?

   _____
   _____
   _____

5. How was the work divided among team members?

   _____
   _____
   _____

6. What challenges did your team face during the problem-solving process? How did you overcome them?

_____
_____
_____

7. Describe any conflict within the team during the problem-solving process. How did you resolve it?

_____
_____
_____

8. Based on your experience, summarize what you learned about teamwork and collaboration.

_____
_____
_____

2-2 Workplace Ethics

A *code of conduct* identifies the manner in which employees should behave while at work or when representing the company. Conduct a search on the Internet using a job title of your choice and the phrase *code of conduct* (e.g., *salesperson code of conduct*).

1. Describe the type of information you found regarding a code of conduct for your desired occupation.

_____
_____
_____

2. List two potential ethical situations you may encounter in your desired occupation and describe how you intend to approach them.
   Ethical Situation #1:

_____
_____
_____

   Ethical Situation #2:

_____
_____
_____

2-3 Digital Citizenship

As a professional, you will be expected to demonstrate appropriate behavior while using technology at work. This includes the correct use of intellectual property. The Internet provides numerous sources for obtaining text, images, video, audio, and software. Even though this material is easily accessible, it does not mean you can use it as you choose. Intellectual property laws must be followed. The following table contains a list of issues related to intellectual property. Work in small groups to learn more about these issues. Provide descriptions along with examples demonstrating inappropriate usage related to each issue.

Intellectual Property		
Issue	Description	Inappropriate Use
Infringement		
Plagiarism		
Copyright		
Licensing agreement		
Public domain		
Piracy		

Netiquette is also an important component of digital citizenship. It is a professional requirement in the workforce. Most work is completed on a computer, so it is imperative that employees understand and practice netiquette. Continue working in small groups to create two netiquette behavior examples in the workplace. For each behavior, create one example that shows incorrect netiquette usage and then rewrite it to show correct netiquette usage.

1. Netiquette Behavior #1:
   Incorrect usage:

   _____

   _____

Correct usage:
_____
_____

2. Netiquette Behavior #2:
   Incorrect usage:
   _____
   _____

   Correct usage:
   _____
   _____

2-4 Certification Options

Conduct an Internet search for a list of certifications in your desired industry. List available certifications in the left column of the following table. In the right column, explain how each certification could help further your career. Then, answer the questions that follow.

Certifications in My Industry	
Certification	**How it will further my career?**

1. Which certification are you most interested in obtaining and why?
   _____
   _____

2. What will be required of you to earn this certification?
   _____
   _____

CHAPTER 3
Personal Brand

Learning Outcomes

3.1 **Summarize** the importance of a personal brand.

3.2 **List** steps for creating a personal brand statement.

3.3 **Explain** the purpose of a personal commercial.

CONNECT TO YOUR CAREER

Workplace Connection

3-1 Personal Brand
3-2 Personal Brand Statement
3-3 Personal Commercial

OVERVIEW

As a professional in the workplace, the way you conduct yourself plays a part in establishing your reputation. Your reputation is also known as your *brand*, which is who you are, how you differentiate yourself from others, and how others see you.

A self-assessment is the process of evaluating your own abilities, behavior, and performance in order to understand your strengths and weaknesses. A personal brand, on the other hand, is the way you present yourself to the world, including your reputation, image, and unique value proposition. The two intersect in that a strong self-assessment can help you understand and communicate your unique value, which in turn can strengthen your personal brand. Additionally, building a personal brand can help you be more aware of your strengths and weaknesses, leading to a more effective self-assessment. Ultimately, the two concepts can work together to help you become more successful in your personal and professional life.

airdone/Shutterstock.com

3.1 Your Personal Brand

As a professional, you will work to develop your personal brand. A **personal brand** is an individual's reputation. It is a concept that defines a person's professional aptitudes, skills, abilities, personality, and values. Your brand helps to positively distinguish you from others.

There are several factors that contribute to a great personal brand. These factors can include:
- *Clarity:* Your personal brand is clear and concise. It clearly communicates who you are and what you stand for.
- *Authenticity:* A personal brand is authentic and genuine. It reflects your true personality, values, and beliefs.
- *Consistency:* Your personal brand should be the same across all channels and platforms. It presents a consistent image and message to the world.
- *Relevance:* A great personal brand is relevant to your target audience. It addresses the needs, wants, and concerns of the people you want to reach.
- *Differentiation:* A unique personal brand sets you apart from others in your industry or field. It highlights what makes you different from others.
- *Authority:* A personal brand establishes you as an expert or thought leader in your field. It conveys a sense of knowledge, experience, and credibility.
- *Engagement:* A convincing personal brand encourages engagement with your audience. It fosters a sense of community and connection with the people you want to reach.

In Chapter 1, you completed a self-assessment, which will help you have a better idea of your strengths and weaknesses. The self-assessment process is one of many important tools that will help you understand what you *think* your reputation is as a professional and how you see yourself. You can then work on your personal branding to create the reputation you *want* as a professional and the way you want *others* to see you. Personal branding can help you build the reputation, or brand, that you desire and will help you be successful in a career.

CONNECT TO YOUR CAREER

Complete 3-1 Personal Brand, pg. 52

3.2 Personal Brand Statement

A **personal brand statement** is one sentence that describes what a potential job candidate offers an employer. It reflects the aptitudes, skills, abilities, personality, and values a person will provide to a company in exchange for an agreed-upon salary. It is, in a sense, a tagline or slogan designed to persuade a company to hire that person. The goal of a personal brand statement is to give an employer an idea of how an individual would contribute to the company.

A brand statement clarifies your most important values. Consider individuals who possess time-management skills. Their personal brand statement may use keywords such as *efficiency* and *expectations*.

Businesses often use slogans and logos as a branding strategy to convey their company values. For example, Apple used the slogan "Think different" in advertisements to make their customers feel as though the use of Apple products set them apart from the rest of the world.

Creating a Brand Statement

A personal brand statement should be concise, using the keywords that best reflect how you want to be known in your industry. The number of keywords in a brand statement should be limited for maximum effect, and you should brand yourself as the professional you want to become, not necessarily the professional you are at the moment. Examples of brand statements are listed in **Figure 3-1**.

FIGURE 3-1

A personal brand statement is one sentence that describes what a potential job candidate can offer an employer.

Personal Brand Statements
• A creative problem-solver who can combine mathematics skills and science expertise to help develop sustainable energy sources.
• A writer who is able to blend communication and critical-thinking skills to illustrate solutions to common problems.
• A driven team player who uses leadership skills to motivate others and exceed goals.
• A customer-service professional with excellent communication skills committed to market-driven collaboration and idea sharing in an effort to achieve 100 percent customer satisfaction.
• A product development coordinator with impeccable time-management skills dedicated to prioritizing promotion of outside-the-box thinking to stay competitive in tomorrow's marketplace.
• A production manager who implements soft skills to continually promote client-based, customer-directed deliverables while maintaining the highest standards.

Goodheart-Willcox Publisher

The Best App for That

Handshake

Handshake is a career development and job search platform that connects students and recent graduates with employers. The app provides a platform for job seekers to discover job opportunities, build their professional networks, and gain insights into different industries. Employers can use the app to connect with top talent, post job and internship opportunities, and participate in virtual and in-person events. Handshake offers a personalized experience, with features such as career advice and customized job recommendations based on the user's interests and skills. Additionally, the app provides resources such as résumé reviews and interview preparation to help students and recent graduates in their job search. Handshake is widely used by universities and colleges, and is designed to help students and recent graduates take the next step in their careers and find meaningful employment.

When writing a personal brand statement, choose words that best describe your aptitudes, skills, abilities, personality, and values. These words will become your *brand keywords* and help create a memorable statement. You can find keywords to use by researching the industry in which you would like to work and looking for terms that reflect the core of the occupations in that industry. For example, school administrators typically seek teachers who have passion, enthusiasm, sensitivity, empathy, and a sense of humor. Including these keywords makes it more likely your brand statement will yield employment opportunities. The creation of a personal brand statement can be accomplished in four steps.

Step one: The first step in writing a personal brand statement involves defining yourself. What is your reputation? Consider what other people say about you and how they would define you, and list as many descriptive adjectives as you can. For example, you may list educator, thinker, manager, problem-solver, or hard worker as words that describe you.

Step two: The next step is to list your skills. Focus on the soft skills and hard skills you possess that are relevant to your industry. For example, if your goal is to work in advertising, identify skills you possess that will help you obtain a job in an advertising field, such as creativity and work ethic. These skills will help paint a picture of your background and demonstrate your value to an employer.

Step three: The next step is to create short, descriptive phrases that describe how you work, what you are capable of accomplishing, and what you can offer an employer. What sets you apart from the rest of the workforce? Why should a company hire *you* over another applicant? For example, you may work with urgency to deliver results despite obstacles. Include that description in your list of phrases.

Step four: The final step is to compile the words and phrases you have listed to create a succinct statement that provides an overall description of you as an employee. Using the examples given in each of the previous steps, a personal brand statement could be "A creative problem-solver with copywriting experience who works with urgency and grace under pressure to deliver results, even when obstacles present themselves."

Applying a Brand Statement

After you are comfortable with your brand statement, use it whenever appropriate. This means adding it to your career-search tools, including your résumé, cover letter, professional social media accounts, and portfolio. Your brand statement is your slogan, and you are advertising yourself. Just as notable individuals use their personal branding to reach their audiences, you can use your brand to further your career and expand your network.

CONNECT TO YOUR CAREER

Complete 3-2 Personal Brand Statement, pg. 52

3.3 Personal Commercial

During the job-search process, there will be many opportunities to communicate your personal brand. One of the first applications of your personal brand should be developing a personal commercial. A **personal commercial**, also known as an *elevator pitch*, is a rehearsed introduction that includes brief information about a person's background and a snapshot of their career goals.

It is suggested that a 30- to 60-second commercial is an appropriate length. Keep your commercial brief, as if you could recite it while riding on an elevator going from one floor to the next with professional contacts.

Career Persona

Automotive Service Technician

Responsibilities

An automotive service technician is responsible for diagnosing and repairing various issues with vehicles. Daily tasks may range from performing routine maintenance, such as oil changes and tire rotations, to more complex repairs involving a vehicle's electronic system. It is important for auto technicians to stay current with industry developments and advancements in technology through ongoing training and education. Automotive service technicians typically perform the following activities:

davooda/Shutterstock.com

- Use diagnostic tools and equipment to inspect and test parts and systems
- Repair or replace faulty parts and components
- Perform repairs that meet manufacturer specifications
- Follow checklists to ensure no steps are missed when examining parts or diagnosing problems
- Communicate with customers to explain problems and proposed solutions
- Keep records of work and maintain a clean and organized workspace

Qualities and Skills

- *Technical knowledge:* Automotive service technicians need knowledge of mechanical, electrical, and electronic systems in vehicles, including both gas-powered and electric.
- *Diagnostic skills:* Service technicians must be able to determine mechanical or operating errors using computerized diagnostic equipment.
- *Attention to detail:* An eye for detail is important to ensure that inspections and repairs are completed thoroughly and accurately.
- *Problem-solving skills:* Auto technicians and mechanics must have the ability to think critically and identify the best solution to resolve vehicle issues.
- *Dexterity:* Service technicians must have steady hands and good eye-hand coordination to assemble and attach auto parts.

Education

- Completion of vocational program in automotive service technology
- Certifications, as required by employers, such as those offered by ASE (National Institute for Automotive Service Excellence); OEM (Original Equipment Manufacturer); and SAE (Society of Automotive Engineers)

Next Steps

To become an automotive service technician, research the industry to learn about the various jobs available and to understand the qualifications and experience required for different roles. Begin taking courses in automotive repair, electronics, computers, and mathematics to establish a strong background in this field. Search out apprenticeship programs that offer training and job placement services. Working in an entry-level job at a local auto shop can help you get real-world experience and on-the-job training.

Connect to Your Community

Building a personal brand is a great way to connect to the community and make a positive impact. A personal brand represents your values, skills, and personality, and is an effective tool for creating connections with others who share your interests and goals. To use your personal brand to connect to the community, start by identifying your core values and the issues that are important to you. Next, get involved in organizations and activities that align with your values, such as volunteering, attending community events, or participating in local initiatives. Additionally, make use of social media to share your thoughts and experiences, and engage with others online. By leveraging your personal brand to connect with others, you can build relationships, establish yourself as a thought leader, and create a positive impact in your community. Whether you are seeking to advance your career, grow your network, or make a difference, building a strong personal brand is an effective way to achieve your goals and connect with the people and organizations that matter to you.

LightField Studios/Shutterstock.com

Chances are you will not recite your speech verbatim. However, there is value in being prepared with a concise message that promotes who you are and your abilities. A personal commercial makes the most of the few seconds you may have when you meet a potential networking contact.

Developing a Personal Commercial

When developing a personal commercial, it is important to be succinct and clear in your purpose. Your listener must understand why you have created this commercial and what your career goal is. If your goal is to network for a job, include the
- title of the job you are seeking;
- skills required for the job that you possess; and
- general location of your target geographical area.

There are situations in which you may be seeking advice or guidance rather than networking for a specific job. You may be searching for a person who can educate you on potential career choices or skills necessary for a future job. If your goal is to network for advice, include
- a clear example of what kind of advice or information you are seeking;
- the specific topics you want to discuss; and
- your availability to meet.

A personal commercial, like a personal brand statement, can be created by performing the following steps:

Step one: Review your personal brand statement. Your brand statement is who you are and reflects your professional qualities, values, and goals. It will be the basis of your elevator pitch.

Step two: Summarize your education, soft skills, and hard skills. Write a brief paragraph that identifies the highlights of your education. It may be the type of degree you earned, area of concentration, or school you attended. Review the earlier self-assessment you made of your soft skills and hard skills. Select one or two of each that demonstrate your best skills.

Step three: Determine exactly what you are seeking from the networking contact you may meet in the elevator in impromptu situations. You may be looking for a job or looking for information about an industry. The elevator pitch is a networking tool for finding information and making a connection with someone who can help you in your career.

Step four: State your motivations for your career direction. It may be that you want to inspire others through teaching or learn all you can about technology so you can make a future career decision.

Step five: Write your elevator pitch. As you summarize the material, remember that your brand statement is your guiding force. **Figure 3-2** illustrates the narrative for two 30-second commercials. Notice that the first column shows the personal brand statement that is used as the basis for the commercials.

CONNECT TO YOUR CAREER

Complete 3-3 Personal Commercial, pg. 53

FIGURE 3-2

A personal commercial is a rehearsed introduction that includes brief information about a person's background and a snapshot of their career goals.

Examples of Personal Commercials

Personal Brand Statement	Personal Commercial
A marketing professional who is dedicated to creating jaw-dropping promotions.	I am Susan Roskowski, an assistant marketing product manager **<current job title>** with a degree in marketing communications from Baylor University. I am located in the greater Houston area **<target geographical area>** and looking for a career in an advertising agency **<job title goal>**. My skills include writing promotions that capture the attention of the target audience based on their demographics **<hard skills required for the job>**. I am proficient at ad creation and social media marketing. I am flexible and skilled at working with others **<soft skills required for job>**.
A compassionate healthcare professional who has the skills, knowledge, and commitment needed to help patients achieve or improve quality of life.	I am Samuel Lopez, a physical therapist **<current job title>** with over five years of experience in the field. I specialize in a range of physical therapy services, including sports injury rehabilitation, post-surgery recovery, and chronic pain management **<hard skills required for the job>**. I am looking for a position within the tri-state area **<target geographical area>** at a well-respected healthcare facility that prefers to use a holistic approach to physical therapy **<job goal>**. I am compassionate and skilled at communicating with patients **<soft skills required for job>** to ensure they understand and follow their personalized treatment plan and recover from their injuries.

kornn/Shutterstock.com
Artco/Shutterstock.com
Goodheart-Willcox Publisher

Rehearsing a Personal Commercial

To be prepared when an unexpected networking opportunity presents itself, it is necessary to practice your personal commercial. Rehearsing your commercial will help you achieve the goal of making a positive impression on the person with whom you are speaking. If your commercial is not polished and ready to present, a career opportunity can be missed.

Begin by practicing in front of a mirror and rehearsing your speech. Do not read your commercial word-for-word, even while you are practicing. The goal is to make the interaction conversational and comfortable for the person with whom you meet. Time your commercial and remember to keep it within 30 to 60 seconds.

When you are satisfied with the content and delivery of your commercial, ask a friend or family member to record you as you deliver it. Ask for feedback from your listeners and record it multiple times until you are satisfied with the final product.

You may decide to post the final version of your commercial to a website such as YouTube or Instagram. The link to the video can then be added to your résumé, e-mail, or portfolio.

Summary

3.1 Summarize the importance of a personal brand.
A personal brand is an individual's reputation. It is a way to express one's identity and differentiate oneself from others. It describes what value a potential job candidate offers to an employer. A personal brand reflects an individual's professional aptitudes, skills, abilities, personality, and values.

3.2 List steps for creating a personal brand statement.
Four steps that can be taken to create a personal brand statement are defining who you are as a professional, listing your soft skills and hard skills, creating short phrases describing how you work, and compiling the information to make a concise statement.

3.3 Explain the purpose of a personal commercial.
A personal commercial is a rehearsed introduction that includes brief information about a person's background and a snapshot of their career goals. Also known as an elevator pitch, a personal commercial can be delivered in person, or a candidate can stand out from the crowd by recording a personal commercial, posting it online, and including a link on employment documents.

Glossary Terms

personal brand   personal brand statement   personal commercial

Review

1. How can performing a self-assessment help when defining your personal brand? (3.1)

2. When creating a personal brand statement, what types of words should be chosen? (3.2)

3. How can you find brand keywords that will help you create your personal brand statement? (3.2)

4. List and describe the steps for creating a personal brand statement. (3.2)

5. Provide examples of ways a personal brand statement can be applied once it is created. (3.2)

6. What is an appropriate length for a personal commercial? (3.3)

7. What are three items that should be included in your personal commercial if you are looking for a job opportunity? (3.3)

8. What three items should your personal commercial contain if you are seeking information or advice? (3.3)

9. List and describe the steps for creating a personal commercial. (3.3)

10. What are some recommendations for practicing a personal commercial? (3.3)

Application

1. What is your *current* reputation as a professional? Why? (3.1)

2. What do you want your *future* reputation as a professional to be? (3.1)

3. What message do you want to convey to your audience through your personal brand? (3.1)

4. Who is your target audience for your personal brand, and how can you best reach and connect with them? (3.1)

5. How will you measure the success of your personal brand, and what steps will you take to continuously improve and evolve it? (3.1)

6. List examples of keywords you will use when you create your personal brand statement. (3.2)

7. In what ways will you apply your personal brand statement when searching for a career? (3.2)

8. How can you use your personal brand statement to effectively network and further your career goals? (3.2)

9. How can you incorporate your personal brand into your personal commercial? (3.3)

10. You should be prepared to network at all times. Why do you think you might need more than one rehearsed personal commercial? (3.3)

CONNECT TO YOUR CAREER

Workplace Connection

3-1 Personal Brand

Working with a small group, conduct an Internet search using the phrase *personal branding*. Read about the importance of a personal brand and how a personal brand statement can help you market yourself. Then, answer the questions that follow.

1. List five things you learned about personal branding.

   _____
   _____
   _____

2. Why is personal branding so important when preparing for a career?

   _____
   _____
   _____

3. Provide an example of someone who has successfully established a personal brand. This could be a well-known individual or someone you know personally. Explain how this individual's personal brand aligns with their reputation and image.

   _____
   _____
   _____

3-2 Personal Brand Statement

Use the four-step process described in this chapter to build a list of qualities and characteristics that will be included in the development of your personal brand statement.

Step one: Define yourself and your reputation.

_____
_____
_____

Step two: List your hard and soft skills.

_____

_____

_____

Step three: What sets you apart from other workers?

_____

_____

_____

Step four: Compile your brand statement.

_____

_____

_____

3-3 Personal Commercial

Work with a partner to conduct an Internet search using the phrase *elevator pitch*. This phrase is often used interchangeably for *personal commercial*. Read about expectations for a personal commercial. Using your research, list a set of guidelines you can follow when creating your own personal commercial. For example, consider how long it should be, how many words it should include, etc.

Guideline #1:

_____

_____

Guideline #2:

_____

_____

Guideline #3:

_____

_____

Guideline #4:

_____

_____

Using the guidelines you established in the first part of this activity, follow the five-step process outlined in the chapter to draft a personal commercial that you can use in your job search. Each partner should draft their own personal commercial.

Step one: Review your personal brand statement. What does it say about your professional qualities, values, and goals?

_____

_____

_____

Step two: Write a paragraph that highlights your education and skills.

_____

_____

_____

Step three: Summarize what actions you want your networking contact to take.

_____

_____

_____

Step four: Succinctly summarize your career motivation.

_____

_____

_____

Step five: Write your elevator pitch.

_____

_____

_____

_____

_____

After you have completed your commercial, practice it with your partner and get feedback. Incorporate the feedback to improve your pitch. Once you have perfected your pitch, have your partner record a video of you delivering it so that you may post it to your social media sites.

UNIT 2 Online Presence

Chapter 4 Managing Your Online Presence
Chapter 5 Networking for Your Career
Chapter 6 Protecting Your Identity

Dzmitry Abrazhevich/Shutterstock.com

Why It Matters

The landscape for finding a job has experienced trends and changes. Jobs are harder to find, there are fewer jobs available, and the competition is fierce. The Internet drives the job-search process, and career seekers learn how to use it as a strategic tool to reach an employment goal.

Online job-search strategy starts with creating and developing your online presence. When employers search for your name on the Internet, will they find positive or negative information? After you have established your online presence, you can use it to develop a professional network that will help you make connections in the workplace. However, remember to always be cautious with your Internet activity because protecting your identity is an important aspect that should not be ignored in the job-search process.

CHAPTER 4
Managing Your Online Presence

Learning Outcomes

4.1 **State** ways a job seeker can create and maintain a positive online presence.

4.2 **Explain** the importance of a professional e-mail account.

4.3 **Describe** how a LinkedIn account can be used in the job-search process.

4.4 **Describe** how a Twitter account can be used in the job-search process.

4.5 **Describe** the use of Instagram as a job-search tool.

4.6 **Explain** the importance of positive thinking during the job-search process.

CONNECT TO YOUR CAREER

Workplace Connection

4-1   Online Presence
4-2   Professional E-mail Account
4-3   LinkedIn Account
4-4   Twitter Account
4-5   Instagram Activity
4-6   Positive Thinking

OVERVIEW

The career-search process starts with your online presence. People learn many things on the Internet—current events, news, weather, social issues, and much more. Potential employers will explore the Internet to see what they can find about you. Although your name might not be the subject of millions of search engine trends, your name and the online results that it returns are important considerations during your job search.

An online presence can help to inform professionals in your field about your skills, qualifications, and talents. Additionally, it can reveal information about your character based on the websites associated with your name. How will you stack up against other candidates?

Rawpixel.com/Shutterstock.com

4.1 Creating Your Online Presence

One of the first steps in the job-search process is to evaluate your online presence. An **online presence** is what an Internet search reveals about someone. In today's workforce, an online presence can influence success for a job seeker in the career-search process. Hiring managers often conduct independent research on job applicants to determine if the interview process should move forward.

Most people retain Facebook, Twitter, and Instagram accounts to socialize and maintain relationships with friends and family. These are important aspects of online communication. However, since the Internet can reveal private information to unapproved parties, a potential employer may be able to view private exchanges without the account owner's knowledge or consent. Discretion should be used when posting to social websites, as these activities might appear when a search is conducted for your name.

Most personal social media sites offer privacy customization so the user can designate who can and cannot visit specific pages. Privacy settings for personal accounts should be set so that potential employers, or the public, cannot view personal photos or information of the owner of the account. Photos or comments posted online will become part of a person's digital footprint. A *digital footprint* is a data record of an individual's online activities. Items posted to the Internet cannot be completely hidden or deleted. What is posted online today could risk personal and professional opportunities in the future.

Most employers enter an applicant's name in a search engine to see what the online presence reveals about the person. This search will yield a positive, negative, or nonexistent online presence. It could also reveal a shared online presence if someone else has an account with the same name. **Figure 4-1** lists each type of online presence.

A *positive online presence* can lead to employment opportunities. This occurs when a hiring manager enters a name into a search engine and discovers results such as links to well-written articles or blog posts, a professional portfolio, or memberships to business networking sites. As a result, an employer's impression of a potential employee can be positively influenced, even before an interview.

A *negative online presence* can harm an individual's professional reputation and minimize a person's chances for potential job interviews. Inappropriate photos, improper behavior, or lewd remarks on social media sites can eliminate a person from employment opportunities.

A *nonexistent online presence* denotes lack of technology skills or abilities, or lack of motivation or proactive thinking. It implies that a person does not stay up to date, which can be a reflection of who the person might be as an employee.

Entering your own name into a search engine is the best way to evaluate your personal online presence. If the results are anything but positive, consider what you can do to reflect a more positive image. If the results are nonexistent, consider participating in positive online activities that will get your name as a professional in circulation.

If the search results show multiple accounts by other people with a shared name, consider examining the results. A hiring manager will likely not know what you look like, so it is possible for the wrong profile to be selected, which may generate a poor first impression. If possible, think of how to differentiate your name in your online accounts. This can be accomplished by using a middle initial, for example. This way you have a unique online presence when someone conducts an Internet search for your name.

CONNECT TO YOUR CAREER

Complete 4-1 Online Presence, pg. 70

FIGURE 4-1

An online presence is what the public can learn about a person from viewing their Internet activities.

Online Presence	
Type	**Search Results**
Positive	Search engine results reflect your professional accomplishments.
Negative	Search engine results reflect activities that negatively impact your chances of getting hired.
Nonexistent	A search engine returns no results that match your name.
Shared	Search engine results are an exact match to your name; however, the results are not about you, but about someone with your same name.

Goodheart-Willcox Publisher

4.2 Professional E-mail Account

Before beginning the career-exploration process, a professional e-mail account should be created to keep your personal and professional activities separate. This e-mail account should be used during the job-search process. Businesses use e-mail to communicate available jobs and schedule interviews with job candidates. A separate e-mail account will enable you to manage communication for the job-search process and other professional business. Examples of e-mail addresses are shown in **Figure 4-2**.

Recruiters and human resource departments may sort job applicants by names that appear in the e-mail address. An e-mail address is a reflection of the owner of the e-mail account. An employer expects to see the e-mail contact's name, not an unprofessional e-mail address. For that reason, consider using your first name and last name separated by a period or underscore. If your name or a variation of it is not available from the selected provider, try using your first initial and last name or other combinations that reflect your legal name. If all combinations fail, consider switching providers.

A secure password is needed for an e-mail account. A **secure password** is a code used to access a private account or other private information, such as an e-mail account or computer network. A secure password is typically between 8 and 20 characters long and a combination of letters, numbers, and special characters. The safest password combinations are those that are unpredictable. Password strategies and examples are shown in **Figure 4-3**.

Less secure, predictable passwords often contain the following data:
- address
- birthday or anniversary date
- names of family members or pets
- favorite numbers, repeated numbers, or numbers in a sequence

Unauthorized users should not be able to easily identify or guess your password. To protect your identity, never share a password with others.

After you have created your e-mail account using a secure password, the next step is to create a signature block. A **signature block** is the full name, phone number, and e-mail address of the owner of the account. Most e-mail accounts have a field that automatically adds a signature each time a new e-mail is created, or a response is made to a previous message. You may choose to include a job title under your name in your signature block. If you do not have a permanent position, you can designate a job title that describes your skills, such as *Welder*, until you find a permanent position. You may also choose to use your brand statement. **Figure 4-4** shows examples of professional

FIGURE 4-2

A professional e-mail account should be created to keep personal and professional activities separate.

Sample E-mail Addresses	
Personal E-mail Address	**Professional E-mail Address**
hockeystar@e-mail.com sassy55555@e-mail.com totallyrockin_thehouse@e-mail.com	kevin.jones@e-mail.com carol_smith@e-mail.com jdouglas@e-mail.com

Robbiya/Shutterstock.com
Goodheart-Willcox Publisher

FIGURE 4-3

A secure password is a code used to access a private account or other private information.

Creating a Password	
Strategy	**Example**
Start with a memorable sentence.	I will exercise more.
Remove the spaces and punctuation.	Iwillexercisemore
Capitalize or lowercase an unexpected letter.	iwilleXercisemore
Create a memorable, unique misspelling.	iwilXercisemor
Add numbers and symbols.	#iwilXercisemor2

Goodheart-Willcox Publisher

FIGURE 4-4

A professional signature block includes a person's full name, phone number, and e-mail address in a readable size and font.

Signature Blocks

Shelley Jones
Junior Accountant
(212) 555–1234
sjones@e-mail.com

Rakesh Singh
Lab Assistant
(623) 555–4023 | rsingh@e-mail.com
www.websiteurl.com

Santiago Dunn
Assistant Developer, Point n' Click Web Design
(312) 555–3997 | santiagodunn@e-mail.com
Twitter: www.twitter.com/sdunnweb

Tinicia Henson
Social Media Associate | AgriCo
(215) 555–1601 | hensont@e-mail.com
LinkedIn: www.linkedin.com/in/tiniciahenson
Twitter: www.twitter.com/TiniciaAgriCo
Instagram: www.instagram.com/AgCoProd

Goodheart-Willcox Publisher

signature blocks. It is important to use a readable font style and size.

CONNECT TO YOUR CAREER

Complete 4-2 Professional E-mail Account, pg. 71

4.3 LinkedIn Account

Networking plays an important role in the career-search process. **Networking** is talking with people and establishing relationships that can lead to career growth or potential job opportunities. It is the process of creating new contacts with a goal of giving and receiving support while building relationships. To build and expand your professional network, it is essential to learn to network online.

LinkedIn is a professional social networking site that provides static communication regarding business and employment opportunities. This professional networking site is used by more than 800 million people in the global workforce for purposes of making new contacts and building business relationships. It is limited to closed groups and individual contacts. LinkedIn offers users space for posting and finding jobs that might not be advertised publicly.

LinkedIn's basic account type is a freemium model. *Freemium* means you can take advantage of basic services without paying. When first joining LinkedIn, the freemium model is a good choice. As your career advances, you might wish to purchase account upgrades which provide premium services and features. There are several upgrade plans from which to select.

The advantage of establishing an account on LinkedIn is that the site promotes your profile through search engine optimization. **Search engine optimization (SEO)** is the process of indexing a website so it will rank higher on the list of returned results when a search is conducted. When someone searches for a person who has a LinkedIn account, that person's name will appear either at the top or near the top of the search results list.

LinkedIn for Students is a resource site for college students who want to begin a career with professional resources and support. It is LinkedIn's student-centric handbook for kick-starting a career that includes information for helping and preparing them to sign up for LinkedIn. The significant difference and advantage of LinkedIn for Students is that the site hosts and advertises student-specific jobs, such as internships and job-shadowing opportunities.

The student LinkedIn site encourages students to be active with the creation and revision of their profiles. It is recommended that students continue to create, edit, and improve the profile information regularly. Some of the resources that help students successfully build a profile and network with potential employers include:
- a profile checklist
- job-hunting handbooks
- ideas for how to build a professional brand
- tips on communicating effectively on LinkedIn
- tips on using LinkedIn to find a job or internship

LinkedIn for Students offers suggestions, such as searching for CEOs in a target area who have attended the same college or university, and encourages students to create connections with various alumni. This includes networking with fellow students, current employees, and executives who are alumni of the same school.

Create an Account and a Profile

To use LinkedIn, an account must be created. To do this, navigate to www.LinkedIn.com and provide the information requested, including your professional e-mail address. Once your account is created, LinkedIn generates a URL address, or link, that navigates directly to your page. You can add your LinkedIn URL to your e-mail signature block and résumé.

Career Persona

Welder

Responsibilities

A welder's daily tasks typically include preparing and setting up welding equipment, reading and interpreting blueprints or schematics, and welding metal components together using various welding techniques such as MIG, TIG, or stick welding. Welders are also responsible for inspecting completed work to ensure that it meets quality standards and making any necessary repairs or adjustments. Some additional responsibilities of a welder include the following:

matsabe/Shutterstock.com

- Maintain and repair welding equipment and tools
- Follow safety procedures and guidelines
- Work with other tradespeople as part of a team to complete projects
- Communicate with supervisors and other team members to ensure smooth workflow and timely completion of projects
- Continuously learn new welding techniques and technologies to improve skills and stay current with industry developments

Qualities and Skills

To be successful as a welder, the following qualities and skills can be useful:

- *Attention to detail:* Welding requires precision and accuracy, and welders must pay close attention to their work to ensure that the final product meets quality standards.
- *Physical dexterity:* Welding can be physically demanding, and it requires good hand-eye coordination, manual dexterity, and the ability to work in awkward positions.
- *Problem-solving skills:* Welders must be able to identify and troubleshoot problems in their welding processes, such as warping or cracking, and determine the best solution to fix them.
- *Safety awareness:* Welding can be a hazardous job, and it is crucial for welders to follow safety protocols and use personal protective equipment to prevent accidents.
- *Technical knowledge:* Welders must have a solid understanding of welding techniques, metallurgy, and welding codes and standards.

Education

- Completion of a welding program at a vocational school or community college
- On-the-job training under the supervision of an experienced welder
- Certifications such as those offered by the American Welding Society (AWS)
- Occupational Safety and Health Administration (OSHA) training on electrical safety

Next Steps

For those interested in pursuing a career as a welder, one of the first steps to take is to enroll in a welding program at a vocational school or community college. These programs typically cover a range of welding techniques and provide hands-on experience with the equipment and tools used in the field. Taking courses in blueprint reading, shop mathematics, mechanical drawing, and electrical applications will be helpful. Conduct research to learn about state licenses and certifications required.

The next step is to create a LinkedIn profile. A **profile** is information that describes who a person is professionally. An account profile is a career snapshot and is part of an individual's professional online presence. Potential employers can use the information in a profile to learn more about a job candidate's professional background. Tips for creating a LinkedIn profile are as follows:

- *Use an attention-getting headline.* Use a job title or promote an area of expertise. Keep it short.
- *Add a high-quality, professional profile picture.* This helps you make a good impression on potential connections and recruiters. Statistics show that LinkedIn members who have a photo get more profile views than those with no photo.
- *Include a summary about yourself.* The *About* section of your profile should describe your professional background and objectives in one to two paragraphs. This is a good place to include your personal brand statement.
- *Add work experience, education, and skills.* Use relevant keywords that describe your skills and experiences. This can help you appear in search results for those keywords, making it easier for recruiters to find you.
- *Include endorsements.* Your connections will be able to *endorse*, or verify, that you have the skills listed. This provides recognition of your skills and builds credibility, helping make you a viable job candidate.

CONNECT TO YOUR CAREER

Complete 4-3 LinkedIn Account, pg. 72

Connections

The purpose of creating a profile is to share who you are as a professional. The best way to accomplish this is to make connections. **Connections** are people in an individual's network who are added only by invitation. By accepting your invitation, your connections agree to share their network with you. Those who are connected can view each other's profiles without limits. However, those not connected will only have a limited view of each other's profiles. If you are not connected, your name may not be found by an important contact. Therefore, it is advantageous to gain as many connections as possible.

LinkedIn users connect by sending invitations to other LinkedIn members. You can search for a person you know on LinkedIn by using the search function. Once you see the profile for which you are looking, select the **Connect** button to send an invitation.

Connections are categorized as first, second, or third degree.

- A *first-degree connection* is a direct connection, mutually agreed upon by you and another LinkedIn member. You are able to view the entire profile of someone who is your first-degree connection, and that person can see your entire profile. Additionally, you can see their e-mail address and connections, unless hidden.
- A *second-degree connection* means you are not directly connected to the other member, but you have a first-degree connection in common. You can see the full profiles of your second-degree connections, but you will not be able to see their e-mail address or message them directly. You can send them an invitation to connect.
- A *third-degree connection* is someone who is connected to one of your second-degree connections. You have a limited view of the profiles of your third-degree connections.

LinkedIn Tips

There are many ways you can use LinkedIn as a tool to help build career success. Tips for effectively using LinkedIn are as follows:

- *Connect with people you know.* LinkedIn is a great way to stay in touch with colleagues, classmates, and other professionals. Reach out and send connection requests to people you know and trust.
- *Join relevant groups.* There are many groups on LinkedIn focused on specific industries, professions, or interests. Joining and participating in these groups can help you network with like-minded professionals and stay up to date on news and trends in your field.
- *Share relevant content.* Share articles, blog posts, and other content that is relevant to your industry or profession. This helps establish you as a thought leader and can help you attract more connections and job opportunities.
- *Engage with others.* LinkedIn is not a one-way street. Be sure to comment on and share other people's content and participate in discussions in groups. This helps you build relationships and show that you are a collaborative and engaged professional.
- *Use LinkedIn for job searching.* LinkedIn has a powerful job-search function that allows you to search for jobs based on location, industry, and other criteria. Be sure to regularly check for job openings and consider using LinkedIn's "Easy Apply" feature to quickly apply for jobs that interest you.

Workplace Skills

Netiquette is etiquette used when communicating electronically. It is also known as *digital etiquette*. Netiquette includes accepted social and professional guidelines for Internet-based communication. These guidelines apply to e-mails, social networking, and other contact with customers and peers via the Internet. Netiquette dictates proper usage of Standard English, grammar, and professionalism when communicating. It also involves avoiding spamming other people. *Spamming* is intentionally sending numerous, unwanted e-mails or social media messages.

- *Use LinkedIn to showcase your work.* LinkedIn allows you to create a portfolio of your work, including writing samples, presentations, and other media. This can be a great way to show off your skills and accomplishments to potential connections and recruiters.
- *Update your LinkedIn profile.* Keep your LinkedIn page current. Make updates to reflect new work experiences, training, and skills.

4.4 Twitter Account

Twitter is an online news and social networking site for professionals and nonprofessionals to communicate in real time. Since Twitter communication occurs in real time, it can be much faster than e-mail. The purpose of networking on Twitter is to follow available job posts, as well as people's ideas, stories, opinions, and information. Twitter is a place where employers can post jobs and job seekers can visit to find employment opportunities.

Twitter communication consists of user-driven postings called *tweets*. This makes Twitter-based communication a form of micro-blogging. A **microblog** is short communication limited to a certain number of characters per post. Setting a character limit not only necessitates brevity, but encourages users to make succinct, memorable posts, as well.

Twitter can be a useful tool for finding job opportunities, as many companies and recruiters use the platform to advertise open positions and connect with potential candidates. Here are some ways you can use Twitter to find job openings:

- *Follow companies and recruiters.* Follow the companies you are interested in working for, as well as recruiters and staffing agencies in your industry. This will allow you to see any job openings they tweet about and stay up to date on company news and culture.
- *Use Twitter's search function.* Look for keywords related to your job search, such as "job openings," "hiring," or the name of your industry. This can help you find job openings that might not be widely advertised.
- *Network with others.* Twitter can be a great way to connect with other professionals in your field. Engage with other users by commenting on their tweets, sharing their content, and starting conversations. This can help you build relationships and learn about potential job openings.
- *Use hashtags.* Many companies and recruiters use specific hashtags (#) to advertise job openings on Twitter. Some examples might include #jobopening, #hiring, or #careers. Search for these hashtags to find job openings that are actively being promoted on the platform.

CONNECT TO YOUR CAREER

Complete 4-4 Twitter Account, pg. 72

Create an Account and a Profile

To join Twitter, you must sign up for an account by navigating to www.Twitter.com. Once you have created your account, you can connect with people you know in Twitter by providing access to your e-mail address book. Twitter accounts can be set as public or private. Tweets from public accounts are viewable by anyone, even those without a Twitter account. To view tweets from a private account, a user must request and gain permission from the account owner.

Creating a profile on Twitter differs from creating a profile on LinkedIn. A Twitter profile consists of just two details: a username and bio. Even though a Twitter profile contains less information than that of LinkedIn, create it in a way that highlights who you are as a professional.

Username

Twitter allows its users to create a unique username or use an e-mail address as a username. The username limit is 15 characters. Usernames on Twitter are unique

Time Management

Effects of Poor Time Management

Poor time management can lead to negative consequences and symptoms that can significantly affect an individual's life. Here are some of the most common symptoms of poor time management:

- *Procrastination:* A common symptom of poor time management is the tendency to constantly put things off until the last minute. This can lead to feeling overwhelmed and stressed.
- *Missed deadlines:* When individuals are unable to properly manage their time, they may frequently miss important deadlines. This can result in a loss of credibility and professionalism.
- *Chronic stress:* Poor time management often results in constantly feeling behind and stressed, which can lead to physical and mental health problems.
- *Disorganization:* People with poor time management skills often struggle with disorganization. They may have a cluttered workspace, forget important appointments, and struggle to keep track of their schedule.
- *Burnout:* When people consistently fail to properly manage their time, they may experience burnout. This can result in feelings of exhaustion and a lack of motivation.
- *Interpersonal conflicts:* Poor time management can also lead to conflicts with family and friends, as commitments may be consistently missed or pushed back.
- *Poor work performance:* In a professional setting, poor time management can result in a decline in work performance. This can result in lower productivity and a decrease in job satisfaction.

in that they feature the @ symbol as a prefix. Your username becomes your Twitter account URL address. Create a professional-sounding username on Twitter so recruiters will follow your posts. For your professional Twitter account, focus on including your legal name with an occupation, professional designation, or geographic area. This helps make it memorable and marketable. Consider the following examples:

- name with profession, such as a welder: @BobCross_Welder
- name with professional designation, such as writer: @KayJones_Writer
- name with general location, such as NYC: @AmyMackNYC

Bio

A Twitter bio is similar to a LinkedIn headline. In their bios, users display information about who they are and what they do. A Twitter bio is limited to 160 characters. Tips for creating a bio include the following:

- Consider using your personal brand statement as part of your bio.
- Use keywords in your bio so your account will appear in search results for those words.
- Upload a professional photo. In an effort to stay recognizable across networking platforms, consider using the same photo used for your LinkedIn account.
- Include a link to your portfolio, website, or blog. This will provide those who view your profile with a direct link to your work.

Followers

Where LinkedIn has connections, Twitter has followers. **Followers** are Twitter members who view another user's tweets in their own Twitter feed. When you post a new tweet, your followers will see it first. Users are permitted, and often encouraged, to follow as many public profiles as they choose.

By changing an account's settings to private, account owners will have the ability to approve or deny who follows their tweets. To follow someone with a private profile, a user must send a request and wait for approval. For both public and private profiles, an individual has the option of "blocking" a particular user. Users cannot view profiles from which they have been blocked.

Posting to Twitter

Gaining popularity on Twitter can be achieved through the consistent use of hashtags. A **hashtag** is a searchable keyword that links users to all tweets marked

with the same keyword. If a user searches for a specific hashtag that is included in your tweet, then your tweet will appear in the search results. Hashtags can be placed anywhere in a tweet. Any word or string of words can be turned into a hashtag by adding the pound symbol (#) immediately before the word with no space between the symbol and the word(s). Some examples of hashtags include the following:
- #careermanagement
- #careers
- #consultingjobs
- #greenjobs
- #hireme
- #ITjobs
- #jobpostings

You can also conduct a search for these or similar hashtags to find available jobs. When appropriate, include a link to your portfolio, website, or blog in your tweets. This can help potential employers learn more about you.

4.5 Instagram Account

Instagram is a mobile-centric, media-sharing site that allows users to share pictures and videos publicly or privately. Although originally designed as a social networking tool, it has become a powerful tool for job seekers who want to establish and maintain an online presence and promote a personal brand.

Instagram can be a useful tool for finding a job, especially in industries such as fashion, design, and photography where visual content is important. Many companies use Instagram to showcase their products and services and may post job openings on their profile. By following companies that interest you and engaging with their content, you may be able to learn about job opportunities that are not widely advertised.

Create an Account and a Profile

Similar to other social and professional networking sites, you will need to create an account to activate a profile. It is recommended that you use your Twitter profile name for your Instagram account name. This makes it easier for people to find you on Instagram, and it ensures that any item in which you are tagged on Instagram will also show in your Twitter feed. Just as you did with your LinkedIn and Twitter accounts, upload a professional photo and create a bio. There are only 150 characters allowed for the bio, so it is a great place to record your personal brand statement. After you have set up your account, you can include your Instagram link in your professional correspondence, portfolio, e-mail signature, and LinkedIn and Twitter profiles.

Posting to Instagram

As a career self-promotion tool, you can upload photos that highlight professional accomplishments, such as a picture of an award or honor. Instagram is a great way to build a portfolio of videos and photos that demonstrate skills and talents that will catch the eye of an employer. A good way to demonstrate your talents to a potential employer is to post before and after photos of a project. This gives an immediate snapshot of your skills and what you are capable of accomplishing.

You can also upload short videos that allow an employer to see how you work in your chosen industry. For example, if you are a welder, you can upload a video of work being done on a project to illustrate your ability with a given tool or material.

After you have uploaded a photo or video, you can use a hashtag so it can be found by other users. Similar to Twitter, users can search for a specific hashtag, and all posts with that tag will be listed under the search results. This helps to increase the number of people who view your profile.

CONNECT TO YOUR CAREER

Complete 4-5 Instagram Activity, pg. 72

4.6 Positive Thinking

Connecting to a career is a long-term adventure and should be approached as such. It will not be over in one day, or even in one week. Often, it may take months to find a career with which you connect.

The way you approach the career-search process reveals who you are as a potential employee. Be positive during the job-searching journey. Concentrate on qualities you possess that other candidates may not. Believe you are the right person for each job for which you apply, and maintain positive thoughts throughout the process, such as the following:
- I have capabilities that other candidates do not.
- I am a self-starter.
- I demonstrate critical-thinking skills.
- I have great judgment skills.
- I work well with other people.
- I can do this job.
- I will be able to find the work that I enjoy.
- I am a valuable employee.

There are many online tools to help you communicate and demonstrate your positive qualities. Remember, you want to create a positive online presence to make a good impression on prospective employers. Add details to your online profiles that reflect your best qualities. Post tweets that promote your personal brand. Post photos or videos demonstrating your top-notch skills.

Searching for a job is a process. Not every attempt will lead to an interview or job offer, but continue to be optimistic. Negative experiences can lead to negative thoughts. If this occurs during the job-search process, manage your emotions carefully. Negative thoughts or actions should never be a part of your online presence. Derogatory, distasteful, or controversial posts can be harmful to your reputation.

Self-talk is internal thoughts and feelings about oneself. Negative self-talk messages sometimes invade the thoughts of job candidates. To change negative self-talk to positive, challenge your thoughts by focusing on what you do well. Tips on how to transition from negative self-talk to positive are shown in **Figure 4-5**. Often, just changing your train of thought or stepping away will help you escape the negative self-talk and give you a moment of clarity. Instead of being your worst critic, become your biggest supporter.

CONNECT TO YOUR CAREER

Complete 4-6 Positive Thinking, pg. 73

FIGURE 4-5
Remaining positive and using positive self-talk can help you retain an optimistic outlook in your career search.

Self-Talk Tips	
Main Ideas	**Suggestions**
Stay healthy.	Taking care of your body and mind can help you better handle stress and negative influences. Make sure to eat nutritious foods, exercise regularly, and get enough sleep.
Keep a cheerful outlook.	Use any stress you may be experiencing in a positive way to help you set and achieve your goals. Remember that your career search is a process, and it is important to stay optimistic and focused.
Find ways to relieve stress.	When you feel overwhelmed, try taking deep breaths or taking a short break to focus on something else. This can help you clear your mind and feel more refreshed.
Discuss your problems.	Sometimes it can be helpful to talk to a trusted friend, family member, or counselor about your stressors and concerns. They may have a unique perspective and be able to offer advice or support.
Cooperate with others.	When working with others, try to approach conflicts with a spirit of compromise rather than confrontation. This can help you avoid unnecessary stress and anxiety.
Manage your time well.	Make a list of all your tasks and prioritize them based on their importance. Try to tackle the most urgent tasks first and check them off as you complete them. This can help you feel more organized and in control.
Know your limits.	It is important to recognize when a problem may be beyond your control and to practice acceptance until you can find a solution. This can help you avoid feeling overwhelmed or helpless.
Take time to relax and have fun.	Remember to take breaks and engage in activities that you enjoy. This can help you recharge your batteries and feel more balanced and fulfilled.

Goodheart-Willcox Publisher

Summary

4.1 State ways a job seeker can create and maintain a positive online presence.
A positive online presence can be established through the creation of well-written articles or blog posts, a professional portfolio, or memberships to professional networking sites.

4.2 Explain the importance of a professional e-mail account.
A professional e-mail account is essential so a person can keep professional activities separate from personal activities. Most businesses use e-mail for employment-related communication. A professional e-mail address that contains or reflects the applicant's legal name is expected by an employer. An unprofessional e-mail address could be eliminated at the beginning of the application process.

4.3 Describe how a LinkedIn account can be used in the job-search process.
LinkedIn is a professional social networking site that allows job applicants and companies to communicate. It offers applicants space for creating a profile to showcase their skills, work experience, education, and other important qualifications to help them seem viable as a job candidate. It also offers companies space to post jobs that may not be advertised publicly. Staying active and updated on LinkedIn can not only help people network with others in their industry, but also find new employment.

4.4 Describe how a Twitter account can be used in the job-search process.
Twitter is an online news and social networking site on which users can communicate with their followers in real time. Often, employers will post job openings to their Twitter feeds before posting to a publicly accessible job-search website. Users can search hashtags such as #careers and #jobpostings to find recent employment opportunities that have been posted to the website.

4.5 Describe the use of Instagram as a job-search tool.
Instagram is an online mobile-centric, media-sharing site that allows users to share pictures and videos publicly or privately. When used correctly, Instagram can enhance a person's credibility as a potential employee by offering proof of abilities through photos and videos. Users can also search for businesses on Instagram. By following companies of interest and engaging with their content, users may be able to learn about job opportunities.

4.6 Explain the importance of positive thinking during the job-search process.
It is important to stay positive during the job-searching journey. Job seekers should focus on their capabilities and qualifications. There are many online tools available to help communicate and demonstrate one's positive qualities to make a good impression on prospective employers. Practicing positive self-talk, while learning to avoid or ignore negative self-talk, is key for an individual to maintain an optimistic outlook.

Glossary Terms

connection
follower
hashtag
microblog
networking

online presence
profile
search engine optimization (SEO)

secure password
self-talk
signature block

Review

1. Explain the importance of a professional online presence. (4.1)

2. List and explain the steps to create a professional e-mail account. (4.2)

3. Explain the importance of networking during a job search. (4.3)

4. Why is search engine optimization an important aspect of LinkedIn? (4.3)

5. List tips for creating a LinkedIn profile. (4.3)

6. Differentiate three types of connections on LinkedIn. (4.3)

7. What is a hashtag and how is it used in Twitter? (4.4)

8. How can Twitter be used in the job-search process? (4.4)

9. How can Instagram be used as a career self-promotion tool? (4.5)

10. Evaluate the importance of positive thinking during the job-search process. (4.6)

Application

1. When considering you for a job, why do you think it is appropriate for potential employers to take into account what they read about you online? Where might an employer look online to learn more about you? (4.1)

2. How do you manage your online presence across multiple platforms, such as a website, LinkedIn, Twitter, and Instagram? (4.1)

Chapter 4   Managing Your Online Presence

3. Create a list of characteristics that most employers would consider negative online presence and explain your reasoning for each. (4.1)

_____

_____

_____

4. What should you consider when creating a suitable e-mail address for professional communication? (4.2)

_____

_____

_____

5. What elements did you add when you created a signature block for your e-mail account? How does your signature block strengthen you as a job candidate? (4.2)

_____

_____

_____

6. Search for jobs in your field using the search feature in LinkedIn. Notice that some of the same words are used in job posts from different employers. List ten of these repeated words that could be important in your job search. (4.3)

_____

_____

_____

7. Search for LinkedIn profiles of people you know. What ideas did you gain for your own profile? (4.3)

_____

_____

_____

8. How can you use Twitter to promote your personal brand? (4.4)

_____

_____

_____

9. How can you use Instagram to visually showcase your work, build a professional brand, and engage with potential employers and recruiters in your field? (4.5)

___

10. Explain how you practice positive self-talk in situations that could be perceived as negative. How can this improve your chances of success when looking for a job? (4.6)

___

CONNECT TO YOUR CAREER
Workplace Connection

4-1 Online Presence

Enter your name in the following search engines: Google, Bing, and DuckDuckGo. If you find you have a shared online presence, try entering your name and city to narrow the results.

1. What was displayed when you entered your name? Record the top three entries for each search engine.

Google

___

Bing

___

DuckDuckGo

___

2. Search engines do not always display the same results. Compare and contrast your findings from each search engine. What information is the same from one search engine to the next? What information is different?

   Similar Information:

   _____

   _____

   Different Information:

   _____

   _____

3. An interviewer may visit social media profiles of job seekers to find information. What type of information or photos should be removed or changed before the interviewing process begins?

   _____

   _____

4-2 Professional E-mail Account

If you have not already done so, create a professional e-mail account. Once an account is established, read the Terms of Service. If you already have an account, visit the website and read the terms again.

1. What did you learn about the Terms of Service for your e-mail account?

   _____

   _____

2. Since many users never read the Terms of Service, they do not know that e-mail is owned by the host company. Potentially, the e-mail provider can read or track communication sent and received without the user's permission. Do you think this is a violation of privacy? Why or why not?

   _____

   _____

4-3 LinkedIn Account

If you have not already done so, create a LinkedIn account. If you already have an account, revisit the items below and make improvements as needed to ensure your profile accurately represents you.

1. Create a LinkedIn headline, including your full name, title, location, and industry. If you do not have a permanent position, write a title that succinctly describes your skills. You may choose to include your brand statement. Write your headline in the space provided.

   _____

   _____

   _____

2. Complete the other sections of the profile. Make certain your profile is 100 percent complete. Did you have problems completing any of the sections? If so, explain why.

_____

_____

_____

3. LinkedIn automatically creates a URL for your profile. Customize the link to fit your needs and write the URL in the space provided.

_____

4-4 Twitter Account

If you have not already done so, create a Twitter account. If you already have an account, revisit the items below and make improvements as needed to ensure your profile reflects your personal brand.

1. Write your chosen username for your professional Twitter account here.

_____

2. Create a bio for your Twitter account in the space provided. It should be a professional description. Consider including your personal brand statement. Keep in mind you can only have 160 characters.

_____

_____

_____

3. What will you tweet about to look for employment? What hashtags do you plan to use?

_____

_____

_____

4-5 Instagram Activity

If you have not already done so, create an Instagram account. Remember to upload a professional photo and create a bio. Then, work in small groups to review each other's Instagram accounts and provide feedback. Consider whether the account presents a professional image.

1. Based on the feedback, list the top three most helpful tips you received about your Instagram account.

_____

_____

_____

Chapter 4   Managing Your Online Presence

2. What did you learn by looking at other group members' Instagram accounts?

___

3. Describe any updates you will make to your Instagram account.

___

4-6 Positive Thinking

Positive thinking improves mental and physical health. It is a skill that can be practiced and developed over time. For this activity, work in small groups to practice your positive thinking skills.

1. Brainstorm negative thoughts individuals might experience as they start the job-search process. For example, job seekers may think, "I'll never find a job." As a group, select and list three negative thoughts.

___

2. Apply a positive interpretation to the three negative thoughts selected. For example, if the negative thought is "I'll never find a job," a more positive interpretation could be "I may not have found a job yet, but I have skills and experience that are valuable."

___

3. As a team, list five tips individuals can follow to actively practice positive thinking, such as writing down three things to be grateful for each day.

___

CHAPTER 5
Networking for Your Career

Learning Outcomes

5.1 **Discuss** the importance of professional networking.

5.2 **Describe** important etiquette necessary while networking.

5.3 **Define** *professional reference*.

CONNECT TO YOUR CAREER

Workplace Connection

5-1 Business Card or Contact Information

5-2 Your Professional Network

OVERVIEW

Networking is a term used frequently in the workplace to describe the action of talking with people and establishing professional relationships. Anytime people interact, they are networking. It can happen virtually anywhere: in an office, on a train, or at a conference. Expanding your list of professional contacts who may be able to assist you in advancing your career is an important element in a job search. Sometimes, who you know can be just as important, if not more, than what you know.

Networking for your career can be done formally by attending meetings or events or informally through conversations with someone you meet at work or at a social event. These professional relationships can also be established through e-mail communication or through professional social media accounts. *Any communication that leads to career discussions can yield a new member of your professional network.*

Mike Flippo/Shutterstock.com

5.1 Professional Networking

As you begin your job-search process, you will find that the more people you know, the greater your odds will be for finding job leads. *Networking* is talking with people and establishing relationships that can lead to potential career or job opportunities. You probably already have a personal network that includes your friends and family. These are the people with whom you socialize and build personal relationships.

As you begin your career, you will develop a professional network. A **professional network** consists of people who support an individual in career and other business endeavors. Consider asking the career development director at your school or your favorite instructor to be part of your professional network. These people have come to know you during your formal education. Through your interactions with them, they may have become mentors or other respected sources of advice. Call on these individuals to help guide you through the career-search process.

Networking requires confidence and the ability to market oneself. Tentativeness is a networking obstacle. When others ask, let them know your career goals. This may lead to an opportunity to share your career-search activities. When stating your career goals, clearly communicate your skills and expertise, as well. Clear and concise self-promotion is critical for professional networking. There is no value in networking with others if they are unclear about your career potential and goals.

Networking can help you find jobs that may not be advertised to the public. Knowing someone at a company who has information about a job opening can lead to contact with a hiring manager. A person in your professional network may help you get an interview or give you good advice about a company that may lead to a job opportunity.

Conducting informational interviews is an important networking activity that can provide insight into your profession. **Informational interviewing** is a strategy used to interview and ask for advice and direction from a professional, rather than asking for a job opportunity. This can lead to networking opportunities and better prepare you for the job-search process. By talking with someone in your desired field, you can learn more about what is expected, types of jobs available, and other inside information about an industry.

Resist becoming a self-centered networker that only *receives* information. Networking involves supporting others. Therefore, your support and assistance should be reciprocated when possible. Self-centered networkers face the chance of being rejected. Networking begins at the pre-career stage and becomes a permanent part of socialization throughout your career. Your network will evolve and might include thousands of individuals over your lifetime.

Face-to-Face Networking

Face-to-face networking can begin anywhere you meet with individuals or groups of people. An opportunity to connect with someone who can share information that may help you in your career should never be discounted. Informal opportunities might start with people in your social network. By initiating a conversation about career topics, you may find that you are connected by a mutual friend to someone who may eventually become part of your professional network.

Business cards are a valuable tool for networking and promoting your business. They provide a tangible way for individuals to remember your name, contact information, and company details. They can serve as a reminder of your conversation and can be easily shared with others. Business cards can also help establish credibility and professionalism, making them an essential part of any business's marketing strategy.

An example of a traditional business card is shown in **Figure 5-1**. Your full name should be placed on the first line, followed by a job title that describes your skills, such as *Master Chef*. Without a title, the person to whom you give the business card may not remember the field or type of position in which you are interested. The job title is followed by a phone number and e-mail address. To protect your personal information, avoid including a physical address. If you have a LinkedIn account, the URL for your page should be included, as well. In addition, you might choose to use your personal branding statement.

FIGURE 5-1

A business card should include important contact information.

Betty Hernandez
Master Chef
(605) 555-3462 | b.hernandez@e-mail.com
www.linkedin.com/in/bettyhernandez
www.hernandezinstruction.com

An experienced chef with a passion for creating outstanding food.

Goodheart-Willcox Publisher

Workplace Skills

Protocol is customs or rules of etiquette. *Etiquette* is the art of using good manners and polite behavior in any situation. *Business etiquette* is applying good manners in the workplace. It requires employees to show respect and courtesy when interacting with coworkers, customers, clients, or other business contacts. Employees who do not follow protocol or practice etiquette are often not employed very long.

There are several alternatives to traditional professional business cards that you might consider:
1. **Digital business cards:** These are electronic versions of traditional business cards that can be shared via e-mail, text, or social media. They often include links to your website, LinkedIn profile, and other online profiles.
2. **QR codes:** QR (Quick Response) codes are a type of barcode that can be scanned with a smartphone to access information or a website. You can create a QR code that links to your digital business card or other online profiles.
3. **Video business cards:** These are short, personalized video messages that can be shared online. They can be a fun and engaging way to introduce yourself and share your contact information.
4. **Social media profiles:** Many professionals now use their social media profiles (e.g., LinkedIn, Twitter, Instagram) as a primary way to share their contact information and connect with others.

Ultimately, the best alternative to a traditional business card will depend on your needs and preferences, as well as the expectations of your industry and target audience.

Online Networking

Networking is not limited to face-to-face opportunities. Online networking refers to the use of the Internet to connect with other people, both professionally and personally. This can take many forms, such as social media platforms, professional networking sites, and online forums. Online networking has become increasingly popular in recent years, as more and more people have access to the Internet and the number of online platforms grows.

There are many benefits to online networking, both for individuals and for businesses. Perhaps the most obvious benefit is that it allows people to connect with others from all over the world. This is particularly useful for professionals who want to expand their network beyond their immediate geographic area. For example, a freelance writer in the United States might connect with an editor in the United Kingdom, or a startup founder in India might connect with a potential investor in Silicon Valley.

Another benefit of online networking is that it allows people to connect with others who share similar interests or are working in similar fields. This can be especially useful for people who are looking to learn more about a particular industry or profession, or for those who are looking to collaborate on a project. For example, a graphic designer might connect with other designers on a social media platform to share tips and tricks, or a software developer might join an online forum to discuss the latest programming languages and tools.

Online networking can also be a great way for businesses to promote their products or services. By creating a profile on a professional networking site or social media platform, a business can connect with potential customers and partners from all over the world. This can be especially useful for small businesses or startups that might not have the resources to invest in traditional marketing or advertising campaigns.

Online networking is a powerful tool that allows individuals and businesses to connect with others from all over the world. Whether you are looking to expand your professional network, learn more about a particular industry or profession, promote your products or services, or stay in touch with friends and family, online networking has something to offer. By leveraging the power of the Internet, you can make valuable connections, gain new knowledge, and create new opportunities for yourself and your business.

5.2 Networking Etiquette

Etiquette is the art of using good manners in any situation. There are rules of networking etiquette that should be followed, both in person and online. Your professional reputation will be molded by the way you treat others.

Connect to Your Community

Connecting to community events is a great way for you to expand your social circle, gain valuable experience, and potentially find new opportunities. One effective way to connect is to start by researching local events and organizations that align with your interests. This can be done through social media, university bulletin boards, or community websites. Attending or participating in these events and introducing yourself to other attendees can lead to making new connections and possibly even finding mentorship opportunities. Another option is to get involved in on-campus clubs and organizations, which provide a space to meet like-minded individuals and develop skills outside of the classroom. Additionally, attending career fairs and networking events can help you build relationships with professionals in your field of interest. By actively seeking out these opportunities and being open to new experiences, you can begin building your professional network.

TZIDO SUN/Shutterstock.com

Respect is an important part of networking etiquette. When you are reaching out to connect with others, invite people with whom you are familiar. If you want to extend an invitation to others you do not know but who have similar interests or connections, include a message stating why you would like to add them to your network.

When networking, try to be brief and polite. It is considered rude to dominate a person's time with long conversations either in person or online. Remember, you are making an impression with a person who can potentially help build your career.

It is acceptable to let others know that you are seeking employment, but remain sensitive to each person's reaction when you do so. If a person does not respond offering a known job opportunity, quickly close the topic with a phrase such as, "If you hear of anything, please let me know," and move the conversation in a new direction. If a person responds positively, it is acceptable to send an e-mail that reminds the contact of the details of the conversation and include your résumé.

In-Person Etiquette

On the day you will be meeting with a person who could become a member of your network, select attire that will match the appropriate dress code for the appointment and company while reflecting who you are as a professional. It is acceptable to arrive early for a meeting, but no more than 15 minutes prior to your scheduled meeting time. It is not acceptable to arrive late. Plan to come to the meeting alone; bringing an uninvited guest is considered unprofessional. If you rely on someone else for transportation, instruct the person to wait in the vehicle for the duration of your visit.

Prior to entering the building, mobile devices should be silenced or turned off and placed out of sight. Maintaining eye contact is important not only during the handshake, but throughout the rest of the meeting. A lack of eye contact can make you seem rude and uninterested.

During conversation, good communication skills should be used. This means avoiding slang or unprofessional language. You should not monopolize the conversation. It is important to demonstrate your interest not only in the job and information, but also in the person with whom you are talking. Your focus and attention should be on the person and what is being said.

When the meeting has ended, offer one of your business cards, and ask for one in return. It is a good idea to make notes on each business card you have collected. These notes can be as simple as a physical feature or detail you learned about the person, or they can consist of what a typical day in that position entails. Before leaving, initiate another handshake if socially acceptable and thank your networking contact for meeting with you.

A follow-up e-mail should be sent thanking the person for their time. This reinforces your professionalism and acknowledges the conversation you have had. It will also keep your name on the radar of the people with whom you met, which could potentially lead to further networking or career opportunities.

Career Persona

Culinary Professional

Responsibilities

Culinary professionals are responsible for preparing and cooking food according to recipes, menu plans, and customer preferences. They work in a variety of settings, including restaurants, hotels, catering companies, and institutional settings such as schools and hospitals. Culinary professionals must:

Puchong art/Shutterstock.com

- Use a variety of kitchen and cooking equipment
- Enforce food safety regulations, such as proper storage and handling of food, to ensure the safety of customers and staff
- Collaborate with other culinary professionals, such as chefs and bakers, to create new dishes and menus
- Continuously develop culinary skills and research new techniques and ingredients to keep up with the latest culinary trends
- Maintain the kitchen equipment and facilities, including overseeing the cleaning and sanitation of the kitchen area

Qualities and Skills

A culinary professional is someone who is trained in the art and science of cooking. To be successful in this field, they should have certain qualities and skills, including:

- *Creativity:* A chef must have a creative mind and a passion for experimenting with different ingredients, flavors, and cooking techniques to create unique and delicious dishes.
- *Attention to detail:* In the kitchen, every detail matters, from the way ingredients are cut and arranged to the final presentation of a dish. A chef must be meticulous to ensure consistent quality and presentation.
- *Physical stamina:* Cooking can be a physically demanding job, and a chef must have the endurance to stand for long hours, lift heavy pots and pans, and handle hot and sharp kitchen equipment.
- *Knowledge of food and cooking techniques:* A chef must have a deep understanding of various cooking techniques, ingredients, and cuisines, and be able to apply that knowledge to create delicious and visually appealing dishes.
- *Time-management skills:* A busy kitchen is a fast-paced environment, and a chef must be able to manage time effectively to ensure that all dishes are prepared and served on time.

Education

- Formal culinary education
- Apprenticeship or on-the-job training
- Work Experience

Next Steps

For those who want to enter the culinary world, it is important to complete a culinary education program. Students can also seek out part-time job opportunities to gain on-the-job experience in a professional kitchen. Culinary professionals often must spend years working in kitchens to advance to head cook positions. Students can continue their education and obtain professional certifications offered by the American Culinary Federation. For example, certifications are offered for various levels of chefs, such as sous-chefs and executive chefs.

CONNECT TO YOUR CAREER

Complete 5-1 Business Card or Contact Information, pg. 85

Online Etiquette

Etiquette is as equally important for online communication as it is for face-to-face contact. Positive, professional communication leads to positive online networking experiences. Writing negative posts that rant or vent about an individual or company is ill-advised. If you are communicating via e-mail, follow the rules of grammar and proper formatting. Negative or poorly written online communication could influence a potential hiring manager to eliminate you as a job candidate.

People value their time, and professional networking is no exception. It is appropriate to send e-mails asking for job-search strategies or leads. However, do not flood a person's account with comments, questions, and other communication. One or two skillfully worded questions or comments spread over a period of time are enough to grab someone's attention. When a person does not reply immediately, it is best not to persist. It may be a matter of time before a response is received. However, lack of communication may imply that they are not interested in communicating. If one person does not reply, find someone else who can be beneficial.

Although networking online can provide many new insights into the careers of people, remember to respect their privacy. Sending unsolicited e-mails, connection requests on LinkedIn, and other online communications to people you do not know could be perceived as spam. If there is a person you do not know but want to add to your network, send a note that provides a good reason to connect. Another option is to ask for an introduction from someone in your network who knows that person.

5.3 Professional References

A **professional reference** is a person who knows an individual's skills, talents, or personal traits and is willing to provide a recommendation. These are people who can comment on your qualifications, work ethic, and personal qualities, as well as the work-related aspects of your character. This could include past supervisors, colleagues, or clients. It's also important to have a diverse group of references, because having a variety of perspectives can add credibility to your references. Having a list of three to five professional references is recommended.

When submitting a list of professional references, create a document and add your name and the phrase *Professional References*. List each person and their contact information, as shown in **Figure 5-2.** By creating a strong group of professional references, you will be able to demonstrate your qualifications and credibility to potential employers or clients and help increase your chances of success in your career.

When searching for potential references, there are some guidelines and tips you should follow:

1. *Choose people who know your work well.* It is important to choose people who can speak to your skills and experience in a meaningful way. Consider selecting people who you have worked with closely, such as supervisors, colleagues, or clients.
2. *Seek permission.* Before listing others as a reference, be sure to ask for their permission and provide them with a copy of your résumé or a summary of your work history. This will help them to be better prepared to speak about your qualifications.
3. *Provide contact information.* Be sure to provide potential employers with the name, job title, organization, phone number, and e-mail address of each of your references.
4. *Let your references know what to expect.* Inform your references of the specific position or opportunity for which you are applying and provide them with any relevant information or materials (e.g., the job description, your résumé).
5. *Thank your references.* Be sure to thank your references for their time and assistance. This could be as simple as sending a thank-you note or e-mail.

It is helpful to create a spreadsheet of people you meet and note whether they are part of your professional network. For those whom you consider to be in your network, note each person's name, contact information, industry, date you met, and any other important information. Also include whether this person can be used as a reference. This will make it easy to tailor your résumé and references each time you submit them. Your spreadsheet should be updated regularly to reflect changes in your network. Consider saving your spreadsheet with a cloud-based storage service; that way you can access it from your mobile device whenever you have an Internet connection.

CONNECT TO YOUR CAREER

Complete 5-2 Your Professional Network, pg. 86

FIGURE 5-2

Creating professional references is an important step in building a strong personal brand and establishing credibility in your industry.

Francis Massuro
Professional References
(218) 555-1234
fmassuro@e-mail.com
www.linkedin.com/in/fmassuro

Joan Lawrence, Executive Director
Village Plus Corporation
139 South Broad Street
Madison, WI 53558
(608) 555-8792
joan_lawrence@villageplus.com

Bryon Thornton, Public Relations Specialist
Chem-Rite
2020 Main Street
Bemidji, MN 56601
(218) 555-0784
bthornton@chemrite.org

Jason Akiyama, Research Associate
Vivalab Industries
47 Euclid Avenue
St. Cloud, MN 56301
(320) 555-0516
akiyama@vivalab.com

Cheryl Finley, Copywriter
On-Point Media Specialists
903 Joseph Drive
Duluth, MN 55804
(218) 555-1204
finley@onpoint.com

Goodheart-Willcox Publisher

Summary

5.1 Discuss the importance of professional networking.
Networking is talking with people and establishing relationships that can lead to potential career or job opportunities. A professional network consists of people who support an individual in their career and other business endeavors. Networking can help a person find jobs that may not be advertised to the public. A person in one's network not only may have information about job openings, but also may be able to arrange for an interview.

5.2 Describe important etiquette necessary while networking.
Etiquette is the art of using good manners in any situation. Your professional reputation will be molded by the way you treat others, so the rules of etiquette should be followed when networking in person and online. Arrive on time, silence all mobile devices, use good communication and listening skills, make eye contact, and do not dominate conversations when networking in person. When networking online, respect others' privacy, avoid writing negative posts, and make network connection requests appropriately.

5.3 Define *professional reference*.
A professional reference is someone who knows an applicant's skills, talents, or personal traits and is willing to recommend that individual. References are members of a person's professional network who can vouch for that person's qualifications, work ethic, and personal qualities, as well as work-related aspects of their character.

Glossary Terms

etiquette
informational interviewing
professional network
professional reference

Review

1. Why is professional networking important to a career? (5.1)

2. How can a personal social contact lead to a professional network connection? (5.1)

3. Describe the differences between networking online and networking in person. (5.1)

4. Explain why acting as a self-centered networker does *not* help your career. (5.1)

5. How do business cards support networking and demonstrate in-person etiquette? (5.1, 5.2)

6. Why is etiquette important when networking? (5.2)

7. Describe appropriate networking etiquette when meeting with someone in person. (5.2)

8. What are some behaviors that are *not* acceptable when networking online? (5.2)

9. Why is it important to have a list of professional references? (5.3)

10. How can you generate a list of professional references? (5.3)

Application

1. How can you ensure that you are dressed appropriately for networking events? (5.1)

2. What is the best way to introduce yourself at networking events? (5.1)

3. How do you show respect for others' time and attention when networking? (5.1)

4. How would you follow up with someone you met while networking? (5.1)

5. Consider the traditional business card and the alternatives to a business card discussed in the text. Which method would you prefer to use when networking? Explain your answer. (5.1)

6. Make a list of events that you might attend in the next few weeks that would be beneficial for networking. Why did you select these activities? (5.1)

_____

_____

_____

_____

7. Explain your strategy for networking online. (5.1)

_____

_____

_____

_____

8. Recall a situation in which you met someone in your industry who did not follow professional etiquette. What was your impression of this person? (5.2)

_____

_____

_____

_____

9. What are some reasons why you should consider tailoring your list of professional references, depending on the job for which you are applying? (5.3)

_____

_____

_____

_____

10. How would you choose people to be professional references for you? (5.3)

_____

_____

_____

_____

CONNECT TO YOUR CAREER
Workplace Connection

5-1 Business Card or Contact Information

1. Conduct an Internet search using the industry in which you work or would like to work and the phrase *business cards or business card alternatives*. For example, if you work in hospitality, type the phrase *hospitality business cards*. Review the results. Note any common design elements or specific information.

   _____
   _____
   _____
   _____

2. Record the information you will include on your business card. Include your full name, job title, phone number, e-mail address, LinkedIn URL, and other important information.

   _____
   _____
   _____
   _____

3. Once you have recorded all information to be included on your business card, you must determine how it should be presented. In the space provided, sketch a design concept for your business card.

4. Describe your plan for publishing your contact information. Remember that you may be networking in person as well as online.

_____
_____
_____
_____

5-2 Your Professional Network

As you begin your career search, there will be many face-to-face networking opportunities. To make the most of these opportunities, you should be prepared. Work with a partner to complete this activity to practice your networking skills. Follow the steps below.

1. Create a networking scenario, such as a networking event at a career fair or an industry trade show, an informational interview with a professional, or some other situation.

2. Practice your networking etiquette with your partner. Each partner will assume the role of either the job seeker or the professional contact and act out the scenario Think about how you would greet the person, the ways to maintain a professional conversation, and how to end your interaction.

3. Present your scenario to the class. Have the class give feedback on your performance, focusing on areas such as the use of proper networking etiquette, effective communication, and overall confidence. List helpful feedback shared by your classmates for all group presentations.

_____
_____
_____
_____
_____
_____
_____
_____
_____
_____
_____

CHAPTER 6

Protecting Your Identity

Learning Outcomes

6.1 **Define** identity theft.

6.2 **Explain** how to recognize and report employment scams.

6.3 **Identify** potential risks that can be encountered when using the Internet.

6.4 **Define** malware and list examples.

6.5 **Summarize** how to create and maintain a security plan.

CONNECT TO YOUR CAREER

Workplace Connection

6-1 Identity Theft
6-2 Employment Scams
6-3 Malware

OVERVIEW

The job-search process can take place almost exclusively online. As you establish and refine your online presence, it is important to know how to stay safe on the Internet. You must be aware of the ways in which you can prevent your identity from being stolen. In simple terms, do not provide private information to people you do not know.

Limiting the amount of personal information you post online is only half of the battle. You should also be wary of employment scams, which may seem harmless at first. Furthermore, understanding the types of malware that exist to jeopardize your computer and the data that is stored on it is increasingly important in today's society. Create, maintain, and, most importantly, use a security plan to protect yourself, your identity, and your computer.

Inspiring/Shutterstock.com

Copyright Goodheart-Willcox Co., Inc.

6.1 Identity Theft

Identity theft is an illegal act that involves stealing someone's personal information and using that information to commit theft or fraud. Each time you connect to the Internet, there is a risk that your computer or mobile device can be hacked and your identity stolen.

During the job-search process, it is especially important to be diligent in protecting your privacy. Avoid being lulled into a false sense of security when communicating with others, especially with those whom you do not know personally. This includes communication via phone calls, e-mail, and social media.

Use caution and common sense when posting information to sites with which you have registered an account. Determine which personal details are appropriate and safe to share with strangers and resist the urge to share too much information. For example, rather than listing a personal address on application forms or e-mail, provide your professional e-mail address as contact information.

While it may seem harmless to post information such as your date of birth to your social media accounts, you may be potentially setting yourself up for identity theft. If someone manages to bypass the security of these sites, your date of birth can be stolen.

If a job application includes a field for a Social Security number, place all zeros in the spaces provided. You are *not* under obligation to provide this information anywhere when searching or applying for a job.

If you suspect your identity has been stolen, visit the Federal Trade Commission website for guidance (www.identitytheft.gov). Time is of the essence, so if this happens to you, act immediately.

CONNECT TO YOUR CAREER

Complete 6-1 Identity Theft, pg. 99

6.2 Employment Scams

When you begin to apply for jobs online, you will visit many websites that are unfamiliar. While most of the sites will be legitimate, some might be designed to gain personal information for the purposes of compromising your identity. Those who are trying to commit identity theft have mastered the art of creating fake job ads to lure visitors to their websites.

If you post your résumé on a website, there is a chance you will receive unsolicited e-mails from companies

---

Time Management

Productivity

Finding ways to be productive can be as easy as reaching for your mobile device. Smartphones can be great time-management tools. Many smartphones come with built-in apps that can help you with the following tasks:

- *Scheduling:* Calendar apps allow you to schedule appointments, set reminders, and create to-do lists, making it easier to plan your day or week. Using your mobile phone to organize and prioritize tasks helps you stay on top of things.

- *Tracking time:* There are a variety of time-tracking apps available for smartphones that can help you monitor how you spend your time and identify areas where you may be able to improve your productivity.

- *Avoiding distractions:* Constant notifications from social media, e-mail, and other apps can be major distractions. Consider turning off notifications for nonessential apps during work hours. Blocking distracting websites during specific times of the day can help you stay focused on your work. The "Do Not Disturb" feature on your phone can silence all notifications and calls, giving you a distraction-free environment.

- *Taking notes:* A note-taking app can help you capture ideas and thoughts as they come to you, so you don't forget them later.

- *Taking breaks:* It is important to take regular breaks to rest your eyes and clear your mind. Use your phone's timer or alarm to remind you to take a break.

Next time you need help managing your time, consider the many time-saving apps available on your smartphone.

asking you to apply for a job. To protect your privacy, research the company to make sure the posting is legitimate before responding.

Recognizing Employment Scams

There are multiple signs that indicate an employment scam, starting with the e-mail address listed on a job advertisement. For example, if the ad claims to be from a corporation but the contact e-mail address is a Yahoo address, something is wrong. Companies typically have their own URL that is a part of the e-mail address.

Another way to identify fraudulent employment advertising is to look for misspelled words and grammatical errors in the listings. Reputable companies sometimes make errors, but fraudulent advertisements are known for poorly written content. If a job advertisement contains a high number of spelling or grammatical mistakes, chances are it is not legitimate.

One common type of employment fraud happens when criminals create fake employment ads and contact people using information they find online in résumés. After contact has been made, the applicant is informed that, in order to proceed with employment, the company needs to set up a direct-deposit account. Unfortunately, many unsuspecting people provide bank or PayPal account numbers, convinced they are dealing with a legitimate company. Criminals use many variations in payment-forwarding scams. Never provide any bank account or payment information in preparation to obtain a job.

Under no circumstances should an applicant pay a potential employer. Legitimate companies do *not* request payment of any kind during the application process. However, a fraudulent company might insist that you pay for a background check or pay fees related to the application process. The request may include asking for a credit card number to cover these fees. An applicant should never pay for an interview or for any portion of employment verification. Beware of anyone who requests a credit card during an application process.

Carefully evaluate job advertisements to determine whether they are legitimate. Job ads that make grandiose claims are usually not genuine. Avoid any job posting that advertises making large amounts of money for little work or over a short period of time. A good rule of thumb to remember is that if the job seems too good to be true, it probably is.

It is easy to become distracted when finding the perfect job advertisement on a website. Before you start submitting personal information, slow down and investigate the site. A legitimate website will list a physical address and additional information about the business. If you are unfamiliar with the organization, search for its name online, and evaluate what you find. Sometimes, conducting a search for the name of the business plus the word "scam" can reveal whether the business is legitimate.

The *Better Business Bureau (BBB)* is a nationwide, nonprofit agency dedicated to providing free business reliability reviews. The BBB gives businesses a rating of A+ through F. If you have suspicions about a company, you can check its rating with the BBB. It is possible that other people have also had negative experiences with the same company in the past. As a result, its rating can reveal whether you should get involved with the company.

Reporting Employment Scams

If you encounter a suspicious business or website when searching for jobs online or are the victim of an employment scam, report the incident immediately. Reporting the incident helps law enforcement track down scammers and thieves. There are several agencies that are dedicated to the protection of job seekers from such scams.

The *Internet Crime Complaint Center (IC3)* is a government organization that was established as a means to receive complaints of Internet-based crimes and report them to the appropriate local, state, or federal law enforcement agency. The IC3 is a partnership between the Federal Bureau of Investigation (FBI) and the National White Collar Crime Center (NW3C).

Another federal organization that handles claims of online scams is the *Federal Trade Commission (FTC)*, which is a government agency that focuses on consumer protection. The FTC addresses complaints regarding identity theft, business practices, work-at-home cons, and job scams, among others.

The Best App for That

Google Drive

Google Drive is a cloud-based file storage service offered by Google to Google account holders. Google Drive allows users to store, synchronize, and share files across devices and platforms. The app enables you to store résumés, cover letters, portfolio materials, and other important employment documentation in your Drive. Each file is available on your mobile device when you are away from your computer and need it. Account holders are given 15 gigabytes of free storage with the option of purchasing additional storage plans.

CONNECT TO YOUR CAREER

Complete 6-2 Employment Scams, pg. 100

6.3 Internet Usage

Each time you access a search engine or visit a web page, your computer's identity is revealed. Your name might not be visible to the public, but the computer's Internet protocol (IP) address is shown. The **Internet protocol address**, known as an *IP address*, is a number used to identify an electronic device connected to the Internet. While your personal information, such as your name and address, cannot be easily discovered, an IP address can reveal your approximate geographic location based on your Internet service provider. Any e-mails you send from your computer or mobile devices have that device's respective IP address attached to them, so use caution when doing so.

One way to protect your online identity is to ensure that you are only transmitting data over secure web pages. Before uploading documents to a website, ensure the site is secure by checking that the URL begins with https. The *s* stands for secure. This is not 100 percent foolproof, but generally is a sign of protection. Secure websites may also display an icon, such as a padlock symbol, somewhere in the browser to indicate the communication is secure. Be wary of uploading applications, résumés, cover letters, or any material that contains personal information to sites that do not display such protection.

In general, it is a good idea to avoid public Wi-Fi hotspots. While convenient, these networks are generally not secure and put your computer devices at risk for being hacked, therefore inadvertently exposing data. Hackers are able to create "fake" hotspots in locations where free or paid public Wi-Fi exists. For example, a hacker could create a local Wi-Fi hotspot from the parking lot of a restaurant and use the name of the restaurant as the name of the network. Patrons then unknowingly connect to the fake network, which allows the hacker access to any data being transmitted over that connection.

The Wi-Fi signal with the best strength may not always be a legitimate hotspot. An easy way to avoid fake hotspots is to check with an employee of the business providing the Wi-Fi to get the name of the network and the access key. If a Wi-Fi authentication screen is asking for credit card information, confirm that the Wi-Fi is legitimate. For example, hotels will generally not ask for a credit card number when guests are logging into Wi-Fi, because they already have a card number on file.

Cookies

Cookies are bits of data stored on a computer that record information about the websites a user has visited. Cookies contain information about where you have been on the Internet and the personal information you enter on a website. Some advertisers place them onto your computer without your knowledge or consent. Most cookies are from legitimate websites and will not harm your computer. Marketers use the information for research and selling purposes. However, if a hacker gains access to the cookies stored on your computer, you could be at risk. Cookies are encrypted by the sites that place them on your computer, but if they are decrypted, they can be used to steal personal information you have entered on a website, such as credit card numbers. Cookies also can be used to target you for a scam based on your Internet history.

As a precaution, there are ways to protect your computer from cookie-based attacks. One way is to opt out of accepting them. Some Internet browsers allow you to change your system settings to either *accept* or *never accept* cookies. This may be referred to as *incognito* or *private browsing* mode. Check your browser for specific instructions. Some websites will require a user to allow cookies in order to view the website. In this situation, the browser settings can be configured to temporarily accept cookies or accept cookies only from a list of approved websites.

Another way to protect your computer is to delete cookies. Depending on the version of the browser, you may be able to select an option in the **Settings** menu that will automatically delete the cookies on a regular basis or each time the browser is closed. Still another way to remove them is to run a disk cleanup on your computer.

In addition to cookies, temporary files containing information about the websites you have recently visited are stored on your computer. These files slow down your computer system, and they can potentially put you at risk. To delete temporary files, go to your **Settings** menu to clear your browsing history or data.

Session Hijacking

Session hijacking occurs when an unauthorized person takes control of a user's computer to monitor Internet sessions privately. It is also called *cookie hijacking*. If successful, a hacker could gain access to personal information. The user whose computer is being hijacked has no way to detect that a hijacking has occurred. Because one method of hijacking involves the interception of cookies, regularly deleting them from a computer can help prevent it from happening.

Phishing

Phishing is the use of fraudulent e-mails and copies of valid websites to trick people into providing private and confidential personal data. The most common form of phishing is done by sending a fake e-mail to an individual or group of people. The e-mail message looks like it is from a legitimate source, such as an employment agency. The e-mail asks for certain information, such as a Social Security number or bank account information, or it provides a link to a web page. The linked web page looks real, but its sole purpose is to collect private information that is then used to commit fraud. It is important to never open an e-mail attachment that you are not expecting. It is better to send an e-mail asking about the attachment before opening it.

6.4 Malware

Malware, short for *malicious software*, is a term given to software programs that are intended to damage, destroy, or steal data on a computer. The purpose of malware can be to disrupt your productivity, gain access to your personal data, or to compromise your online identity.

Beware of an invitation to click on a website link for more information about a job advertisement. A large percentage of websites contain malware. One click can activate a code, and your computer could be hacked or infected. An illegitimate website may encourage visitors to download applications or templates that contain malware. Malware comes in many forms, including software viruses, adware, spyware, and ransomware.

Software Viruses

A **software virus** is a computer program designed to negatively impact a computer system. A virus may destroy data on the computer, cause programs on the computer to malfunction, or collect information and transmit it to some other location. Viruses can be introduced onto a computer by downloading virus-infected programs from an e-mail or from a website.

Adware

Adware is a form of software that displays or downloads advertisement material automatically without the user's knowledge. While navigating the Internet, you may have an unwanted advertisement that pops up on your screen and interrupts your session. Some of these ads are made in the hopes the user will see it and click on it. This type of advertisement itself is usually harmless to your computer and is no different from a television commercial. However, certain types of adware are programmed to collect data with the consent of a user, which is unknowingly given by clicking on the ad. After you have clicked on it, the advertisement will record specific information, such as your computer's IP address, approximate geographic location, and browsing habits. Some adware even logs keystrokes entered by the user, such as passwords and banking information. This information then goes to the owner of the ad.

The goal of most adware programs is to customize future advertisements to better reach potential consumers. For example, if you click on a travel advertisement, you will notice more travel, airline, car-rental, and hotel advertisements as you browse the Internet. There is a fine line between adware and computer spying. If an advertiser does not notify you that it is gathering information about clicking habits, it is considered spying.

Spyware

Spyware is software that spies on a computer. Spyware can capture information such as Internet activity, e-mail messages and contacts, usernames, passwords, bank account information, and credit card information. Often, affected users will not be aware that spyware is on their computer.

Ransomware

Ransomware is a software program that takes over a computer system and locks it until the owner pays a sum of money to regain control of their computer system. Ransomware can target any computer user, including corporations and governments, as well as personal PC users. Anti-ransomware software protection, similar to other virus-protection software, can be purchased for a computer system to protect users against this threat.

CONNECT TO YOUR CAREER

Complete 6-3 Malware, pg. 100

6.5 Create and Maintain a Security Plan

Fortunately, there are steps you can take to protect yourself while applying for jobs online. If you have any suspicions about communicating with someone or providing your information via a website, do not proceed. Investigate the person or the company with whom you are dealing. You may be able to avoid a scam before it is too late.

Your online identity is yours alone. When your information becomes public, it becomes vulnerable to identity theft. Hackers hope to gain access to personal bank account or credit card numbers, as well as personal information, such as a Social Security number, birth date, or physical address. In order to protect your identity online, a multitiered security plan should be developed. **Figure 6-1** shows a security plan checklist that can be used to develop your own security plan.

Antivirus Software

Virus-protection software, also referred to as *antivirus* or *antimalware* software, can be purchased from a reputable company to help protect a computer. New computer viruses are being created every day, and the only way to ensure your antivirus software will recognize them is to update its database regularly. Once installed, adjust the settings so the software runs on a regular basis, such as every day or once a week. By selecting this option, the software updates itself with the latest virus programs, scans the computer for viruses, and deletes them from the computer. Some antivirus programs perform this function automatically.

Your virus-protection software should also have a firewall. A **firewall** is a program that monitors information coming into a computer and helps ensure only safe information gets through. Firewalls function by following a set of rules that determines what can and cannot pass over a computer network. Think of a firewall as a traffic light; it controls what can safely pass and what gets stopped by the network.

Mobile Security

Mobile devices are not entirely safe from hackers. In fact, as mobile devices become more advanced, they become just as susceptible to malware as desktop and laptop computers. Consider downloading and running antivirus software for your mobile device.

It is also wise to put a plan in place to protect your mobile device from theft. If you become careless and leave it in an unexpected location, your device can be stolen as well as your identity. You may also be stuck with a large phone bill.

Some digital devices have thumbprint readers or retina scanners that allow the owner to unlock the phone with *biometric verification*, or verification by biological traits. Other devices can be protected by creating a passcode. A *passcode* is similar to a password but uses numbers instead of words. An example of a passcode is a banking PIN. This code should be kept in a safe place so that if the unexpected happens, you can contact your service provider. Your provider may be able to track the phone through GPS or remotely delete private information before it is stolen and used maliciously.

You rely heavily on your mobile device, so it is important to guard it against theft and viruses that could disrupt your primary means of communication.

Secure Passwords

Recall the strategies discussed in Chapter 4 for creating secure passwords. Implement these strategies when you create a password for an online account. Passwords are grouped into categories: weak, medium, and strong. **Figure 6-2** describes these three levels of password strength.

To protect your identity while applying for jobs online, remember to do the following:
- Change your passwords often.
- Use at least 10 characters with an unpredictable capitalization, a number, and a symbol.
- Record your passwords on a dedicated hard-copy document to keep track of them and the accounts for which they are used. Include an abbreviation of the account name, the password, and the date that you created the password. Store this document in a secure location. Alternatively, use password manager software to store passwords for online accounts.

FIGURE 6-1

In order to protect your identity, develop a multitiered security plan.

Security Checklist
- ☐ Secure passwords created for computer
- ☐ Secure passwords created for mobile device
- ☐ Password information stored in a safe place
- ☐ Antivirus protection software installed and running
- ☐ Data backup completed
- ☐ Internet browser updated
- ☐ Security settings set to high
- ☐ Windows automatic updates in *on* position
- ☐ Pop-up blocker turned on
- ☐ Suspicious e-mails deleted
- ☐ Unknown links avoided
- ☐ Cookies deleted
- ☐ Firewall turned on
- ☐ Wireless router password set
- ☐ Flash drives checked for viruses before using
- ☐ Automatic wireless connections disabled
- ☐ Free public hotspots avoided
- ☐ Public hotspots or wireless connections used with caution
- ☐ Privacy settings on for social networks

triutamis/Shutterstock.com

Goodheart-Willcox Publisher

FIGURE 6-2

Passwords are grouped into categories: weak, medium, and strong.

Password Strength	
Strength	**Description**
Weak	Contains one easy-to-remember word, uses lowercase letters with no symbols, usually six to eight characters in length
Medium	Contains one uppercase letter in a lowercase word and one number or symbol, usually eight characters in length
Strong	Contains a mixture of uppercase and lowercase random letters, numbers, and symbols and is 10 characters or longer

Goodheart-Willcox Publisher

- Record security questions that you answered to create an account and note how the account system will contact you if you forget your password.

Multifactor Authentication

If given the option, enabling multifactor authentication can help strengthen the security of all your online accounts. **Multifactor authentication** is a process in which a website requires multiple identity verifications before granting access to an account. For example, when logging into a LinkedIn account, you may have to enter a password then retrieve a verification code or one-time password from either an e-mail or text message. Some websites may require you to answer verification questions rather than sending an access code.

Security Settings

Before using the Internet, become acquainted with the security settings and features of your browser. Within the **Settings** menu, locate your web browser's security features. Change your settings to protect your computer and your information. Enabling a *pop-up blocker* prevents your web browser from allowing you to see pop-up ads, which often contain malware.

If your computer or mobile device has a built-in web camera, consider keeping it covered or deactivated when not in use. Even if they are not actively being used, these cameras can be accessed remotely by unauthorized users, essentially gaining access to a live stream of your day-to-day life.

Cloud-Based Backups

An important part of a security plan is backing up the data on your computer. If a virus invades your computer or the hard disk crashes, it may be too late to retrieve your files. Having a backup can prevent losing files.

Creating cloud-based backups refers to the practice of storing and maintaining copies of data on remote servers that are accessible over the Internet. These servers, also known as *cloud storage*, are owned and operated by third-party companies and can be accessed from any location or device with an Internet connection. The main advantage of cloud-based backups is that they provide an off-site location for data storage, which can protect against data loss due to physical disasters such as fires or floods. Additionally, cloud-based backups can be automated, making the process of backing up data more convenient and efficient.

There are several steps you can take to utilize cloud-based backups for your computer files:

1. Sign up for a cloud storage service, such as Google Drive, Dropbox, or Microsoft OneDrive. These services allow you to store files on their servers and access them from any device with an Internet connection.
2. Install the cloud storage software on your computer. This will create a special folder on your computer that is synced with your cloud storage account.
3. Move the files that you want to back up into the cloud storage folder. The files will be automatically uploaded to the cloud and will be available for access from any device.
4. Set up automatic backups. Most cloud storage services allow you to set up automatic backups of specific folders or file types. This way, you don't have to remember to manually upload your files.

It is important to note that while cloud-based backups are a convenient and effective way to protect your data, they are not a replacement for a local backup solution. It is still a good idea to periodically create copies of your important files and store them on an external hard drive or USB drive in case of a disaster.

Career Persona

Carpenter

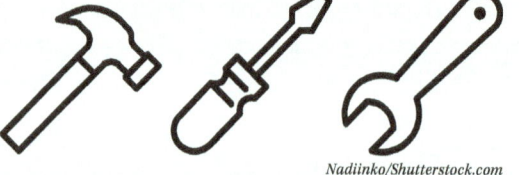
Nadiinko/Shutterstock.com

Responsibilities

Carpenters construct frameworks and structures from wood and other materials. They may work indoors or outdoors while constructing homes, commercial buildings, and even tall structures. The daily tasks for carpenters can vary depending on the specific project they are working on and their specific role and level of experience. Some responsibilities of carpenters include the following:

- Read and interpret blueprints and drawings
- Measure to make accurate cuts
- Use hand and power tools to cut, shape, and join wood and other materials
- Assemble and install structures and fixtures made of wood, such as walls, roofs, and decks
- Inspect and maintain tools and equipment to ensure they are in good working condition

Qualities and Skills

To be a successful carpenter, one should possess the following qualities and skills:

- *Physical dexterity:* Carpentry requires manual dexterity and hand-eye coordination to handle tools and materials with precision.
- *Attention to detail:* Carpentry involves precise measurements and cuts, so it is essential to pay close attention to detail and have an eye for accuracy.
- *Strength and endurance:* Carpentry is a physically demanding job that requires strength and endurance to lift and maneuver heavy materials.
- *Knowledge of building codes and safety regulations:* Carpenters must be knowledgeable about local building codes and safety regulations to ensure their work meets all relevant standards.
- *Familiarity with tools and equipment:* Carpenters must have a thorough understanding of the tools and equipment they use, including hand tools, power tools, and measuring instruments.

Education

- High school diploma or equivalent
- On-the-job training or apprenticeship sponsored by trade unions or contractor associations
- Associate's degree in carpentry from vocational or technical school is optional
- Certifications available, including those from the National Association of the Remodeling Industry and the National Wood Flooring Association

Next Steps

If you are interested in becoming a carpenter, research the field to learn about the different types of carpentry. Taking courses such as mathematics and mechanical drawing can be useful. Attending a technical or vocational school can help future carpenters learn the specific skills and techniques required for the trade. Taking a job as a construction laborer or helper who assists experienced workers provides valuable on-the-job experience with tasks similar to those of carpenters.

Summary

6.1 Define identity theft.
Identity theft is an illegal act that involves stealing someone's personal information and using that information to commit theft or fraud. Common sense should always be used when deciding what information is shared online. An individual's personal address or Social Security number should never be included on online employment forms.

6.2 Explain how to recognize and report employment scams.
There are multiple signs that indicate an employment scam. These signs include an e-mail address that does not have a company URL, poorly written content with misspelled words and grammatical errors, job ads that request payment, and grandiose claims. A good rule of thumb to remember is that if the job seems too good to be true, it probably is. Employment scams should be reported to *Internet Crime Complaint Center (IC3)* or the *Federal Trade Commission (FTC)*.

6.3 Identify potential risks that can be encountered when using the Internet.
Potential risks that can be encountered when using the Internet include transmission of data over unsecure web pages, fake Wi-Fi hotspots, theft of cookies, session hijacking, and phishing.

6.4 Define malware and list examples.
Malware is a term given to software programs that are intended to damage, destroy, or steal data on a computer. Malware comes in many forms, including software viruses, adware, spyware, and ransomware.

6.5 Describe how to create and maintain a security plan.
The creation of a multitiered security plan can help protect a person's identity online. This includes downloading, installing, and running virus-protection and firewall software; setting security parameters on mobile devices; establishing secure passwords; using multifactor authentication; becoming acquainted with security settings of a browser; and regularly backing up a computer.

Glossary Terms

adware	**Internet protocol address**	**ransomware**
cookies	**malware**	**software virus**
firewall	**multifactor authentication**	**spyware**
identity theft	**phishing**	

Review

1. Describe methods of avoiding identity theft. (6.1)

_____
_____
_____
_____
_____

2. List and explain three ways to recognize an employment scam. (6.2)

3. What type of information can be revealed by a computer's IP address? (6.3)

4. Describe two methods of removing cookies from a computer. (6.3)

5. What is *phishing*? (6.3)

6. What is the purpose of malware? (6.4)

7. How does malware infect a computer or device? (6.4)

8. List and describe four types of malware. (6.4)

9. What are some best practices for creating a security plan? (6.5)

_____
_____
_____

10. Why is it important to back up your computer both on the cloud and locally? (6.5)

_____
_____
_____

Application

1. What are some reasons a hacker would want to obtain a person's identity online? (6.1)

_____
_____
_____

2. How could you confirm a company's information before applying for a job? (6.1)

_____
_____
_____

3. What types of information should you avoid supplying on a job application or during the job-search process? (6.1, 6.2)

_____
_____
_____

4. Recall a job advertisement you have seen that looked suspicious. What caused you to suspect that it might be a scam? Explain. (6.2)

_____
_____
_____

5. Make a list of Internet activities that could possibly put your online identity at risk. What can you do to safeguard your identity? (6.3)

6. What are some red flags to look for when receiving e-mails or messages from unknown sources? What precautions would you take? (6.3)

7. How would you know if your computer has a virus? (6.4)

8. What are some best practices for protecting a computer from malware? (6.4)

9. Security settings may be found in different locations on different types of Internet browsers. Describe how to find the security settings on the Internet browser you use. (6.5)

10. How can you protect your digital devices and personal information when using the Internet? (6.5)

CONNECT TO YOUR CAREER
Workplace Connection

6-1 Identity Theft

Identity theft can cause serious, ongoing problems affecting your credit and other areas of your life. Working in small groups, visit the Federal Trade Commission (FTC) website at www.identitytheft.gov to learn more about identity theft.

1. Read the information that pertains to reporting identity theft and summarize the steps that should be taken if this should happen to you.

   _____
   _____
   _____

2. On the same website, read about identity theft victims' rights. Summarize your findings.

   _____
   _____
   _____
   _____

3. What computer-security steps does the FTC suggest you take if you are a victim of identity theft?

   _____
   _____
   _____
   _____

4. Create a list of common ways that identity thieves obtain personal information, such as phishing scams.

   _____
   _____
   _____
   _____

5. Select one of the scams from your list. Create a poster or presentation outlining strategies for preventing this type of attack. Share it with the class.

6-2 Employment Scams

Conduct an Internet search using the phrase *avoiding employment scams*. Record three facts you learned.

Fact #1:

___

___

___

___

Fact #2:

___

___

___

___

Fact #3:

___

___

___

___

6-3 Malware

Conduct Internet research on the latest antimalware software. Recommend five software programs you would consider using on your computer. In the table provided, list the name of each program, its cost, and the features included, such as Internet security, adware protection, etc. Then, answer the questions that follow.

Here are some helpful tips as you conduct your research:
- Look for reviews and comparisons of different antimalware software options from reputable sources such as technology websites and magazines.
- Consider the specific features and capabilities of each software, such as real-time protection, scheduled scanning, and quarantine functionality.
- Check the software's compatibility with your device's operating system and any additional requirements such as hardware specifications.
- Consider the software's pricing and any subscription or renewal fees.
- Look for customer support options such as a FAQs, user forums, and contact information for customer support.
- Check the software's update frequency and the company's history and reputation.
- Read user reviews and feedback for the software.

Antimalware Software		
Software Name	**Cost**	**Features/Capabilities**

1. List the make and model of your mobile device(s). Visit your service provider or manufacturer's website, and conduct a search to find current information about malware that may affect your device.

    Make:
    _____

    Model:
    _____

    Potential malware:
    _____
    _____
    _____
    _____

2. How susceptible to viruses is your device?

3. Conduct Internet research regarding how to protect your mobile device against malware. What did you find?

4. In the space provided, outline your personal security plan for your digital devices.

UNIT 3 | Job-Application Process

Chapter 7 Résumés
Chapter 8 Cover Letters
Chapter 9 Applying for Jobs

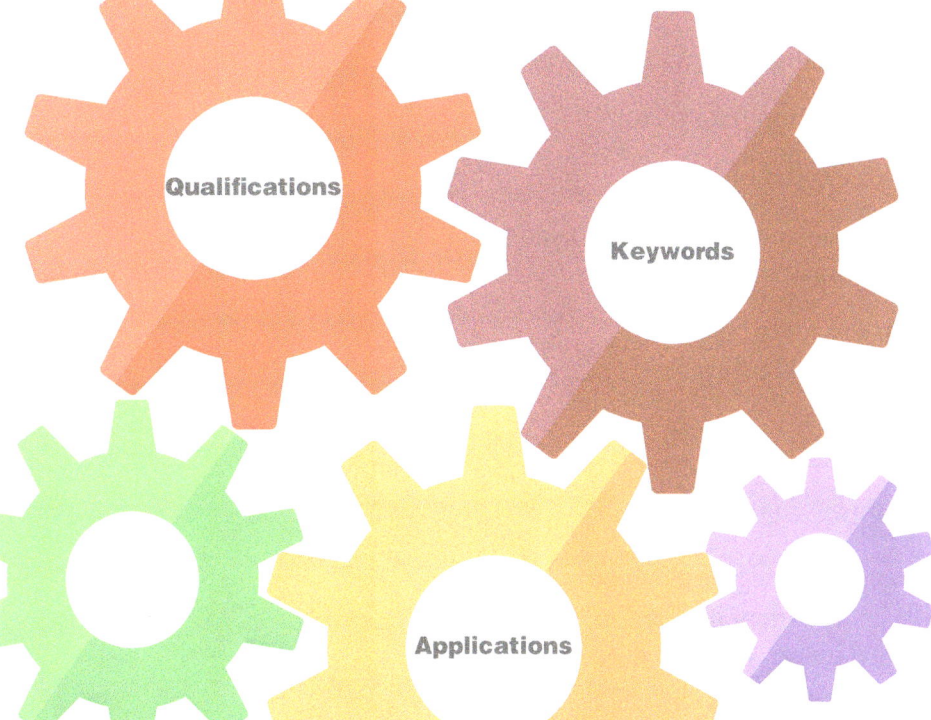

Dzmitry Abrazhevich/Shutterstock.com

Why It Matters

One of the first challenges you will face as a job seeker is showing a potential employer that you are the perfect candidate for a position. In most cases, your résumé will be the key to this process. Once you identify a job opening, you must create a résumé that convinces the employer to invite you for an interview. Along with the résumé, you will submit a cover letter. If you are required to complete a formal application form, it should be as presentable as your résumé and cover letter.

Company websites, professional networking sites, and job-search websites will be valuable sources for finding advertisements for positions. You can make these resources work for you by adopting a Sunday Evening Plan. The plan includes updating your online presence on a regular basis and managing the application process.

CHAPTER 7: Résumés

Learning Outcomes

7.1 **Explain** the purpose of a résumé.

7.2 **Discuss** the importance of keywords.

7.3 **Identify** sections of a résumé.

7.4 **List** three types of résumés.

7.5 **List** three formats that can be used to resave a master résumé.

7.6 **Discuss** two examples of a nontraditional résumé.

CONNECT TO YOUR CAREER

Workplace Connection

7-1 Résumé Templates
7-2 Résumé Keywords
7-3 Résumé Heading and Summary
7-4 Résumé Experience, Education, and Special Skills
7-5 Master Résumé
7-6 Nontraditional Résumés

OVERVIEW

When a person is seeking employment, the résumé is an important first step in getting an interview. A job applicant gets one chance to impress a potential employer, so a résumé must make a strong and positive statement about who they are. The candidate must persuade the employer that the skills and experience listed on the résumé fit the position they are seeking to fill.

A good résumé is a marketing tool that sells an individual as the perfect candidate for a position. What makes a good résumé? First, it must be well-written and presented in an organized manner. Second, it must have searchable keywords. Finally, it must have content that entices the reader to request an interview.

NPFire/Shutterstock.com

7.1 Résumé

A **résumé** is a written document that lists an individual's qualifications for a job, including work experience and education. It is a glimpse into a candidate's professional preparation and pertinent qualifications for work. Its chief purpose is to convince a potential employer that an applicant's experiences and skills match the qualifications of the job. Think of a résumé as a powerful summary of *who* a person is and *why* that person would be an asset as an employee. It is often the first impression most employers will have about a job applicant prior to a first meeting.

When creating a résumé, consider using a template to get the process started. A *résumé template* is a pre-formatted, word-processing document that contains a standard layout with adequate margins of white space. Templates look balanced on a page and include pre-selected fonts, bullet points, headers, footers, and, sometimes, separator lines. They are documents designed to give a résumé a professional look and feel. It can be easier to use a template and customize it for personal needs rather than to start from scratch. If you choose to start with a template, remember to customize it so that it looks original and reflects your personality.

When reviewing the many available templates, consider the following:
- adequate white space and margins
- font that is black in color
- headings that are larger than the body text
- plain styling without elaborate headings, text boxes, or tables

There are a myriad of free templates available from Microsoft, Google Docs, and other online resources that can be saved as editable documents.

As you progress in your career, you will take on new responsibilities and experience changes in your jobs, education, and interests. Therefore, you will have to continually update your résumé for subsequent job applications. Keep in mind that a résumé should be well-written, free of errors, and organized in a way that highlights your skills and qualifications. It is worth spending the time to perfect your résumé. It is the gateway for a potential interview and, ultimately, to a great job.

CONNECT TO YOUR CAREER

Complete 7-1 Résumé Templates, pg. 123

7.2 Keywords

As you begin sifting through job ads, you will notice certain words that are used frequently. These repeated words often include specific terms related to the position, such as *leadership*, *degree*, and *specialist*, to list a few. These are known as *keywords*. As explained in Chapter 1, keywords are words that relate to the functions of an open position. Most keywords are nouns or noun phrases, not verbs. Examples of keywords are shown in **Figure 7-1**.

FIGURE 7-1

Keywords are words that specifically relate to the functions of a position for which an employer is hiring.

Keywords			
• Accounts payable	• Energy efficiency	• Inventory management	• Refrigeration
• Automotive repair	• Event planning	• Kitchen management	• Reporting
• Baking	• Fabrication	• Leak detection	• Research
• Bilingual	• Fact checking	• Logistics	• Reservations
• Blueprints	• Financial planning	• Marketing	• Safety regulations
• Bricklaying	• Food and beverage service	• Masonry restoration	• Sales and marketing
• Clinical procedures	• Food safety	• Medical terminology	• Stonemasonry
• Compassion	• Front desk operations	• Menu planning	• Storytelling
• Concrete work	• General maintenance	• Multimedia production	• Teamwork
• Cooking	• Health and safety	• News writing	• Tiling
• Cost controls	• HIPPA regulations	• Patient care	• Vehicle diagnostics
• Customer service	• Housekeeping	• Patient privacy	• Web design
• Drain cleaning	• Information technology	• Pipefitting	• Welding
• Electronic health records (EHR)	• Interviewing	• Plasma cutting	• Welding inspection
		• Recipe development	

Goodheart-Willcox Publisher

Employers use keywords in job advertisements to describe the duties associated with requirements for open positions. Employers select keywords that are important to the job and then look for those words in the résumés submitted by candidates. This can help identify potential matches for a job opening. The job advertisement in **Figure 7-2** uses several keywords, as highlighted.

Reading job advertisements and identifying keywords to use in your résumé can be a helpful exercise. Using the right combination of keywords is the best way to become visible to an employer or recruiter. One way to ensure visibility is to include the same keywords that employers use in the advertisement for the job for which you are applying.

Résumés with the correct keywords trigger responses, while those without matching keywords are ignored. A lack of keywords associated with a specific job decreases the chances of an applicant being flagged during the early stage of the screening process.

Trending

Trending refers to keywords and phrases that have the highest number of online searches on any given day. Many Internet search engines list what is trending, as do social media websites. Trending information is saved, and the data are tabulated. These tabulations are ranked and posted on the sites. For example, if you conduct a search for "technology jobs," the search engine will rank your search terms and offer the most popular results for the job posting keyword phrase. If enough employers use consistent wording for job posts, search engines will categorize those posts and record how often they are repeated. In addition, as job seekers enter terms into search engines to find open positions, those terms are also tabulated. For example, if a candidate is looking for an accounting job, a search engine will list keywords associated with accounting jobs that are most popular at the moment.

As the needs of employers change, keywords related to a job will also change. For example, as the result of damage and destruction caused by a natural disaster, employers might be looking for stone, block, or brick masons. Keywords in a job advertisement for a mason in a residential area may include *cement repairs* or *chimney repairs*.

Consider the job for which you are applying and determine the appropriate keywords to use on your résumé to match what is trending.

Applicant Tracking System Software

Applicant tracking system software is a tool that allows employers and recruiters to keep track of job postings, applications, and résumés on job boards. It typically enables companies to post and manage job listings, track applicant activity, and schedule interviews.

Applicant tracking system software is used by employers and recruiters to sort through résumés and flag the ones that match the keywords for which they are looking. Over the last decade, the hiring process has transitioned from a manual process of reading print résumés to an automated process of using computer programs to scan electronically submitted résumés for keywords. With hundreds of résumés and job postings available online, it may be difficult for a person to read each résumé that is received. For that reason, some larger companies rely on computer programs to scan the content for keywords to expedite the screening process.

In order to know which keywords will result in software finding a résumé quickly, research can be

FIGURE 7-2

Using an appropriate combination of keywords in a résumé is the best way to become visible to an employer or recruiter.

Essential Duties and Responsibilities
- Reading and interpreting blueprints and schematics to determine the specific welding requirements for a project.
- Setting up and maintaining welding equipment, including selecting and installing torches, torch tips, and filler rods.
- Selecting the appropriate welding process for a job, such as MIG, TIG, or Stick welding.
- Operating manual or semi-automatic welding equipment to fuse metal segments using high heat and pressure.
- Inspecting completed welds to ensure they meet specifications and standards.
- Maintaining a clean and organized workspace to ensure safety.
- Performing routine maintenance on welding equipment to ensure it is in good working order.
- Adhering to safety protocols and wearing personal protective equipment as needed.
- Staying up to date with new welding technologies and techniques.
- Working with other team members to complete projects efficiently and effectively.

Goodheart-Willcox Publisher

conducted on trending keywords in a given career field. For example, for an entry-level office position, one might think of the words *clerk* or *receptionist*.

CONNECT TO YOUR CAREER

Complete 7-2 Résumé Keywords, pg. 124

7.3 Sections of a Résumé

Résumés have standard sections employers expect to see. Some sections, however, are optional and should be included only if they apply to you and the position you are seeking.

As you apply for positions, you will find the need to customize your résumé to fit the job for which you are applying. You may apply for more than one type of job or job title at any given time. For example, a qualified marketing professional might find several positions for which to apply. One position may be for a marketing manager, a second might be for a communications manager, and another may be for a promotions manager. If the applicant is qualified for all three, three résumés will need to be created. Each version will have different keywords and profiles, but the core material will likely remain the same.

Keep in mind that customizing may simply mean changing a few keywords. On the other hand, it could mean major rewrites to sections of your résumé. It is important to be flexible and cognizant about what an employer wants.

When deciding how to format each section, consider the overall length of the final document. Will it be one page or two? Typically, a recent graduate should have a one-page résumé, while those with several years of experience may have two pages. Regardless of page count, adequate white space should be allowed on the page for readability.

Heading

A **heading** is a person's full name, phone number, e-mail address, and geographic location. This is a standard part of a résumé and is the most prominent feature that identifies a job applicant. At a quick glance, a potential employer can learn the geographic location or proximity to the job location and the personal contact information of the person applying for a job.

The first line of a heading is your legal name. Nicknames and abbreviations are *not* acceptable. However, it *is* acceptable to use only a first name and last name. Middle names or initials are optional.

On a résumé that is printed and physically submitted for a job application, an exact street address can be listed followed by a phone number beginning with the area code. On a résumé that is submitted electronically, the exact street or home address should *not* be added to the heading, as shown in **Figure 7-3**. It is likely that the résumé will be posted on the Internet, so it is unnecessary, and possibly unsafe, to list an exact street address and city. It is acceptable, and recommended, to use a general geographic area, with or without the zip code. For example, you can provide a major city or a general metropolitan area in close proximity to where you reside.

Next, list the telephone number at which you can be contacted. There is no need to indicate whether the number is a mobile or land line. It is obvious that it is the preferred phone number. If you are uploading your résumé to an online job board, such as Indeed, do not add your phone number to your résumé. Use your professional e-mail address only. An **online job board** is a website that hosts job postings for employers and allows applicants to apply for jobs seamlessly.

A professional e-mail address should appear next, followed by links to your professional social media accounts. Links to profiles such as LinkedIn, Twitter, and Instagram make it easy for employers to verify a candidate's digital footprint. Remember that social media searches are sometimes an employer's first choice to screen candidates.

FIGURE 7-3

A heading is a person's full name, phone number, e-mail address, and geographic location.

Sample Résumé Headings	
Submitted in Person	**Submitted Electronically**
Shelley Jones	Shelley Jones
111 Main Street	Greater Baltimore Area 21202
Baltimore, MD 21202	555-555-1234
555-555-1234	sjones@e-mail.com
sjones@e-mail.com	www.linkedin.com/in/shelley-jones
www.linkedin.com/in/shelley-jones	

Goodheart-Willcox Publisher

Summary

After creating the heading for a résumé, prepare a summary that gives employers a quick glance of your qualifications. It should briefly describe your core strengths and skill sets, helping employers see why you are the best candidate for the job. A summary may determine whether an employer continues reading the résumé. A summary may consist of the following:

- *Brief overview of qualifications*: This section concisely summarizes a candidate's specific area of expertise and most valuable skills.
- *A personal brand statement*: As you learned in Chapter 3, a personal brand statement is one sentence that describes what a potential job candidate offers an employer. It should be a brief, catchy statement that encapsulates the applicant's unique skills, abilities, and values in a way that differentiates the applicant from others. It should also be closely related to the job opening.

CONNECT TO YOUR CAREER

Complete 7-3 Résumé Heading and Summary, pg. 124

Experience

Most often, experience is included as the next section on a résumé, immediately followed by education. However, if you are a recent graduate without much work experience, you may consider the reverse and list your education first, followed by experience. This is a personal preference, and there is no right or wrong way to present this information.

Past and current jobs or internships comprise the experience section of a résumé. List each position held and the name of the company or organization, including the city and state. If you work remotely, you can list "Remote Work" in place of the city and state. Additionally, note the start and end dates of employment. If still employed with a company, use the word "present," such as "August 20-- to present" or "20-- to present," replacing "--" with the year. Then, follow with a description of the work experience. Volunteer work may also be listed. Employers often are interested in community-oriented applicants who perform charitable activities.

Use keywords when possible to trigger a match for job-related search criteria. For example, if a job recruiter is looking for an accountant, scanning software will search for résumés on the Internet that include keywords such as *ledger accounts*, *balance sheets*, *financial audits*, *operational data*, and *reconciling discrepancies*. Keywords that are unrelated to the job description should not be used.

It is also helpful to list your key accomplishments while on the job. Use strong action words to showcase your accomplishments, such as *managed*, *supervised*, *completed*, etc. Using specific numbers and statistics helps demonstrate the impact of your accomplishments.

Education

Most often, education is included on a résumé immediately following work experience. However, as noted earlier, if you are a recent graduate without much work experience, you may consider listing your education first, followed by experience.

The label of this section can be changed from "Education" to "Relevant Coursework" or "Certifications." If you are still in school, indicate the number of years you have attended and provide your expected graduation date. List the courses you have taken that are most relevant to the position for which you are applying. Include any training, workshops, or seminars you have completed, even if you participated in classes for a previous employer.

If you are no longer a student, your education should be listed beginning with the most recent diploma or degree earned. Include colleges as well as business or technical schools. Graduates should indicate the year a degree or diploma was earned, type of degree received, major subject, and minor subject, if any. Also, any certifications earned, special courses or training programs completed, or any other related educational achievements should be included. If you have earned multiple degrees, each degree should be listed separately. If you are an outstanding scholar in your college career, or if you have achieved other academic recognition or awards, add them to your résumé.

College students have an implied high school diploma or GED, so adding high school information is optional. High school information should only be added when there are outstanding achievements or honors and awards to highlight.

Special Skills

The *special skills* section of a résumé is an opportunity to focus the reader's attention on the skills gained in school or from previous jobs. These skills may not be noted or highlighted in other sections of a résumé. Job postings will likely include hard skills, which are job-specific skills, and soft skills, which are transferable skills. Soft skills may include teamwork, organization, management, or other workplace skills an employer might look for in a candidate. The goal is to list top skills that will entice employers to schedule an interview.

Career Persona

Stonemason

Responsibilities

A mason is responsible for constructing, maintaining, and repairing structures made of brick, stone, and other masonry materials. Tasks include mixing and applying mortar, laying bricks and other materials, and shaping and finishing surfaces to create a smooth and durable finish. Some of the responsibilities include the following:

FishCoolish/Shutterstock.com

- Prepare and lay bricks, concrete blocks, stone, and other masonry materials to construct or repair walls, foundations, partitions, arches, and other structures
- Mix, apply and spread mortar, cement, or other bonding agents
- Repair and maintain masonry structures
- Read blueprints and drawings to understand and follow specifications and building codes
- Inspect and maintain masonry equipment and tools

Qualities and Skills

Masonry is a skilled trade that requires a combination of physical abilities, technical knowledge, and craftsmanship. Successful masons possess qualities such as:

- *Attention to detail, precision, and patience:* Masons must be able to visualize the finished product and understand the steps required to achieve it.
- *Good communication skills:* To work effectively with clients, contractors, and other tradespeople, masons need to be able to communicate clearly and concisely.
- *Problem-solving skills:* Masons must be able to troubleshoot issues and come up with creative solutions to challenges that arise during the construction process.
- *Physical strength and manual dexterity:* Masonry work can be physically demanding, requiring endurance, strength, stamina, and balance while using hands and arms to install, position, and move materials.

Education

- Vocational or technical school program in masonry
- Apprenticeship program through a union or contractor association
- OSHA 10-Hour Training Certification
- National Center for Construction Education & Research (NCCER) Certification

Next Steps

If you are interested in pursuing a career in masonry, there are several steps you can take to prepare yourself for the job market. Finding a technical school that offers a program in masonry will be a step in the right direction. Learn more about apprenticeship programs offered by the Home Builders Institute and International Masonry Institute. Getting on-the-job experience by working alongside experienced masons is another way to learn masonry basics.

A bulleted list of points might reflect your technical skills, communication skills, problem-solving skills, and job-specific skills, or those related to a specific profession.

Carefully review a job advertisement for the job you are seeking and focus on the required skills. If you have the relevant experience, use the same words to describe it. Only use the keywords that fit your background. Do not stretch the truth.

CONNECT TO YOUR CAREER

Complete 7-4 Résumé Experience, Education, and Special Skills, pg. 125

7.4 Résumé Formats

After you finish gathering information for your résumé, you are ready to select a format. Depending on the industry and job for which you are applying, you may find that it is best to use one format over the other. Three types of common résumé formats are timeline, skills, and combination.

Timeline Résumé

A **timeline résumé**, also known as a *chronological résumé*, is a résumé that emphasizes employers and work experience with each. Work experience is listed in reverse chronological order, with the most recent information first. If your most recent work experiences are the best qualifications you possess when applying for a job, use this résumé format. An example of a timeline résumé is shown in **Figure 7-4**.

On a timeline résumé, beginning dates and end dates should be listed for each job under the *Experience* section of the résumé. One of the following options should be used to format the dates:
- month and year: September 20--
- month, day, and year: September 1, 20--
- year only: 20--

Remember that a résumé presents a broad overview of your experience to an employer and is the vehicle to gain an interview. The exact duration of your work at a particular job might be of interest to a potential employer later. However, at the résumé stage, your task is to display information accurately without giving an employer an initial negative impression. For example, if you worked at an organization for only two months, you might want to state just the year, such as "2023" as opposed to "November 2023 to December 2023." Indicating two months is not necessary if you want to emphasize the skills you gained as an employee, rather than the fact that you were employed as seasonal help.

Skills Résumé

A **skills résumé**, also referred to as a *functional résumé*, is a résumé that lists work experience according to categories of skills or achievements rather than by employer. It lists work experiences according to relevant achievements rather than by time. For example, if you have floral arrangement skills but your last job was as a restaurant server, you might want the floral arrangement experiences to be the first information seen by the potential employer. In this case, a skills résumé is a good choice. Use a skills résumé to highlight your skills over your most recent work experiences. An example of a skills résumé is shown in **Figure 7-5**.

Skills résumés typically have the dates of employment omitted. If you have significant gaps in your employment history, it is appropriate to create and submit this type of résumé. It also presents an opportunity to focus on the skills and experiences you are capable of utilizing, even if they are not applicable to your current job. List your strongest experience or skills first, followed by the least-developed skills or experience.

Combination Résumé

A *combination résumé* is exactly as it sounds—a combination of both the timeline and skills résumés. This format is used when you want to emphasize that your skills are your strengths against the backdrop of more recent work experience.

Workplace Skills

Leadership is the process of influencing others or making things better. It is a soft skill that reflects professionalism. Certain traits such as honesty, competence, self-confidence, communication skills, problem-solving skills, and dependability are examples of leadership characteristics. Setting goals, following through on tasks, and being forward-thinking are also important leadership abilities. *Leaders* are those who guide others to a goal.

FIGURE 7-4

A timeline résumé is a résumé that lists work experiences in reverse chronological order with the most recent information first.

PIERRE DUPONT

123 Main Street, Redwood City, CA 94061   573-555-4321
pierre.dupont@e-mail.com   www.linkedin.com/in/pierre-dupont

SUMMARY

Highly skilled stonemason with over five years of experience in the construction industry. Proficient in all aspects of masonry work, including bricklaying, concrete pouring and finishing, stone veneering, and more. Able to follow plans and specifications accurately while demonstrating a strong attention to detail. Capable of working effectively as part of a team or independently, and comfortable taking on leadership roles when needed.

EXPERIENCE

Stonemason, 20-- to present
Elysium Enterprises, Redwood City, CA
- Work on a variety of commercial and residential projects, including new construction and renovations.
- Read and assess construction blueprints and technical drawings.
- Use stone cutting, shaping, and binding tools.
- Lead a team of three to five masons on larger projects.
- Demonstrate strong problem-solving skills and ability to adapt to changing jobsite conditions.

Apprentice Mason, 20-- to 20--
Eon Solutions, Redwood City, CA
- Assisted lead masons with all aspects of masonry work.
- Learned various masonry techniques and best practices.
- Participated in on-the-job training and completed a formal apprenticeship program.

EDUCATION

Associate of Science in Construction Technology
Horizon Tech, Baltimore, MD
- Graduated: June 20-- with honors
- Coursework: masonry, construction materials, and building codes

SPECIAL SKILLS

- Operating cranes, hoists, and other heavy machinery.
- Ability to use both modern power tools and traditional hand tools.
- Bilingual: Fluent in English and French.

Goodheart-Willcox Publisher

FIGURE 7-5

A skills résumé is a résumé that lists work experiences according to relevant achievements rather than by date.

KIM YAN

New York City Area 10002   kimyan@e-mail.com
www.linkedin.com/in/kim-yan

SUMMARY

Experienced florist with a passion for creating beautiful and unique floral arrangements for a wide range of occasions. Skilled in using a variety of flowers and foliage to create stunning and creative designs. Possess a strong attention to detail and ability to work well under pressure.

KEY ACHIEVEMENTS

- Designed and created award-winning floral arrangements for weddings, funerals, and special events.
- Voted one of the "Top 10 Florists" in the New York City area for providing exceptional customer service and high-quality products and service.
- Partnered with local event planner organization to provide all floral arrangements for weddings, parties, and corporate events.
- Developed inventory management system for flowers, plants, and supplies to ensure freshness and availability.
- Promoted the business through social media and marketing initiatives, resulting in a 20 percent increase in sales over the past year.

SPECIAL SKILLS

- Knowledge of proper care and maintenance techniques for a variety of flowers and foliage.
- Proficiency in a variety of flower arranging techniques, including hand-tied bouquets and traditional and modern arrangements.
- Ability to work with live, dried, and silk flowers and greenery.
- Experience with customer sales and service.
- Collaboration with other professionals to ensure that projects are completed on time and to the client's satisfaction.

EXPERIENCE

Floral Designer, Petals and Posies Floral Creations, New York City, NY
Floral Assistant, Donovan Flowers, Newark, NJ

EDUCATION

FlowerSchool New York, 20--

CERTIFICATIONS

American Institute of Floral Designers (AIFD), 20--
Society of American Florists (SAF), 20--

Goodheart-Willcox Publisher

Connect to Your Community

Volunteering is a way for you to give back to your community while gaining valuable skills and experiences. Many types of volunteering opportunities are available to match a wide range of interests. Volunteering activities related to community service may include working with local organizations that help meet community needs, such as food banks, homeless shelters, or environmental cleanups. Event volunteering involves helping to organize and run local events such as charity walks, concerts, or festivals. Additionally, there are opportunities to volunteer in educational settings, such as participating in tutoring or mentoring programs for younger students. Finally, there are many international volunteering opportunities, such as teaching in another country or working on conservation projects. These opportunities can provide a unique and rewarding experience for those interested in travel and cultural exchange. Overall, volunteering can provide you with meaningful experiences that can help you grow personally and professionally while making a positive impact on your community.

Gustavo Frazao/Shutterstock.com

The organization of a combination résumé consists of your summary, followed by your achievements and/or skills. A list of your work experience should appear next. A combination résumé is illustrated in **Figure 7-6**.

7.5 Saving a Résumé

Once a résumé is created, it is a good idea to save it as a master résumé document. The résumé file should be named MasterResume or something similar. This will be the document to return to when customized versions are needed to apply for different positions. The master résumé is not the file to send to a potential employer. It is a working document to use as a basis for future submissions.

When you have finalized your résumé and are preparing to post it to a website or attach it to an e-mail, you will want to resave the file with a new name to keep your master file intact. Remember to save it as a secondary file with a professional name. There are many naming conventions that can be used. Select the one you are comfortable with and stick to it. Include your first and last name, or last name only, in the file name so the employer can identify your résumé. For example, you could save your master résumé file as FirstNameLastNameResume before sending it to a potential employer. However, you may save three versions of your résumé for three different positions:

- LastNameMktMgrResume
- Last NameComMgrResume
- Last NameProMgrResume

When resaving the file, consider using one of three commonly accepted file formats employers request. These formats are a Microsoft Word document, a PDF, and a plain text file.

CONNECT TO YOUR CAREER

Complete 7-5 Master Résumé, pg. 125

Microsoft Word Document

There will be times when you will attach a résumé to an e-mail when applying for a position. When you created your master file, you more than likely used Microsoft Word. Microsoft Word's default .DOC and DOCX. file extensions are the most common formats for saving a document. To prepare a file for submission, renaming the file as a Word document is one option. A Word file is easy to save by the creator and easy to download by the person receiving it as an attachment. However, one drawback to using a Word file is that it can be changed, either accidentally or on purpose, by the person who opens it.

PDF

While it may seem logical to attach the résumé as a Microsoft Word document, consider attaching it as a PDF file. A PDF file will keep the file intact, including the formatting, and protect it from changes.

FIGURE 7-6

A combination résumé is a combination of both the timeline and skills résumés.

Maria Gomez

Greater San Diego Area
(619) 555–4023
mariagomez@e-mail.com
www.linkedin.com/in/maria-gomez

SUMMARY

Experienced healthcare worker with over five years of experience in providing patient care in a variety of settings. Strong skills in patient assessment, wound care, and medication administration. Highly empathetic and compassionate, with a strong commitment to providing high-quality patient care.

SKILLS

- Patient assessment: Skilled in assessing patient's condition, including taking and monitoring vital signs and documenting symptoms and concerns.
- Wound care: Trained in caring for wounds, including cleaning, bandaging, and redressing wounds and monitoring wound progress.
- Medication administration: Skilled in administering proper medication and doses and monitoring patient response.
- Patient education: Experienced in informing and instructing patients and families about disease management and treatment options.

EXPERIENCE

Staff Nurse (RN), June 20-- to present
Vortex Hospital, San Diego, CA
- Manage patient care and recovery in a busy hospital setting.
- Assess patients' condition and share information with doctors.
- Administer medications and injections.

Patient Care Technician (PCT), June 20-- to June 20--
GHI Clinic, San Diego, CA
- Administered certain medications.
- Drew blood for lab work.
- Performed and managed wound care.

Certified Nursing Assistant (CNA), May 20-- to June 20--
DEF Nursing Home, San Diego, CA
- Discussed and documented patients' health concerns.
- Measured patients' vital signs, including blood pressure and temperature.
- Cleaned and bathed patients.

EDUCATION

Associate Degree in Nursing (ADN), 20--
California State University

CERTIFICATION

Licensed Practical Nurse (LPN)
BLS (Basic Life Support)
ACLS (Advanced Cardiovascular Life Support)

Goodheart-Willcox Publisher

The PDF file can be created in Microsoft Word by resaving the file. Select the **Save As** option in Word to display the Save As dialog box, and then choose **PDF** from the list of options.

Plain Text

There may be times during the job-application process when you are required to copy and paste information from a résumé to an application on an employer's website. In doing this, formatting of a Word document will likely become distorted. Therefore, it will be necessary to prepare a version of your résumé that removes special formatting, such as bulleted lists. This can be accomplished by saving a plain text version of the résumé. When a file in Microsoft Word is saved as plain text, the file name will appear with a .TXT extension. To create a plain text résumé, select the **Save As** option in Word to display a dialog box. Select **Plain Text** from the list of options.

An example of a plain text résumé is shown in **Figure 7-7**. Notice all the formatting has been removed. This will make it easy to cut and paste information into an online form.

7.6 Nontraditional Résumé

Not all résumés will follow a traditional résumé format. For example, if applying for a job as a website developer, you may choose to create an online résumé to showcase your technical abilities. Similarly, if applying for a graphic design position, you can create a résumé that highlights your strengths in a graphical format. Two common types of nontraditional résumés are web-based and visual.

Web-Based Résumé

When preparing a résumé for your electronic portfolio or personal website, you can save the document as a web page in Microsoft Word. Select the **Save As** option in Word to display the Save As dialog box, and then choose **Web Page** or **Single File Web Page** from the list of options. This creates an HTML version of your résumé document, which will open in a web browser when launched. This type of résumé will look similar to the Word version, as it will retain the formatting that was applied in Word. If you decide to save your résumé as a web page, upload it to your electronic portfolio site so all employment documents are in one convenient place.

Rather than just saving your résumé as a web page, you may choose to create a separate, site-based résumé. This type of résumé serves as its own website and can be designed to include various types of content, such as images, sound clips, and video clips. A job seeker can use a web-based résumé to display design abilities, technical skills, or other talents and experience. For example, a musician can post sound or video clips of past performances directly to their résumé website. Similarly, a web developer can include a demo of a program they created. There are many free templates available online that can help you get started.

Before you create this type of résumé, conduct research to make sure this format is appropriate for the job for which you are applying. It is a good idea to have both a web-page résumé and résumé website available for potential employers. If you use a web-based résumé, add a link to it in your professional e-mail signature block.

Visual Résumé

A creative way to highlight your résumé is to create a visual résumé. A **visual résumé** is one that presents information in a graphically appealing format. An **infographic résumé** is a visual résumé in which the content is displayed using a combination of words, icons, and graphics to present information clearly and quickly. Employers can view your information without having to read through multiple lines of text.

There are many websites that offer templates for visual résumés for free or at a minimal cost. This makes it practical for anyone to create a visually appealing document. No graphic design experience is necessary. Similar to other templates, information can be pulled from a master résumé into a new format using charts, tables, and other graphic elements, as shown in **Figure 7-8**. By customizing your résumé to be visually appealing, you can gain an edge on the competition. However, it is important to note that most visual résumés look appealing but are not scannable for keywords. Additionally, it may not be appropriate for your industry or desired position. When you post your résumé online, include both print and visual versions.

Conduct a final check before mailing, posting, or submitting your résumé to make sure every detail of the résumé is complete. This includes proofreading, running a spell check, and reading each line for clarity. Make sure the file is formatted correctly and all other guidelines have been followed. Using the checklist in **Figure 7-9** will help you as you finalize the document.

CONNECT TO YOUR CAREER

Complete 7-6 Nontraditional Résumés, pg. 126

FIGURE 7-7

A plain text résumé does not have special formatting and is helpful when applying for jobs online.

```
JALIA CORTEZ
111 First Street, Redwood City, CA 94061
(650) 555-1234
jcortez@e-mail.com
www.linkedin.com/in/jalia-cortez

Summary
Bilingual, top contributor, and provider of consistent information
to guests. Responds to queries, gives directions, and makes detailed
reservations and recommendations. Utilizes and shares knowledge of local
events and venues in addition to local transportation options. Personable
and engaging in casual conversation with guests.

EXPERIENCE
College of San Mateo, Redwood City, CA
August 20-- to present
Administrative Assistant to the Director of Education
* Screen the director's correspondence and assist with preparation of
responses
* Prepare e-mails, reports, and letters
* Assist with research, editing, and final preparation of reports
* Manage the calendars of five staff members and the director
* Schedule meetings and make special arrangements, such as catering and
A/V equipment
* Maintain up-to-date personnel data for staff members

Jefferson High School, Redwood City, CA
June 20-- to August 20--
Receptionist and Administrative Assistant, Principal's Office
* Scheduled appointments for students, faculty, and parents
* Maintained calendars
* Answered telephones, screened, and directed calls
* Greeted visitors, faculty, and students, and provided assistance as
needed

EDUCATION
Associate of Arts in Office Administration, 20--
Lincoln Community College, Redwood City, CA
SPECIAL SKILLS
Computer: Microsoft Office Suite
Language: Spanish, intermediate-level speaker
General: Excellent verbal and written communication, superior
organizational skills, and multitasking talents
```

Goodheart-Willcox Publisher

FIGURE 7-8

An infographic résumé is a résumé in which the content is displayed using a combination of words and graphics to present information clearly and quickly.

Stephen K. Sunwoo

E-mail: sksunwoo@e-mail.com
LinkedIn: http://www.linkedin.com/in/stephen-k-sunwoo
Seattle area 98103

Seeking full-time, part-time, and freelance graphic design work that is both challenging and engaging.

Essential Information

Work History

20-- –Present — Junior Graphic Designer, Synergy Communications, Tacoma, WA

20-- –20-- — Graphic Design Intern, Definition Designs Seattle, Seattle, WA

20-- –20-- — Layout Apprentice, The Independent Daily, Seattle, WA

Industry Experience

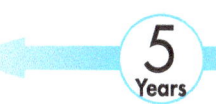

5 Years

Education

Art

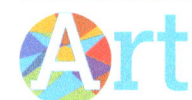

Washington State University,
Art (Digital Media), BA, 20--
Seattle, WA

Programs I Use

PSD, EPS, AI, PNG, PDF, PPT, XLS, DOC, JPG, HTM, CSS

Information About Me

Duties Performed

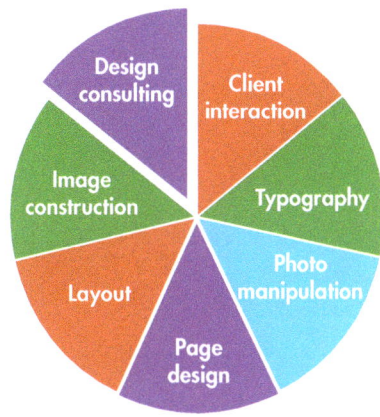

Design consulting
Client interaction
Typography
Photo manipulation
Page design
Layout
Image construction

Where I'm From

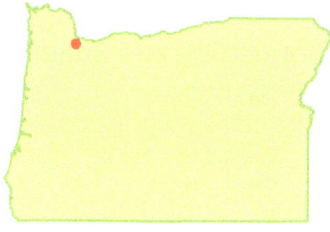

Portland, Oregon

Hobbies

- Tennis
- International cinema
- Fantasy baseball

tele52/Shutterstock.com; Goodheart-Willcox Publisher

FIGURE 7-9

A checklist of items can be used to confirm the résumé is accurate.

Résumé Checklist

Heading
- ___ Full, formal name
- ___ City and state for e-résumés or full address for printed résumés
- ___ Phone number for printed résumés only
- ___ E-mail address
- ___ Personal LinkedIn URL and/or other social media accounts

Summary
- ___ Overview of qualifications
- ___ Personal brand statement

Experience
- ___ Beginning and ending dates of employment
- ___ Company name
- ___ General location of company, such as city and state
- ___ Position held
- ___ Specific descriptions of work performed
- ___ Accomplishments while on the job
- ___ Volunteer work
- ___ Keywords that match the position

Education
- ___ Official college name
- ___ City and state
- ___ Degree obtained or degree title that is in process with expected date of graduation

Special Skills
- ___ Hard skills
- ___ Soft skills

Formatting and Editing
- ___ Single page
- ___ Ample white space
- ___ Keyword check
- ___ Spell check
- ___ Punctuation check
- ___ Grammar check

Saving
- ___ Master version of the résumé
- ___ Customized versions of the master résumé for specific job application

Goodheart-Willcox Publisher

Summary

7.1 Explain the purpose of a résumé.
The chief purpose of a résumé is to convince a potential employer that a candidate's experiences and skills match the qualifications of the job.

7.2 Discuss the importance of keywords.
Keywords are words that specifically relate to the functions of the position for which the employer is hiring. Using keywords in a strategic manner is important, as it can help land an interview. Researching and using keywords that are trending can help better customize a job search.

7.3 Identify sections of a résumé.
Résumés have standard sections that employers expect to see. Standard sections include a heading, experience, education, and special skills. A summary statement can be included as well.

7.4 List three types of résumés.
Three types of résumés include timeline, skills, and combination résumés.

7.5 List three formats that can be used to resave a master résumé.
A master copy of a résumé should be saved as a Word document. Using the master document, the file can be saved as a PDF or plain text file, as opposed to a .DOC or .DOCX file.

7.6 Discuss two examples of a nontraditional résumé.
Web-based résumés work well for electronic portfolios or personal websites. They can be created by saving a master résumé file as a web page instead of a Microsoft Word document or by using online templates. Visual résumés present information graphically. Online templates are also available to help build visual résumés.

Glossary Terms

applicant tracking system software
heading
infographic résumé
online job board
résumé
skills résumé
timeline résumé
trending
visual résumé

Review

1. Explain the purpose of a résumé. (7.1)

___
___
___
___
___

2. Discuss the importance of keywords. (7.2)

3. Describe the relationship between trending topics and keywords. (7.2)

4. Identify and describe sections of a résumé. (7.3)

5. List and describe three types of résumés. (7.4)

6. In what situations would it be more appropriate to use a chronological résumé vs. a skills résumé? (7.4)

7. List three formats that can be used to resave a master résumé. (7.5)

8. How can a master résumé help job seekers in their job search? (7.5)

9. List and describe two examples of a nontraditional résumé. (7.6)

_____
_____
_____

10. In what situations might a nontraditional résumé format be more effective than a traditional one? (7.6)

_____
_____
_____

Application

1. When creating your résumé, will you use a résumé template? Why or why not? (7.1)

_____
_____
_____

2. How can you effectively use keywords and phrases to make your résumé more searchable and appealing to potential employers? (7.2)

_____
_____
_____

3. How can you customize your keywords for your desired industry? (7.2)

_____
_____
_____

4. What skills have you learned from hobbies and other activities outside of school or work that you could include on a résumé? (7.3)

_____
_____
_____

5. How can you tailor your résumé to fit the specific job or industry you are targeting? (7.3)

6. Why is it important to have a clear and concise summary on a résumé? (7.3)

7. Name a job for which you would like to apply. Do you think using a chronological, functional, or combination résumé would be best? Explain why. (7.4)

8. If you were asked by an employer to send your résumé as an e-mail attachment, which file format would you send: a Microsoft Word document, a PDF file, or a plain text file? Explain why. (7.5)

9. Explain the relevance of nontraditional résumés in your industry. (7.6)

10. What is the value of creating a visual résumé? (7.6)

Chapter 7 Résumés

CONNECT TO YOUR CAREER

Workplace Connection

7-1 Résumé Templates

1. Which résumé type will you use when applying for a position—timeline, skills, or combination? Explain how you made your decision.

   _____
   _____
   _____

2. Conduct an Internet search using the phrase *résumé templates*. Record several URLs of templates you would consider using.

   URL #1:
   _____

   URL #2:
   _____

   URL #3:
   _____

   URL #4:
   _____

3. Which template do you prefer? Why?

   _____
   _____
   _____
   _____

4. How would you adapt this template to better fit your résumé needs?

   _____
   _____
   _____
   _____

7-2 Résumé Keywords

1. Research keywords that are used in your preferred industry or career field. Review job advertisements, conduct an Internet search, or use any other resources that will help you create a list of the top five keywords you can use in your résumé.

   _____
   _____
   _____
   _____
   _____

2. Consider your top five keywords. Why do you think these are important to use in your résumé?

   _____
   _____

7-3 Résumé Heading and Summary

1. Create two headings that you might use for your personal résumé. One heading could be used for print résumés, and the other for an electronically submitted résumé. Later, you will transfer this information to your résumé.

   Heading for print résumé:

   _____
   _____

   Heading for electronic résumé:

   _____
   _____

2. Write a summary for your résumé. A summary often consists of a brief overview of your qualifications or even a personal brand statement. (See Chapter 3 for more information on creating a personal brand statement.) Consider what you want to include in your summary and write it in the space provided. You will transfer this information to your résumé in a later activity.

   _____
   _____

7-4 Résumé Experience, Education, and Special Skills

1. Create a list of your work experiences, education, and special skills that you want a potential employer to see. Consider experiences and skills obtained from jobs, internships, volunteer work, and extracurricular activities. Use keywords from the list you created in Workplace Connection activity 7-2. Make sure these sections are accurate, complete, and follow the guidelines in the chapter.

    Experiences:

    _____
    _____
    _____

    Education:

    _____
    _____
    _____

    Skills:

    _____
    _____
    _____

2. Working in small groups, share your lists to get feedback on the information you provided. Based on the feedback, revise your list. You will transfer this information to your résumé in the next activity.

7-5 Master Résumé

Create a master résumé using the drafts from Workplace Connection activities 7-3 and 7-4. Assume this is a résumé that will be submitted electronically and will not include a detailed home address. When you are finished, run a spell-check and proofread the document. Ensure that the master résumé is saved as a Word document.

1. Save your Word document as *FirstnameLastname*_MasterResume.docx (e.g., JohnSmith_MasterResume.docx).

2. Save the master résumé file as a plain text document.

3. Return to the Word version of the master résumé file and save it as a PDF document.

4. Return to the Word version of the master résumé file and save it as a web-page document.

7-6 Nontraditional Résumés

1. Conduct an Internet search using the phrases *visual résumés* and *infographic résumés*. Compare the examples you found. Which résumé do you prefer? Why?

   _____
   _____
   _____
   _____
   _____
   _____
   _____

2. Next, create your own visual or infographic résumé. Use the information in your master résumé to create this new version. Save your document as *FirstnameLastname_InfoResume.docx* (e.g., JohnSmith_InfoResume.docx).

3. Divide into small groups of three or four members. Take turns presenting your visual résumés to the group. Discuss the different approaches and techniques that were used. Describe what you learned from this process in the space provided. Would you make any changes to your visual résumé based on what you learned?

   _____
   _____
   _____
   _____
   _____
   _____
   _____

CHAPTER 8: Cover Letters

Learning Outcomes

8.1 **Explain** the purpose of a cover letter.

8.2 **Identify** sections of a cover letter.

8.3 **Cite** three methods of cover letter submission.

CONNECT TO YOUR CAREER

Workplace Connection

8-1 Cover Letter Template

8-2 Master Cover Letter

OVERVIEW

Writing a cover letter is an important part of the application process. The goal is to convince an employer that you are the best person for the position. A cover letter highlights your abilities while reinforcing your desire to work for the company. More importantly, it is an opportunity to market yourself and convince the employer to grant you an interview.

A professional cover letter presents your personal qualifications in a way that attests to your ability to be a good employee. It shows that you have a genuine interest in the company as well as the position. Once you have captured the potential employer's attention with your cover letter, make it count. Create an impression that will increase your chances for an interview.

Farknot Architect/Shutterstock.com

8.1 Cover Letter

A **cover letter** is formal written communication that accompanies a résumé or a job application to introduce an applicant and express interest in a position. It provides an explanation of why you are the best candidate for the job. It should create an immediate, positive impression of your persuasive communication skills. Effective cover letters are brief, no longer than one page, and written in a way that invites and encourages potential employers to read your résumé. If your letter is ineffective, you may not be considered a viable candidate.

A cover letter is about you and your interest in the company and job for which you are applying. Conduct research about the company and read the job description or posting. Use what you have learned to support your interest in working there. A compelling cover letter succinctly demonstrates to an employer that you would be an asset to the company.

Consider using a template to get the writing process started. Similar to a résumé template, a cover letter template is a pre-formatted, word-processing document that contains a standard layout with adequate margins of white space. Use of a template will establish a balanced look that can be customized for your personal needs rather than starting from scratch. You may also be able to find examples of cover letters online, such as by searching the @opencoverletter Twitter page.

You may need to create different types of cover letters throughout the job-search process. The type of letter you write depends on how you learned about the position for which you are applying. Three basic types of cover letters typically used include application, networking, and inquiry.

An **application cover letter** is a letter used to apply for and provide personal qualifications for a position that has been posted by an employer. The goal of this type of letter is to convince someone in the company to schedule an interview with you. It generally begins with an opening statement in which you introduce yourself and list the specific position for which you are applying. This statement can also include how you learned of the opening. The following is an example of an opening paragraph for an application cover letter:

> My name is Natasha Patel, and I was excited to learn of the opening for an architect at Aurora Industries. I read the job posting on your website and would like to offer my résumé for consideration.

A **networking cover letter** is a letter that introduces an applicant by noting that a person in their network recommended they apply for the position. Ideally, a hiring manager reading this letter would recognize the person referenced in the letter and contact the applicant for more information.

The opening statement for this type of letter is similar to that of an application cover letter but includes the name of the person who recommended you apply for the job. An example of an opening statement for a networking cover letter is as follows:

> My name is Manuel Ramirez, and I recently spoke to Kelly Williams who suggested I forward my résumé to you for consideration for the design architect position in your company.

An **inquiry cover letter** is a letter written to learn if any potential positions are available for which the job seeker would like to be considered. Sending this type of letter is also known as *prospecting*. Generally, these letters are written for positions that have not been posted publicly. In this letter, the applicant is asking to be considered for a specific position if an opening becomes available. The hope is that the company will keep the cover letter and résumé on file for future opportunities.

By default, the opening statement for an inquiry cover letter is different from that of an application or networking letter. This is because there is no specific job opening or person referenced. Instead, the goal is to explain the type of position for which you are looking and offer your résumé for consideration in any potential openings. It should also include a brief summary of how

---

The Best App for That

Monster

The *Monster* job-search mobile app allows you to stay connected to the job-search process at a time and place that are convenient for you. After signing up for a Monster account, you can upload your résumé and apply for jobs directly from the app. You can set criteria to help narrow your job search, such as where you would like to work (e.g., state or city), your desired salary range, the type of occupation or industry you want to work in, and availability date. You will receive notifications for jobs that fit your criteria. You can even browse current job openings by location or job category. Monster strives to connect people to jobs.

you retrieved contact information for the company. The following is an example of an opening paragraph of an inquiry cover letter:

> My name is Fatima Lynn, and I am currently seeking employment as an interior design architect at a reputable company such as yours. I located your contact information through research of the industry, and I would like to provide you with my résumé for future consideration of openings that may become available.

Cover letters are dynamic. The information in each version of the letter changes slightly to match specific job requirements. It is a good practice to create one foundational letter and save it as a master document, similar to creating a master résumé. This document can later be modified each time a résumé or a job application is submitted. **Figure 8-1** provides examples of best practices to consider when writing your cover letter.

CONNECT TO YOUR CAREER

Complete 8-1 Cover Letter Template, pg. 141

FIGURE 8-1

A cover letter is formal written communication that accompanies a résumé or a job application to introduce the applicant and express interest in a position.

Best Practices for Writing Cover Letters	
Do... ✓	**Do Not...** ✗
Customize each cover letter so that it is unique.	Use the same cover letter for each job for which you apply.
Include the exact title of the position and job posting number, if included, for which you are applying.	Omit the position name and job posting number, if included, of the job for which you are applying.
Compose a professional, well-written cover letter that will resonate with the reader.	Compose a hastily written letter because you assume that the reader will understand your intent.
Use Standard English.	Use informal language, slang, jargon, or texting language.
Explain why you are a good fit for the company because you are regarded as a team player.	Omit skills that represent why people would describe you as a team player.
Add job keywords in the cover letter from the job posting.	Omit keywords from the job posting.
Explain why you are applying for the job.	Omit the reason you are applying for the job.
Summarize skills and talents you can bring to the company.	Omit your skills and talents that demonstrate you are a qualified professional.
Add e-mail address.	Omit contact information.
Run spell-check and proofread the letter.	Submit before running spell-check and proofreading carefully.
Add your signature (whether manually or digitally).	Print or key your signature.
Assume that the employer will read all submitted letters.	Assume that the employer will ignore your letter.

Goodheart-Willcox Publisher; Marnikus/Shutterstock.com; Kagan Kaya/Shutterstock.com

8.2 Parts of a Cover Letter

A cover letter includes the following sections, as shown in **Figure 8-2**:
- heading
- date
- greeting
- introduction
- body
- complimentary close
- signature block

Employers expect these sections to be included in every letter that is submitted from a job applicant. Not having the appropriate sections can appear unprofessional and result in a cover letter going unread.

Heading and Date

A cover letter includes a heading that states your contact information. The contact information in the heading should match the contact information found in your résumé. The heading should be formatted so that it looks similar to letterhead, but with simpler elements. Underneath the heading, add today's date.

Greeting

Every cover letter should open with an appropriate greeting that demonstrates professionalism. If you have a contact name, you may use a greeting that begins with "Dear" followed by the person's full name, such as "Dear Chris Scott." It is best to avoid using titles such as "Mr." and "Ms." If you do not have a contact name, do not use "To Whom It May Concern," as it is generally perceived as impersonal. Instead, an approach that is becoming more common is to address the letter to the hiring department or manager. For example, the greeting might be "Hello, Hiring Team."

Introduction

Begin a cover letter with an enthusiastic statement. Follow the statement with a direct opening paragraph that explains exactly why you are sending the communication. For example, "I am applying for the position of assistant architect." In the next sentence, state how you heard about the available position. For example, "I learned about this job opportunity through a job posting on [website] and was immediately drawn to the exciting prospect of joining your dynamic team."

Time Management

Job Search

When searching for a job, managing your time effectively can make the difference between a successful search and a frustrating one. Here are some time-management strategies to help you stay organized and efficient during the job search process.

- *Set aside dedicated time for job searching.* Create a schedule that includes specific blocks of time each day or week for job searching. Treat this time like you would a job and commit to using it solely for job-related activities.
- *Focus on the most important tasks first.* Identify the job-search activities that are most critical to your success, such as networking, customizing your résumé, or researching companies. Prioritize these tasks and tackle them during your most productive hours.
- *Use technology to streamline your search.* Take advantage of online job boards and career search engines to identify opportunities that match your skills and experience. Use job alerts and e-mail notifications to stay informed of new job postings.
- *Keep track of your applications.* Create a spreadsheet or other tracking system to monitor your applications, deadlines, and follow-up tasks. This will help you avoid missing important opportunities or submitting duplicate applications.
- *Make time for self-care.* Job searching can be stressful, so it is important to take care of yourself physically and emotionally. Make time for exercise, healthy meals, and activities that bring you joy and relaxation.

By implementing these time-management strategies, you can streamline your job search process and increase your chances of finding the right opportunity more quickly. Remember to stay organized, stay focused on your goals, and take care of yourself along the way.

FIGURE 8-2

Cover letters are dynamic and should be changed as needed to match specific job requirements.

Kofi Mensah
1006 Mountain View Parkway, San Diego, CA 91932
(619) 555–4023 • kofimensah@e-mail.com • www.linkedin.com/in/kofi-mensah

September 24, 20--

Susan Taylor
Skyline Dynamics
553 Cleveland Street
San Diego, CA 91911

Dear Susan Taylor:

I am writing to apply for the position of Sustainability Consultant Architect at Skyline Dynamics. I learned about this job opportunity through a job posting on LinkedIn and was immediately drawn to the exciting prospect of joining your team. As a multiyear veteran in the architecture industry, I am confident in my ability to contribute to your team and make a positive impact on your projects.

Throughout my career, I have had the opportunity to work on a variety of projects, ranging from residential buildings to commercial structures. This diverse range of experience has allowed me to develop a strong foundation in design and sustainability principles. In my previous role at Zenith Enterprises, I was responsible for leading the design team on a number of successful projects and was praised for my ability to balance creative vision with practicality and cost-effectiveness.

I am excited about the opportunity to join Skyline Dynamics and contribute to your company's mission and vision. I am confident that my skills and experience make me a strong fit for this role, and I look forward to the opportunity to bring my expertise to your team.

Thank you for considering my application. Please contact me to discuss my qualifications further.

Sincerely,

Kofi Mensah

Kofi Mensah
Sustainability Consultant Architect

Goodheart-Willcox Publisher

Next, add a sentence that describes your passion and desire to hold this position. If you have created a personal brand statement, incorporate it in this paragraph. The following is a sample cover letter introduction with a personal brand statement as the closing line:

> I am applying for the position of urban design architect at NimbleTech Solutions. I read your ad for this position on your corporate website. I am a customer-first people person who interacts with urban, town, and city colleagues successfully. Whether providing design recommendations for either small- or large-scale projects, the key is to create positive interaction. My passion is to guide and serve.

Body

The body is the longest part of the letter. Its purpose is to demonstrate that you meet or exceed the qualifications of the job. Do not restate the information in your résumé. Instead, explain why you are qualified for the position. Use pertinent keywords from the job requirements to show the strength of your qualifications. This will help demonstrate why you are a good, long-term fit for the company.

There are two ways the body of a cover letter can be written. You can write it in paragraph form, as shown in Figure 8-2, or you can use a bulleted list of the employer's requirements followed by a list of your matching qualifications, as shown in **Figure 8-3**. If space permits, it is acceptable to place the bulleted list in two columns rather than one column, as shown in **Figure 8-4**.

It is expected that you will ask for an interview in the body of your cover letter. In the closing paragraph, request an opportunity to discuss your qualifications with the reader in a sincere and confident statement. State when you are available and express your eagerness and anticipation to hear from the employer.

Complimentary Close

The **complimentary close** is the sign-off for the letter. Examples include *Sincerely, Best regards,* and *Respectfully.* Only the first word is capitalized.

The complimentary close is followed by the signature block, which includes your name and title. Add a signature to your cover letter above your name. It is preferable to have a cursive signature rather than one that has been typed. *Cursive* is a style of handwriting or font in which each letter of a word is joined to the letters adjacent to it. It is more formal than printing your name.

When you want to add a cursive signature to your cover letter, save your cover letter as a PDF file, and add a cursive signature through the Fill & Sign pane. An example of a signature block with a cursive signature is shown below.

> Sincerely,
>
> *Emily Williams*
>
> Emily Williams
> Product Manager

CONNECT TO YOUR CAREER

Complete 8-2 Master Cover Letter, pg. 142

8.3 Cover Letter Submission

Before submitting a cover letter, it is important to do one final review for accuracy. Your letter should be without grammar, punctuation, or spelling errors. The body should be in a font that is professional and easy to read. Microsoft Word's default font, Calibri, is recommended. The font size should be kept between 11 and 12 points. A font smaller than 11 points will be difficult to read, and a font larger than 12 points will look too aggressive. Margins should be set to 1 inch on all sides, but if your cover letter is short, consider using 1 1/2-inch margins. The checklist in **Figure 8-5** will help you as you finalize the document.

Once perfected, there are a variety of ways to submit a cover letter to apply for a position. The most common methods are submitting by e-mail, uploading to a job board, or submitting a hard copy. A cover letter should be submitted along with your résumé.

Submit by E-mail

When submitting a cover letter and résumé via e-mail, use your professional e-mail account. Include a brief, professional, and clear subject line. Including a subject line can help ensure that your application is properly directed and easily identifiable among other submissions. Make sure that the subject line of your e-mail is concise, professional, and accurately reflects the content of your application. The following is a sample of a subject line:

> Cortez Application for Concierge Position

FIGURE 8-3

The body of a cover letter can include paragraphs as well as bulleted lists.

Jalia Cortez
111 First Street, Redwood City, CA 94061
(619) 555–1235 • jcortez@e-mail.com • www.linkedin.com/in/jalia-cortez

November 30, 20--

Human Resources
Architect ABC
12344 Main Street
Redwood City, CA 94061

Hello Hiring Team:

I am applying for the Architect position at your company. I learned about this job opportunity through a job posting on CareerBuilder. I am confident that my skills and expertise make me a strong candidate for the role. Furthermore, I am drawn to your company's mission and values. I am eager to contribute my talents to this dynamic team and am excited about the opportunity to grow and develop my skills with Architect ABC.

I have reviewed the qualifications posted for this position. I am certain that my skills and talents match the requirements for which you are looking.

Your Requirements
- A professional degree in architecture
- Licensure as an architect
- Strong communication and problem-solving skills
- Ability to manage multiple projects and meet deadlines
- Proficiency in computer-aided design (CAD) software

My Qualifications
- Bachelor's degree in architecture
- California architect's license
- Preparation of comprehensive project proposals, including site analysis, conceptual sketches, and construction documentation, that resulted in successful project bids
- Management of multiple construction sites to ensure adherence to schedules
- Creation of technical drawings for all in-house architects.

I am thrilled at the prospect of contributing my expertise to Architect ABC and collaborating on forward-thinking, eco-friendly initiatives that benefit the people they serve. I have enclosed my résumé for your consideration and would like to set up an interview soon.

Sincerely,

Jalia Cortez

Jalia Cortez

Enclosure

Goodheart-Willcox Publisher

FIGURE 8-4

The body of a cover letter can be two columns to help illustrate a candidate's qualifications.

Jalia Cortez
111 First Street, Redwood City, CA 94061
(619) 555–1235 • jcortez@e-mail.com • www.linkedin.com/in/jalia-cortez

November 30, 20--

Human Resources
Architect ABC
12344 Main Street
Redwood City, CA 94061

Hello, Hiring Team:

I am applying for the Architect position at your company. I learned about this job opportunity through a job posting on CareerBuilder. I am confident that my skills and expertise make me a strong candidate for the role. Furthermore, I am drawn to your company's mission and values. I am eager to contribute my talents to this dynamic team and am excited about the opportunity to grow and develop my skills with Architect ABC.

I have reviewed the qualifications posted for this position. I am certain that my skills and talents match the requirements for which you are looking.

Your Requirements:	**My Qualifications:**
A professional degree in architecture	Bachelor's degree in architecture
Licensure as an architect	California architect's license
Strong communication and problem-solving skills	Preparation of comprehensive project proposals that resulted in successful project bids
Ability to manage multiple projects and meet deadlines	Management of multiple construction sites to ensure adherence to schedules
Proficiency in computer-aided design (CAD) software	Creation of technical drawings for all in-house architects.

I am thrilled at the prospect of contributing my expertise to Architect ABC and collaborating on forward-thinking, eco-friendly initiatives that benefit the people they serve. I have enclosed my résumé for your consideration and would like to set up an interview soon.

Sincerely,

Jalia Cortez

Jalia Cortez

Enclosure

Goodheart-Willcox Publisher

FIGURE 8-5

A checklist of items can be used to confirm the cover letter is accurate.

Cover Letter Checklist

As you create your cover letters, use this checklist to ensure that you add all essential information.

Heading
- ☐ Include full name in the header section
- ☐ Date

Greeting
- ☐ Create a salutation
- ☐ Avoid using "To Whom It May Concern" and titles such as "Mr." and "Ms."

Introduction
- ☐ State why you are writing, e.g., I am applying for the position of _____
- ☐ Add two or three more sentences, such as how you heard about the position and why it interests you

Body
- ☐ Demonstrate qualifications
- ☐ Use job requirement keywords
- ☐ Demonstrate career success
- ☐ Emphasize accomplishments

Closing
- ☐ Thank the reader
- ☐ Create a complimentary closing
- ☐ At the bottom, include a signature block
- ☐ Add your contact information to the signature block, including e-mail and phone number

General
- ☐ Customize the letter for the position desired
- ☐ Format the letter attractively and professionally
- ☐ Proofread and run spell-check
- ☐ Limit to one page
- ☐ Use professional tone throughout
- ☐ Have the letter reviewed by instructor and/or peer

Goodheart-Willcox Publisher

Workplace Skills

Optimism is the expectation that things will turn out well. Optimism enables people to look at the big picture, identify what can be changed, recognize what cannot be changed, and make good decisions. Optimists learn from experiences, accurately identify problems, and try to offer solutions, rather than complaints. Optimistic people are proactive and learn from their mistakes. Optimism can help you maintain a positive attitude during the job-search process.

When creating a subject line in an e-mail, do not:
- use exclamation points
- use all caps
- use a lengthy subject line

The formal content in the body of the e-mail is comprised of the body of your print letter. As with other professional correspondence, it is a good idea to include your e-mail signature block after the complimentary close.

You may opt to attach a cover letter to your e-mail rather than include it in the body of the message. However, not all employers open attachments due to potential exposure to malware. If you choose to attach it, state the purpose of the attachment and reference it in the body of your e-mail message. Save the letter as a PDF file before attaching it to the e-mail.

Some e-mail software includes the option to mark an e-mail as *priority*. You can use this option if you are sending your résumé and cover letter immediately before the submission process is scheduled to close. A high-priority e-mail also indicates that the sender would like the recipient to open the e-mail shortly after it is received.

Upload to an Online Job Board

You may have an opportunity to apply for a position through an online job board. An *online job board* is a website that hosts job postings for employers and allows applicants to apply for jobs seamlessly. If you are applying through a job board, you may be required to upload your résumé and cut and paste your cover letter into a web form. The website will give directions regarding how to complete these tasks. Always follow the directions as specified. It may be necessary to use plain text for your cover letter as the form may omit formatting. In this case, it is better to be safe and use unformatted text. Just like a plain text résumé, you can save and submit a cover letter as a .TXT file.

Submit a Hard Copy

Some employers require submission of a printed cover letter and résumé to be considered for a position. Hard copies should be printed on high-quality white paper. The documents should not be stapled together but may be secured with a paper clip. The documents should be placed, unfolded, into a folder or large manila envelope with the intended recipient's name clearly indicated on the outside. If you are mailing the documents, consider taking the manila envelope containing the documents to the post office to have it weighed so the appropriate amount of postage can be affixed to the package.

Once you secure an interview, if it will be in person, take copies of your documents to present to the interviewer. In this case, it is not necessary to put the interviewer's name on the outside of the folder or envelope, though it *is* necessary to include your own. Be prepared with an adequate number of documents for each person who may be part of the interview team. If you are unsure of how many copies to make, it is appropriate to call the company ahead of time and ask how many people with whom you will be meeting.

Career Persona

Architect

Vector Tradition/Shutterstock.com

Responsibilities

Consider the buildings in which you live, work, shop, and eat. An architect is responsible for designing and planning the layout, appearance, and functionality of these buildings, while also ensuring that the project meets safety codes, zoning regulations, and budget constraints. An architect must:

- Prepare scale drawings with computer software or by hand
- Work closely with clients, engineers, and contractors to ensure the design is properly translated into a finished structure
- Oversee the construction process, including site visits, inspections, and compliance with all relevant building codes
- Conduct feasibility studies and site analysis to determine the best design solution
- Coordinate with other professionals such as structural engineers, mechanical engineers, and landscape architects to ensure the final design is functional, safe, and sustainable

Qualities and Skills

Architects are professionals who design and plan the construction of buildings and other physical structures. Some of the key qualities and skills typically associated with architects include:

- *Attention to detail:* Architects must pay close attention to the smallest details in their designs to ensure that every aspect of the structure is properly planned and executed.
- *Technical knowledge:* Architects must have a deep understanding of building codes, zoning laws, and other technical aspects of construction to ensure that their designs meet all relevant regulations and requirements.
- *Problem-solving skills:* Architects must be able to identify and solve problems that arise during the design and construction process, such as unexpected delays or budget overruns.
- *Passion for architecture:* Finally, architects must have a deep passion for their work, as this is what drives them to continuously improve their skills and create outstanding designs.

Education

- Bachelor's degree in architecture from an accredited university or college
- Practical training as an intern, often through the Architectural Experience Program
- Passage of the Architect Registration Examination (ARE)
- State licensure to practice architecture
- Continuing education requirements as set by the National Council of Architectural Registration Boards (NCARB) and state boards of architecture

Next Steps

To help prepare for a career in architecture, take math courses, including geometry, algebra, calculus, and trigonometry. Science classes such as physics are also beneficial. It is also important to take art classes that explore drawing, painting, sculpting, and photography.

Summary

8.1 Explain the purpose of a cover letter.
The purpose of a cover letter is to provide an explanation of why a person is the best candidate for a job and to create an immediate, positive impression of their persuasive communication skills. There are three basic types of cover letters: application, networking, and inquiry cover letters.

8.2 Identify sections of a cover letter.
Cover letters include a heading, date, greeting, introduction, body, and complimentary close.

8.3 Cite three methods of cover letter submission.
When applying for a position, cover letters may be submitted by e-mail, uploaded to a job board, or delivered as a hard copy.

Glossary Terms

application cover letter
complimentary close
cover letter
inquiry cover letter
networking cover letter

Review

1. What is the purpose of a cover letter and who is the intended audience? (8.1)

2. Why is it a good idea to create a foundational cover letter? (8.1)

3. Identify and describe the goals of each type of cover letter. (8.1)

4. What is *prospecting*? (8.1)

5. Identify and describe sections of a cover letter. (8.2)

6. In which part of the cover letter should you explain why you are qualified for a position? (8.2)

7. Why is the phrase *To Whom It May Concern* not recommended for the greeting of a cover letter? Provide an example of an alternative greeting. (8.2)

8. What should be included in the closing paragraph of a cover letter? (8.2)

9. Describe three methods to submit a cover letter to apply for a position. (8.3)

10. When submitting a cover letter via e-mail, what are some tips for creating a subject line? (8.3)

Application

1. Review the best practices for writing cover letters outlined in Figure 8-1. How would you modify this checklist for your personal job-search process? (8.1)

   _____

   _____

   _____

2. A cover letter describes why you would be an asset to an employer. Write a paragraph that highlights your most important work and personal qualities that would make you an asset to an employer. (8.2)

   _____

   _____

   _____

3. How do you determine which information is best suited for your cover letter vs. your résumé? (8.2)

   _____

   _____

   _____

4. How would you write your cover letter to emphasize your strengths? (8.2)

   _____

   _____

   _____

5. What information would you include in the heading of your cover letter? (8.2)

   _____

   _____

   _____

6. Read the cover letter in Figure 8-2. If you were a hiring manager, what questions would you have for this person after reading it? (8.2)

   _____

   _____

   _____

Chapter 8   Cover Letters

7. Businesses want to hire employees who are excited to come to work. Write an effective sentence that conveys your enthusiasm for the desired position. (8.2)

_____
_____
_____

8. Examples of complimentary closes include *Sincerely, Yours truly,* and *Respectfully.* What closing do you anticipate using that represents who you are and your brand? (8.2)

_____
_____
_____

9. How might the timing of submitting a cover letter affect the candidate's chances of getting an interview? (8.3)

_____
_____
_____

10. Based on the three methods of cover letter submissions (e-mails, online job boards, and hard copies), which do you think you will use the most? Explain why. (8.3)

_____
_____
_____

CONNECT TO YOUR CAREER

Workplace Connection

8-1 Cover Letter Template

1. Working in small groups, conduct an Internet search using the phrase *cover letter template.* Record several URLs of templates you would consider using in the future.

    URL #1: _____

    URL #2: _____

URL #3:
_____

URL #4:
_____

2. As a group, select the template you prefer. Explain why.
_____
_____
_____
_____

3. Based on your research, compile a list of common elements that should be included in a cover letter template.
_____
_____
_____
_____

4. Using your list, create a cover letter template and present it to the class. Then, as a class, decide on the best elements from each template presented and create a final cover letter template.

8-2 Master Cover Letter

1. Using the Internet or other source, search for and select an advertisement for a position that interests you. In the space that follows, record the position title, name of the company, name of the contact person (if available), and e-mail or mailing address.

   Position Title:
   _____

   Company Name:
   _____

   Contact Person:
   _____

   E-mail or Mailing Address:
   _____

2. Write the first draft of each component of an *application cover letter*. Keep it succinct and to the point. Remember to use keywords as you describe your qualifications. Draft the introduction and the body. In the closing paragraph, remember to request the opportunity for an interview.

   Introduction:

   _____

   _____

   _____

   _____

   Body:

   _____

   _____

   _____

   _____

   _____

   _____

   _____

   _____

   _____

   Closing:

   _____

   _____

   _____

   _____

3. Revise your draft letter to create a cover letter in final form. Use the template you created in Workplace Connection 8-1. Run spell-check and proofread the document. When you are finished, save your document as *FirstnameLastname_CoverLetter.docx* (e.g., NatashaPatel_CoverLetter.docx). Alternatively, you may choose to add an additional identifier to the name such as the company name or month to keep track of where or when you are sending letters (e.g., NatashaPatel_CoverLetter_AuroraIndustries.docx). Additionally, save your document in the following formats:
   - Save the master cover letter as a plain text document.
   - Return to the Word version of the master cover letter file and save it as a PDF document.
   - Return to the Word version of the master cover letter file and save it as a web-page document.

CHAPTER 9
Applying for Jobs

Learning Outcomes

9.1 **Explain** how to complete a job application.

9.2 **Describe** the process of applying for a job in person.

9.3 **Describe** the process of applying for a job online.

9.4 **Define** *Sunday Evening Plan*.

9.5 **Explain** methods for managing the application process.

9.6 **Define** a *job-tracking spreadsheet*.

CONNECT TO YOUR CAREER

Workplace Connection

9-1   Job Application
9-2   Job-Search Websites
9-3   Job-Tracking Spreadsheet

OVERVIEW

The job application process does not stop with the résumé and cover letter. You will likely be asked to complete a formal job application form. This form provides information the employer needs during and after the employment process. The application may be a hard copy or online form. Both require the same amount of preparation and care when completing them.

In some cases, you may apply for a job in person. However, you are likely to apply for a job online—one that you might find on a job list or a job board. Both job-search websites and online job boards provide current, up-to-date job advertisements. You can make these job-search resources work for you by adopting a Sunday Evening Plan. This plan involves updating your application documents every week. In addition, managing and organizing the application process will help ease your job search.

Elena Berd/Shutterstock.com

144 Copyright Goodheart-Willcox Co., Inc.

9.1 Job Applications

A résumé and cover letter are not the only documents a person needs when applying for a job. At some point, most companies require a completed job application. A **job application** is a form used by employers to gain more information about a person applying for a job. A portion of a sample application is shown in **Figure 9-1**.

A job application requires personal information, names and addresses of the schools you have attended, and degrees earned. Addresses of your previous employers, supervisors' names, and contact information will also be requested. Some applications require additional information beyond your work experience. Be truthful when answering each question, and do not leave any lines blank. If any requested information is not applicable to you, write "N/A" in the space. You may also be asked for the names and contact information for professional references.

The application may contain a line inquiring as to whether previous employers may be contacted. If a former supervisor is no longer employed where you worked, state that the person is no longer with the company and provide contact information for the human resources department.

After the job application is complete, proofread it and compare it with your résumé. If either document contains conflicting information, edit the documents so they match.

CONNECT TO YOUR CAREER

Complete 9-1 Job Application, pg. 157

9.2 Applying for Jobs in Person

It is not always necessary to wait for a business to advertise employment opportunities. For some businesses, such as retail, it is appropriate to visit and ask for a job application. Some businesses request that applicants take an application with them and return it when it is complete.

If you do not know the employment process of the particular business you plan to target, prepare to stay on-site to complete the application. Bring a quality blue or black pen with you so you will not have to ask to borrow one. Although requesting and completing an application on-site is not a formal interview, dress professionally.

Before your visit, customize a résumé and an inquiry cover letter that best matches the business to which you are applying. Create a separate document that clearly lists professional references and their respective contact information. Print each document and place it in a folder or envelope that you can leave with the human resources manager. If applicable, bring a copy of your portfolio to leave behind.

After you complete the application, sign and date the form. Assemble the application, cover letter, résumé, and list of references in order, and place them in the envelope or folder you brought with you. Make a note in your mobile device that includes the name of the employer and person who took your documents, or to whom you mailed them, along with the date of mailing.

If you have not heard from the company or manager within one week of applying, it is appropriate to call and follow up regarding the application you submitted. From that point, wait for the business to contact you.

While you are waiting, continue applying for as many jobs for which you are qualified. The process of connecting to your career is ongoing. Always apply for jobs and only cease when you are employed.

9.3 Searching and Applying for Jobs Online

Many companies prefer that candidates complete applications online. The online application process is similar to the paper-based method. The process of applying for employment online starts with reading and sorting through available job postings. After finding an employment opportunity that fits your skills and desires, submit an electronic application and necessary employment documents.

Searching for Jobs Online

One way to find available openings is by using a job-search website. A **job-search website** is a website on which multiple employers post employment opportunities on a daily basis. These sites allow users to view openings anywhere in the world. LinkedIn, Twitter, and ZipRecruiter are examples of hosted job-search websites. For the most part, using these sites is free, as they are intended for public viewing. In some cases, users are not required to register or create a username or password to take advantage of these sites. However, some sites, such as LinkedIn and Twitter, do require people to register for an account. There are two basic types of job-search websites: aggregate job boards and non-aggregate job boards.

Aggregate Job Board

An **aggregate job board** is a job-search website that collects data from multiple online sources and combines the results. Think of this popular type of job-search website as a search engine similar to Google.

FIGURE 9-1

A job application is a form used by employers to gain more information about a person applying for a job.

Job Application

Personal Information

Last Name		First Name	Middle Initial
Address	City	State	Zip
How long at present address?	Phone Number		

What date will you be available for work?

Type of employment desired:
　　　_____ Full-time only　　　_____ Part-time only　　　_____ Full- or part-time

If hired, can you furnish proof that you are legally entitled to work in the United States?

What position are you applying for?	What are your salary requirements?

Hours you will be available to work:

Have you ever been convicted of a felony?

If yes, please explain:

The XYZ Company is a drug-free employer and you will be required to pass a drug screening as a condition of employment. I understand and agree to participate in testing. (_____) initials

Educational Information

Name and Address of School	Course of Study	Diploma or Degree
High School		
College Education		
Graduate Education		
Other Education/Training		

Goodheart-Willcox Publisher

A search query is entered, and the website searches across the Internet for items matching it. Instead of a user searching through job boards individually, an aggregate job board collects and compiles posted openings onto one site. Examples include Indeed and SimplyHired.

The job listing may indicate where the original advertisement for the position was posted. The advertisement may have been in a local newspaper, individual job board, or other sources. You can go to the original site of the advertisement and apply there. Alternatively, if you prefer, you may apply for employment directly from the aggregate site. However, you may be required to establish an account in order to do so.

Non-Aggregate Job Board

A **non-aggregate job board** is a website on which employers post job openings directly on the board. The main difference between aggregate and non-aggregate job boards is that non-aggregate boards list only what was posted to them by employers; they do not search the Internet for additional posts. Examples of online job boards are Monster and CareerBuilder.

You may be required to register an account and profile. After the account and profile information are completed, it is important to customize the account and privacy settings to reflect your preferences. Be certain that you understand the options before making your decision, because this may limit the employers or recruiters who have access to your information. Once an account is created, some online job boards invite users to upload and store cover letters and résumés. These sites offer a one-click method, whereby an applicant's documents are forwarded by the site directly to the employer or hiring agent.

Tips for the Online Job Search

Read online job postings carefully. Keep in mind that the *required* qualifications must be met, but you do not necessarily have to meet all of the *desired* qualifications. A benchmark should be set to help you determine if you have a real chance at the position or if the job is completely out of your league. A *benchmark* is how many of the employment qualifications you believe are necessary to meet before you apply for a position. For example, your benchmark may be to meet 80 percent of the advertised desired qualifications and 100 percent of the required qualifications in a job posting.

If you find multiple postings for which you want to apply but are unable to do so immediately, forward them to your professional e-mail account. This action sends the company name, job title, description, and submission details to your e-mail. Alternatively, you can bookmark the page that contains the postings in your Internet browser. This will allow you to return to the page later.

Most job-search websites encourage applicants to post résumés to their accounts at no cost. It is a good idea to take advantage of this free service. These websites are often good sources of potential job candidates for employers who may search the site. If an employer finds a résumé of a candidate with whom it wants to meet, the employer will contact that person directly.

When posting a résumé to a job-search website, the same customization rules apply as with an electronically submitted résumé. For safety and privacy concerns, provide a general geographic location instead of a physical address. Additionally, remove all contact information aside from an e-mail address.

There are hundreds of new openings posted online each day. This can seem overwhelming. However, the steps to search for available employment opportunities online follow a pattern. The home page of most job-search websites features a text box in which to enter search criteria. The first step is to enter a job title, keywords, or a company name. The next step is to select the desired location for the position. Some sites offer options for an advanced search. In these cases, criteria that are more specific can be selected to narrow your search. For example, you may be able to set search parameters to find full-time jobs only. To begin searching for jobs, follow these steps:

1. Search for a job title and desired location.
2. Review available job postings and locate the name and e-mail address of a contact person for each job posting. Not every job posting will have a contact person.
3. Research each company name or individual who posts a job advertisement to ascertain whether you are a good fit for that company and position.
4. Determine if each posting is from a legitimate company or individual. Remember, if it seems too good to be true, it probably is.
5. Follow any application-submission instructions listed in the job posting. If no specific or special instructions have been provided, apply directly to the individual listed as a contact person for the job advertisement. If no contact person is included in the post, apply directly to the company by navigating to the company's website and searching the website for a Careers or Employment Opportunities page. Alternatively, you may be able to apply for the job directly through the job-search website on which you found the listing.

CONNECT TO YOUR CAREER

Complete 9-2 Job-Search Websites, pg. 157

Career Persona

Journalist

Responsibilities

A journalist is a professional who gathers, writes, and reports news and information for various media outlets such as newspapers, magazines, radio, television, and online news websites. The career of a journalist typically involves researching, conducting interviews, and writing articles, news stories, and other types of content on a wide range of topics. Some additional responsibilities of a journalist include the following:

- Inform and educate the public
- Examine news items of significance to determine topics to address
- Analyze and interpret information received from various sources
- Review stories for accuracy, style, and grammar
- Meet tight deadlines

davooda/Shutterstock.com

Qualities and Skills

- *Strong communication skills*: Journalists must have good verbal and written communication skills to clearly relay information to others.
- *Curiosity and persistence*: Journalists must have a strong desire to learn about something and the determination to get answers to questions.
- *Integrity and ethical behavior*: Truthful and accurate reporting is the foundation of good journalism.
- *Interpersonal skills*: To develop news contacts and conduct interviews, journalists must be able to build relationships and work well with their colleagues.
- *Research and analytical skills*: Journalists must conduct extensive research to uncover information and then evaluate it before presenting a story to the public.
- *Digital literacy skills*: Knowing how to use digital research tools, such as websites, apps, social media, and search engines, is a job necessity.

Education

- Bachelor's degree in journalism, communications, or a related field
- Internship or work experience with various news/media organizations
- Continuing education and professional development opportunities

Next Steps

To become a journalist, it is helpful to gain knowledge of the media industry. A good way to gain experience is to work on your school newspaper or at a radio or television station. In addition to English courses, studying an array of subjects, such as history and economics, can give you the background needed to cover a range of topics. In all your courses, continue fine-tune your writing, research, and critical-thinking skills.

Connect to Your Community

Working for local organizations is a great way for you to gain valuable experience in your field of interest. For instance, if you are interested in construction, you can gain experience by working for organizations such as Habitat for Humanity, which builds homes for people in need. Similarly, if you are interested in healthcare, you can gain experience by volunteering at a local health clinic or hospital. Those interested in social services can work at a food pantry or soup kitchen, helping to distribute food and other resources to people in need. If you are interested in working outdoors, working for the parks and recreation department can provide opportunities to work on projects such as maintaining hiking trails or landscaping parks. Regardless of the field, there are many opportunities in the community for students to gain work experience and build skills that will be valuable in their future careers.

Stephanie L Sanchez/Shutterstock.com

Applying for Jobs Online

As you begin applying for jobs online, you will find that different postings will take you to various websites on the Internet. Some employment advertisements link directly to corporate websites, while others link to recruiting agents who screen résumés. Regardless of where the job posting ultimately leads you, each posting and application should be given equal weight.

Resist the temptation to hurry through an online application form. Spelling, complete sentences, and grammar rules still apply. Everything should be carefully proofread before submission. Once the application is submitted, you will not be able to make revisions or corrections.

9.4 Sunday Evening Plan

Monday morning is a critical day in the job-search process for potential employees. This is when recruiters use advanced search criteria to find new and updated résumés of potential job candidates. Recruiters begin each week by sorting through résumés with keywords that match the criteria they seek.

In order to get your résumé viewed by recruiters on Monday morning, your information should be updated on Sunday night. This can be easily accomplished with a **Sunday Evening Plan**, which is a routine or schedule that job seekers set for themselves on Sunday evenings to review their job-search progress and plan their job-search activities for the upcoming week. The purpose of a Sunday Evening Plan is to maintain a proactive approach to job seeking, stay organized, and improve the chances of landing a job. Every Sunday evening during a job search, you should update, edit, and proofread all employment documents. After revising your employment information, post these updated documents to active job boards. The timestamp is important. Even if you find that no edits are necessary, delete the existing documents and re-upload them so they are flagged as new. Recruiters are only notified of new and updated documents. By setting aside time each week to evaluate progress and plan ahead, job seekers can maintain momentum and stay motivated throughout their job search.

A Sunday Evening Plan can include the following tasks:
- Review résumés and cover letters, making any necessary updates or revisions.
- Research potential job opportunities, such as job listings, company information, and industry trends.
- Prepare for upcoming interviews, such as by researching the company and practicing answers to common interview questions.
- Make a list of companies to contact and/or apply for jobs.
- Set specific goals and objectives for the next week.

By setting aside time each Sunday to review your job-search progress and plan your activities for the upcoming week, you can stay on top of the job-search process.

9.5 Managing the Application Process

Managing the application process is a job in itself. Writing a résumé and cover letter are just two of the many tasks that are necessary to find a position. The workplace is more competitive than ever. It will be necessary to put effort into finding employment that fits your needs and interests. Tasks for managing the application process include applying time management strategies, staying current in terms of your employment documents, keeping in touch with one's professional network, setting job alerts, and downloading appropriate applications.

Time Management

Time management is an essential skill when looking for a job. Time slips away quickly. The process must be managed so the right position can be found in an amount of time that works for you. Typically, it is helpful to create a schedule that includes an end goal of when you need to be employed. After your goal has been established, fill in the days with the activities that are needed to reach the goal.

Calendar software works well as a time-management tool. It will allow you to set notifications that remind you of various responsibilities you have on certain days. You may prefer a paper calendar. Use what works best for you.

Some of your application-management responsibilities will include the tasks you have learned in this text. You will add others as you progress. Examples of tasks to schedule may include:
- draft a career plan
- develop a personal brand statement
- create professional networking accounts
- manage your online presence
- create a résumé
- draft a cover letter
- complete an application
- prepare for an interview

Without a schedule, it can be challenging to accomplish all the activities needed to become employed.

Stay Current

It is important to keep your résumé, portfolio, and other employment documents up to date to reflect your current situation and abilities. This information should be revised and customized constantly so it is appropriate and current for job applications. Be proactive and look for reasons to revisit your employment documents. Add an alert to your calendar to review items on a regular basis, and continue performing your Sunday evening updates.

Keep in Touch with Your Network

Maintain regular contact with the people in your network. Note when you contact each person and if you should follow up in the future. If you need to follow up, add an alert in your calendar.

Record each person's name, contact information, and any important notes or tips you receive. For example, "Katie works at Procter & Gamble and knows the human resources director." Save a copy of your networking information to your mobile device or in cloud-based storage so you can access it whenever necessary. A spreadsheet stored only on your computer at home will not be useful if you need to refer to someone in your network and are not at home.

Set Job Alerts

Some websites offer the service of electronic job alerts. After registering for an account and making career preferences, you may be able to set alerts that will help you stay on top of new opportunities. These websites will notify you via text or e-mail of employment opportunities that meet specified criteria. After you receive an alert, you can, in many cases, use a mobile device to apply for jobs. If a position you previously applied for is reposted, some websites will notify you of the repost and indicate you have already applied for this job, saving you valuable time.

Download Apps

Using technology to manage the application process is convenient, but you will not always be in front of a computer when a job opportunity presents itself. It is important to be able to update an account or submit a résumé while on the go. Download apps for websites and social media accounts you use regularly in your employment search. Loading the app on your mobile device will save you time when you want to visit the site on the go.

9.6 Tracking Applications

The job-search process can continue for some time. As you submit applications and start interviewing, it will be important to keep track of the details. Mixing details like the names of companies or contact people, job descriptions, or dates and times of scheduled interviews could cost you an opportunity. Organization is essential. Create a job-tracking spreadsheet to help you stay organized. A **job-tracking spreadsheet** is a single spreadsheet with separate sheets for applications, leads, and interviews to record and track the jobs for which you apply. An example of a job-tracking spreadsheet with customized sheet tabs is shown in **Figure 9-2**.

Applications

Tracking job applications requires organization. This is where having a job-tracking spreadsheet can save time and confusion. The applications sheet (tab) within the

FIGURE 9-2

A job-tracking spreadsheet is a spreadsheet with individual sheets for applications, leads, and interviews to record and track the jobs for which you apply.

A	B	C	D	E	F	G	H	I	J
Job Title	Company Name	Company Address	Company URL	Contact Name	Contact Title	Contact Phone Number	Contact E-mail Address	Source of Job Posting	Date of Application
Personal Banker	Bottom Line Bank	87 Madison Ave. Augusta, ME 04333	www.blbank.com	Amanda Aulett	Hiring Manager	207-555-2886	aaulett@e-mail.com	Indeed	3/9/20--
Teller	Onyx Bank	176 College Ave. Waterville, ME 04903	www.onyxbank.com	Kevin Johns	Human Resources Manager	207-555-6699	kevin.johns@e-mail.com	Monster	4/30/20--
Junior Loan Officer	Hoover Bank	1029 Main St. Palermo, ME 04353	www.hooverbank.com	Andrew Guerin	Senior Loan Officer	207-555-4668	aguerin@e-mail.com	Company website	6/11/20--
Apprentice	Johnson & Wheeler Financial	518 South Broad St. Chesterville, ME 04360	www.johnsonwheeler.com	Jessica Downs	Account Executive	207-555-5937	downsj@e-mail.com	CareerBuilder	9/3/20--
Administrative Assistant	Eldertree Financial Services	905 Eastern Ave. Skowhegan, ME 04976	www.eldertree.com	Melissa Foster	Human Resources Director	207-555-3537	melissafoster@e-mail.com	LinkedIn	11/23/20--
Account Assistant	Simmonds and Associates	826 Spruce St. Palmyra, ME 04965	www.simmondsco.com	Joan McFarland	Recruiter	207-555-7467	mcfarland_joan@e-mail.com	Company website	12/4/20--

Goodheart-Willcox Publisher

job-tracking spreadsheet can be used to organize and track the jobs that you have applied for, along with any responses or feedback from employers.

When you submit an application, create columns in the applications sheet that detail the following information:
- job title
- name, address, and URL of company
- name, title, phone number, and e-mail address of a contact person (if applicable)
- source of the job posting
- date of application
- status of application (e.g., "applied," "interview scheduled," "offer received," etc.)

The spreadsheet can also include a column for notes, which you can use to record any important information or feedback that you received from the employer. This can help you to remember details about the job or the company, and to tailor your future applications accordingly.

In many cases after applying online, applicants receive an e-mail response to the submission. Some online job boards monitor application activities and automatically send an e-mail response when an application has been received. Some businesses also send automatic e-mail responses to candidates acknowledging the receipt of their application. Create an e-mail folder and label it "Job Responses" or something similar. Move these e-mails into that folder as you receive them.

There are many people who apply for posted jobs. Most recruiters and employers select a predetermined number of responses, such as 10 or 20 that stand out. As you will recall, most of the applications are screened through applicant tracking system software. A human may not even see the applications until they have been sorted and selected. Ensure your employment documents are up to date and include relevant keywords.

Leads

Once you begin receiving responses to applications, these become *job leads*. When a representative from a company to which you have applied contacts you for more information, create columns in the leads sheet of your job-tracking spreadsheet that detail the following information:
- job title
- name, title, phone number, and e-mail address of the person who contacted you
- date of the communication
- other pertinent information

A representative from the company contacting you provides an opportunity to follow up with that person at a later date. Persistence is important. If someone has recognized you as a qualified applicant and you are still interested in the position, it is important to keep the communication open and ongoing.

Interviews

Tracking interviews is an important step in the job-search process. When a potential employer makes contact with you for an interview, the company's representative will call or e-mail you directly. Therefore, you should closely monitor calls and e-mail messages. All incoming phone calls, e-mails, and voice mail messages should be attended to promptly and professionally during the application process.

As you begin to schedule interviews, continue using your job-tracking spreadsheet. Your spreadsheet will grow as interview opportunities arise. In addition to the information you initially recorded about the job lead, include pertinent facts about the interview. Create columns in the interviews sheet of your job-tracking spreadsheet that detail the following information:
- name and contact information of the person who scheduled the interview
- interview date

Workplace Skills

A *professional image* is the personal image an individual projects in the workplace. It includes a person's honesty, skills, courtesy, and respect for others. A professional image is what people remember about a person they meet. It could be as simple as the way in which a person greets another or the sincerity that is shown in a conversation. Cultivating a professional image can pave the way for a successful career.

- interview location
- name and title of the person(s) conducting the interview
- interviewer's job title
- any other pertinent information for the interview

Ensure this information is stored on, or accessible from, your mobile device so you will have it on the day of the interview.

CONNECT TO YOUR CAREER

Complete 9-3 Job-Tracking Spreadsheet, pg. 158

Staying Persistent

Unfortunately, it is common to apply for jobs and never receive a response. Moreover, it is difficult to determine whether a person even reviewed your résumé and cover letter. According to a report by Glassdoor Economic Research, the average job seeker applies to about 15 to 20 jobs before getting a job offer. This number could be higher in competitive industries. Because of the number of résumés and applications companies receive, companies commonly do not respond to every application or every qualified candidate.

In any event, the best course of action is to continue to apply for as many jobs as possible until you are hired by an employer. Do not apply for one job, then sit and wait for a response. Submitting résumés can seem like a full-time job itself, but it is worth the effort. Remember that the job-search process is time-consuming, and patience is essential. When applying for multiple jobs and not receiving any responses, it's important to stay positive and persistent, continuing to improve your application materials and networking with potential employers. As shown in **Figure 9-3**, you must continue to put all the pieces of the job-search process together until you find the right fit.

FIGURE 9-3

Fitting together all the pieces in the right way to get a job takes persistence.

Job-Search Process

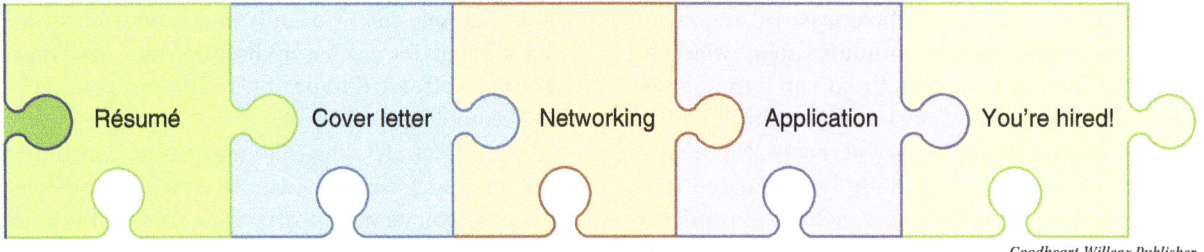

Goodheart-Willcox Publisher

Summary

9.1 Explain how to complete a job application.
A job application includes personal information, names and addresses of schools attended, degrees and certifications earned, addresses of previous employers, supervisors' names, and contact information. It may also ask for references. Job applications can be submitted in person or online.

9.2 Describe the process of applying for a job in person.
Ask for an application and stay on-site to complete it. After completing the application, assemble it, a cover letter and résumé tailored to the company, and a list of references in an envelope or folder. Deliver the folder to a company employee and record the employee's name in a mobile device for addition to a job-tracking spreadsheet. It is acceptable to follow up with the company after one week.

9.3 Describe the process of applying for a job online.
The online application process consists of searching for a job title and desired location, reviewing available postings and taking note of the contact person for each, researching each company to decide if it is a good fit, determining if each posting is from a legitimate company, and applying directly to the company or contact person.

9.4 Define *Sunday Evening Plan*.
A *Sunday Evening Plan* is a routine or schedule that job seekers set for themselves on Sunday evenings to review their job-search progress and plan their job-search activities for the upcoming week. It involves updating employment documents and posting or reposting them on professional networking sites on Sunday evening so they are flagged as new on Monday. Recruiters often begin each week by sorting through résumés with keywords that match the criteria they seek, so updating employment documents on Sunday night can help get an applicant noticed.

9.5 Explain methods for managing the application process.
Methods for managing the application process involve applying time management strategies, staying current on employment documents, keeping in touch with your network, setting job alerts, and downloading mobile apps to your mobile device. Successful management of the application process will keep you in control of your job search.

9.6 Define a *job-tracking spreadsheet*.
A *job-tracking spreadsheet* is a single spreadsheet with separate sheets for applications, leads, and interviews to record and track the jobs for which you apply.

Glossary Terms

aggregate job board	**job-search website**	**non-aggregate job board**
job application	**job-tracking spreadsheet**	**Sunday Evening Plan**

Review

1. Explain the steps involved in completing a job application. (9.1)

_____

_____

_____

2. Describe the steps to apply for a job in person. (9.2)

3. Compare and contrast aggregate and non-aggregate job boards. (9.3)

4. Describe the process of applying for a job online. (9.3)

5. Explain how the use of a benchmark for employment qualifications can aid your job search. (9.3)

6. What is a *Sunday Evening Plan*? (9.4)

7. What does managing the application process involve? (9.5)

8. Summarize the importance of good time management during the job-search process. (9.5)

Chapter 9 Applying for Jobs

9. Describe a job-tracking spreadsheet. (9.6)

10. Why is it important to be persistent when searching for jobs? (9.6)

Application

1. Why do you think companies require a job application in addition to a résumé and cover letter? (9.1)

2. How should you prepare when applying for a job in person? What are some ways to make a good impression? (9.2)

3. What are the advantages and disadvantages of applying for a position in person rather than online? (9.2, 9.3)

4. Types of job-search websites that you can use for your job search include aggregate and non-aggregate job boards. Explain which type you plan on using in your personal job search and why. (9.3)

5. It is important to set a benchmark of how many advertised job requirements you meet before you apply for a job. Review two job advertisements for open positions in your field. What is your benchmark for each? (9.3)

6. Applying for jobs online involves a keyword search. List keywords you will use to search for jobs online. (9.3)

7. Searching for jobs online allows you to set search parameters that include location, salary range, and full- or part-time status, among others. What search parameters will you use when searching for desirable jobs? (9.3)

8. Describe how you will implement a Sunday Evening Plan in your personal job search. (9.4)

9. It is important to keep in touch with your network. Explain how you will keep in contact with your professional network during your job search. (9.5)

10. Staying organized is one of the most important aspects of the application process. Describe how you will customize a job-tracking spreadsheet to benefit you in your job search. (9.6)

Chapter 9 Applying for Jobs

CONNECT TO YOUR CAREER
Workplace Connection

9-1 Job Application

1. Conduct an Internet search using the phrase *sample job application*. Select an application that looks similar to one you might be required to complete for a job opportunity and print it.

2. Complete the application. Refer to your résumé, list of references, or other documents if necessary. Use blue or black ink and your best handwriting. The application must be neat, clean, and free of errors.

3. Proofread your application. Compare it to your résumé and cover letter. If there is any conflicting information, revise your documents appropriately. If you need to correct the job application, print a new copy and start again. Sign and date the form.

4. Next, practice completing the job application electronically by keying your responses directly into the form.

5. Print the completed application. Sign and date the form. Submit it to your instructor along with your handwritten application.

6. Describe what you learned while completing this job application. What information did you have to supply? What information was requested for which you were not prepared to answer?

_____

_____

_____

9-2 Job-Search Websites

1. Conduct an Internet search using the phrase *job-search websites*. Record the URLs for several websites you would consider using.

   URL #1:

   _____

   URL #2:

   _____

   URL #3:

   _____

   URL #4:

   _____

Copyright Goodheart-Willcox Co., Inc.

2. Of the four URLs you listed, which website(s) do you plan to use in your job search, and why?

_____

_____

3. Create an account on the job-search website you plan to use by following the instructions on the website. Upload your master résumé and cover letter as directed.

9-3 Job-Tracking Spreadsheet

A job-tracking spreadsheet is a document that is used to record and track the progress of different job tasks throughout the application process. The spreadsheet can be used to monitor the progress of each task, identify any delays or issues, and ensure that all tasks are completed on time.

1. As a class, brainstorm all the tasks or processes that should be tracked when applying for jobs.

2. Break into small groups and choose one task or process (e.g., interviews, job leads, etc.) to add to a job-tracking spreadsheet. (*Note:* Each group should select a different task.)

3. Create a draft of your part of the spreadsheet for the task or process you selected, including the column headings and any formulas or functions that may be necessary.

4. Present your part of the spreadsheet to the class.

5. Based on feedback and input from the class, make the necessary revisions to your part and share the updated version with all groups.

6. Each group should combine all parts of the spreadsheet into a single document and test the spreadsheet. Enter sample data to confirm that everything works as it should. Make any necessary changes, keeping notes that can be shared with the other groups.

7. Share final feedback with the class to develop the final version of the job-tracking spreadsheet.

8. How can this spreadsheet aid your job search?

_____

_____

_____

9. Do you think using a job-tracking spreadsheet is worth the time and effort? Explain why or why not.

_____

_____

_____

UNIT 4: Landing a Job

Chapter 10 Preparing for the Interview
Chapter 11 The Interview
Chapter 12 Evaluating the Interview

Dzmitry Abrazhevich/Shutterstock.com

Why It Matters

It finally happened—you have been offered an interview. Now, you must prepare for a meeting with an interviewer that may be formal or informal, in-person or virtual. Preparation should include research about the company and job responsibilities and a list of questions you would like to ask the employer. Planning is essential, and it is the key to a successful experience that hopefully will generate a job offer.

After the interview process is complete, take time to reflect on your experience. Use post-interview techniques at the conclusion of each interview to help put things in perspective. What went well? How can you improve for the next interview opportunity? If you are offered a position, take your time and evaluate the compensation package. It is your choice to accept or reject the offer. If you are not offered the position, keep moving forward with the job-search process until you find the right job for you.

CHAPTER 10
Preparing for the Interview

Learning Outcomes

10.1 **Identify** three types of job interviews to which a candidate may be invited.

10.2 **Identify** sources of information for conducting research about a potential employer.

10.3 **Contrast** in-person interviews with virtual interviews.

10.4 **List** types of questions that an interviewer might ask.

10.5 **List** examples of questions that a candidate might ask.

10.6 **Identify** ways to prepare for an interview.

CONNECT TO YOUR CAREER

Workplace Connection

10-1 Informal Interviews
10-2 Company Research
10-3 Virtual Interviews
10-4 Interview Questions
10-5 Questions to Ask
10-6 Mock Interview

OVERVIEW

A job interview is the employer's opportunity to ask questions to determine if you are qualified for the position as well as an opportunity to sell yourself as a potential employee. Keep in mind that your answers to interview questions are important in the employer's decision-making process. In addition, your ability to ask the interviewer insightful questions is also important.

The interview may be formal or informal. It may be an in-person interview or a virtual interview. All interview opportunities require preparation and careful planning in order to make a positive impression. The first step in preparing for a job interview is to learn as much as you can about the job and the company.

Prostock-studio/Shutterstock.com

10.1 Invitation to Interview

At some point in your application process, you will be invited to a job interview. A *job interview* is the employer's opportunity to inquire about details included in your résumé and assess you as a potential employee. An invitation to interview will likely come either as a phone call or e-mail. When you receive a personal phone call from a company representative requesting an interview, ask for necessary details to ensure you arrive at the right place and time. Confirm the location of the interview and the name of the person with whom you will be meeting. Ask if there are any specific documents you should have on hand in addition to your most up-to-date résumé and portfolio. Be polite and reiterate your interest in the opportunity. If you receive an interview invitation via e-mail, netiquette dictates that you respond promptly. Request confirmation of the interview details in your response.

The first interview may be a screening interview. A **screening interview** is a preliminary, informal interview designed to determine if a candidate's skills are good enough to merit a formal interview. Screening interviews are brief and involve questions about your skills, experience, and availability. Any questions you may have about the company or position can also be addressed. These interviews are typically conducted by a recruiter or hiring manager via phone, e-mail, or video conference. This type of interview helps employers narrow the list of potential candidates who will be scheduled for formal interviews.

If all goes well, the next step in the process is a structured interview. A **structured interview**, also known as a *directive interview*, is a formal interview in which a predetermined list of questions is posed to each candidate interviewing for a position. All job candidates are asked the same questions so responses can be compared objectively to evaluate each candidate. These questions range from general to specific.

Rather than a structured interview, an employer may opt to conduct an unstructured interview. An **unstructured interview** is an interview that is less formal and may not necessarily consist of a specific list of questions. The questions asked will typically change from one candidate to the next. Unstructured interviews are typically used to get to know a candidate's personality in a relaxed situation, such as over lunch or dinner.

CONNECT TO YOUR CAREER

Complete 10-1 Informal Interviews, pg. 174

10.2 Company Research

After you have scheduled a formal interview and confirmed the date and time, familiarize yourself with the company, its products, services, size, and potential for growth and expansion. Your first source of information is the company's website. Navigate to the company's

Oleksandr Berezko/Shutterstock.com

Connect to Your Community

Joining local clubs and groups is an excellent way for you to gain valuable skills and experiences that can help you in your future career. For example, joining a local Toastmasters club can help you improve public speaking skills and boost confidence in communicating with others. You can also join job clubs, which provide support and resources for job seekers, such as networking events, résumé workshops, and interview preparation sessions. Joining sports teams can help you improve teamwork and develop leadership skills, which are highly valued by employers. You can also consider joining academic clubs, such as engineering clubs or business clubs, which offer opportunities to learn about your field of interest and connect with like-minded individuals. Other options include volunteering clubs, cultural clubs, and social justice clubs, which can provide opportunities to give back to the community and develop a sense of social responsibility. Regardless of the club or group, joining these organizations can provide you with opportunities to learn new skills, meet new people, and build a strong foundation for your future career.

official website, and search for a section titled About Us, or something similar. Read the contents carefully, and review details about the products and services the company offers. Take notes on the information found here so that you may study them before the interview. If the website includes employees' names, search for your interviewer by name to learn more about that person's role in the company. Additionally, if the company has a page on LinkedIn, it can be useful in your research.

After learning about the company from its website, enter its name in a search engine. Locate news articles, press releases, and comments from customers. Note how the company promotes its brand on social media. If possible, research its competitors; this information will help you to determine how it compares to the rest of its industry. Your research will help you prepare talking points about the company and its mission.

CONNECT TO YOUR CAREER

Complete 10-2 Company Research, pg. 175

10.3 Job Interview

A job interview is one of the most important steps in the job-application process. At the interview stage, you have captured the interest of an employer or hiring manager, and you will have a chance to convince that person to hire you. It is also an opportunity for you to learn if the company and position are the right fit for you.

During an interview, you are the focus. The interviewer will ask questions to uncover information about you as a job candidate. At the same time, it is your opportunity to exhibit your personality while discussing your skills and abilities as a potential employee.

Companies are no longer confined to face-to-face interviews. It is important to remain flexible as the actual meeting may be an in-person or virtual interview.

In-Person Interview

An *in-person interview* is one that is conducted with all of the participants at the same location. Usually, a job candidate is invited to the company office to meet with the hiring manager. In-person interviews can also take place away from company property, such as a restaurant. *Remote-location interviews* are in-person interviews held at an off-site location, such as a college campus or job fair. For some remote-location interviews, it is common to prearrange an interview time, just as you would if you were visiting the company office, and meet the interviewer at the determined location.

You may be interviewed by one person or multiple people. A **panel interview** is an interview in which a candidate talks with multiple interviewers in one room. Each member of the panel might present different angles or questions related to the candidate's ability and the job opening. If you know you will be interviewed by a panel, ask questions about the details before you arrive, such as how many members there will be and the names of each. Some candidates are required to deliver a brief demonstration or presentation for panel interviews. If so, you will have advance notice and time to prepare.

Plan to arrive 15 minutes before the appointment time, but no earlier than that. Allow plenty of time for traveling and wait in your vehicle if you arrive too early. Take into consideration weather, traffic, or other factors that might delay your arrival. It is unprofessional and unacceptable to arrive late to a job interview. If you are unable to make the interview due to an unforeseen circumstance, call your contact at the company to let them know as soon as possible.

It is important to know exactly where the interview is being conducted. Some companies have several locations, and you must be sure that you arrive on time at the correct place on the day of your interview. This information is usually provided by the person with whom you arranged the interview date and time.

If possible, visit the interview location before the day of your interview to gain a sense of the time it takes to get there, including any necessary walking time. If you are unable to visit the company in person, use an online map application, such as Google Maps, that allows you to see the building, parking locations, and other surrounding areas online. Use GPS apps to plot a route to the building and estimate the amount of time needed for arrival.

Some companies have strict visitor protocol. Call the main number for the company and ask about its protocol for visitors. Is there visitor parking? Will a visitor pass be required? Some companies require identification to proceed past the lobby for an interview. Other companies need only the name of the person with whom you have an appointment. Knowing and understanding these policies prior to your arrival can save time and potentially avoid embarrassment and confusion.

Virtual Interview

One advantage of a virtual interview is that the candidate is not required to commute to the employer's location. However, the potential for technical difficulties can be a disadvantage. Be certain to have a strong phone or Internet connection before the interview. It can be difficult to create a strong first impression when troubleshooting technical problems.

It is a good idea to verify that your employment documents and related materials are up to date prior to your virtual interview. This can include updating your LinkedIn profile, blog, or electronic portfolio website. A day or two before the interview, send an e-mail to the interviewer asking if there is any additional material that you will need to submit for the meeting. Attach the most current version of your résumé, portfolio, or other materials with a note explaining that these are the most recent versions of the files. If you want the interviewer to use a website to view your employment documents, provide the URL in your e-mail. Otherwise, the web address you provided in your initial correspondence with the company, which may not have the most recent files, will likely be used. Two types of commonly conducted virtual interviews are telephone interviews and video interviews.

Telephone Interview

For an interview conducted over the phone, the interviewer will arrange to call you, or you will be asked to place the call. If the interviewer is calling you, be at your desk and by the phone at least five minutes early. You should answer the call yourself and identify yourself when the phone rings. If you are placing the call, you will be calling the interviewer's direct line or calling a conference-call number. Place the call no earlier than five minutes before the scheduled appointment time. For conference calls, call in and hold for the moderator.

Even though you cannot be seen, it can be helpful if you are sitting up straight at a desk for the phone call. Treat the phone interview as though it were a face-to-face interview. This will help you maintain your professionalism for the duration of the conversation. It will be necessary to have all the materials you would take with you to an in-person interview, such as your résumé and research notes about the company. These materials should be easily accessible during the interview. Take notes about what the interviewer asks you with pen and paper. Avoid the sound of shuffling papers or the clicking of keys on a keyboard and silence the interview area to eliminate background noise. The interview dialogue should not compete with television, radio, or barking dogs, for example.

Video Interview

Real-time video conferencing using Zoom, Microsoft Teams, Skype, or other technologies requires the use of a web camera, microphone, and an Internet connection for both parties to make visual and audio contact.

Time Management

Prioritizing

Effective time management involves prioritizing tasks to use time efficiently. Setting priorities helps you make progress toward meeting your goals. Priorities keep you on track and on time. Tips on how to prioritize tasks effectively include the following:

- *Make a to-do list.* Start by making a list of all the tasks that need to be done. This may be a daily or weekly list, or even longer term.
- *Identify urgent tasks.* Prioritize the tasks by importance or deadline. Identify tasks that are time-sensitive and require immediate attention. These tasks should be prioritized over less important tasks.
- *Focus on the most important tasks.* Prioritize tasks that will have the most significant impact on your goals or project. Focus on completing these tasks first.
- *Consider the consequences.* Consider the consequences of not completing a task. Prioritize tasks that have the most significant consequences for not completing them.
- *Break down larger tasks.* If a task seems overwhelming, break it down into smaller, manageable tasks. This will make it easier to prioritize and complete.
- *Set realistic deadlines.* Set realistic deadlines for each task. This will help you manage your time effectively and avoid procrastination.
- *Learn to say no.* Do not overload yourself with too many tasks. Learn to say no to tasks that are not a priority or that you do not have time to do.

Prioritizing will help you meet deadlines and fulfill responsibilities. Developing this time-management skill will help you succeed in both your personal and professional lives.

Copyright Goodheart-Willcox Co., Inc.

If you are not familiar with the video-conferencing software being used, take time before the day of the interview to get acquainted with it. Some video-conferencing software requires users to download and install a program, which can be time consuming. To be safe, ensure you have downloaded the necessary program before the day of the interview. On the day of the interview, log on at least five minutes early. It is considered unprofessional to log on at the start time of the interview, and logging in early eliminates the risk of a last-minute connection loss. In all cases, be the first party to access the virtual interview so when your interviewer arrives, you are in position and ready to go.

A video interview requires the same amount of care and preparation as an in-person interview in terms of attire and personal details. Find a quiet place away from traffic noise, the radio, or other distractions. Direct the web-camera so that the interviewer's view reflects a work environment. For example, if your laptop is in your kitchen and the web camera gives a view of dirty dishes, the interviewer will receive the wrong impression. Virtual work environments from a web camera's point of view can be as simple as a plain wall or a wall with framed pictures and a bookcase.

The lighting in the room should be flattering. The interviewer should be able to clearly see you, but you should not appear washed out due to too much light. Overhead or natural lighting tends to work well for use with a web camera. Consider the time of day of your interview, and practice using different light sources.

When participating in a video interview, remember to look into the lens of your camera. This simulates eye contact. Looking at your computer screen to see the interviewer or a mirrored image of yourself leaves an impression similar to looking at the floor during a face-to-face interview.

A virtual interview follows the same pattern as an in-person interview. The conversation might begin with a brief, pleasant question about the Internet connection before starting. The interviewer will then most likely take the lead. Jot down or have the name of your interviewer(s) in front of you and refer to them by name. At the end of the conversation, the interviewer will offer you an opportunity to ask questions. You will have a chance to ask your questions, respond to any further comments, close the interview, and extend your thanks while using their personal names.

CONNECT TO YOUR CAREER

Complete 10-3 Virtual Interviews, pg. 176

10.4 Interviewer Questions

Interview questions are intended to assess your qualifications for a position. By asking questions, the interviewer can evaluate not only your qualifications, but also your personality and fit with other employees in the company. Many commonly asked questions are posed so the hiring manager can learn more about the experience, education, and skills presented in your résumé.

Not knowing how to answer a question can lead to embarrassment and missed opportunities. To avoid such a scenario during an interview, plan, prepare, and practice potential interview questions. Prior to your interview, read the details of the job posting regarding any specific duties or other requirements so you are prepared to answer questions about those topics. Make a list of the required experience, qualifications, and skills. Next to each requirement, list the ways in which you fulfill it.

The types of interview questions asked can vary depending on the type of interview you attend. However, there are common types of interview questions for which you can prepare answers ahead of time. These question types include general information questions, behavioral questions, and stress questions.

General Information Questions

General information questions are aimed at gathering facts about you, such as your education and work experience. Some examples of general information questions and answering strategies include the following:

| What can you tell me about yourself?

Suggested strategy: Succinctly summarize your abilities as they relate to the job qualifications. Do not provide a general life history. Begin with your degree and any related courses. Walk through your pertinent duties at each previous job.

| What jobs have you held?

Suggested strategy: Provide your job title, the name of the company, and a brief summary of the duties involved for each job you intend to discuss. This may or may not be every job listed on your résumé. Focus on jobs with skills that relate to the position you are seeking. Use keywords from the job posting if possible.

| What interested you most about this position?

Suggested strategy: Focus on the duties that interested you in the job and how they align with your previous experience and career goals. If the position is higher in your career path than your current occupation, describe your desire to grow as a professional in your industry. Then explain how this position can help you achieve that goal.

| Why do you want to work for this company?

Suggested strategy: This is a good opportunity to share some information you learned about the company during your research. Relate what you know about the company and why you think you would fit in there. Describe how the company's mission relates to your career goals.

| What is your major strength?

Suggested strategy: Select one of your strengths that relates to the requirements of the position, and explain why you consider yourself strong in that particular area. Provide an example of an occasion where you used it in a previous job. Describe the outcome of this occasion and anything you learned as a result.

| Are you comfortable using the technology required by this position?

Suggested strategy: Share any experience you have with the technology required, including the number of years you have used it and whether you consider yourself a novice, intermediate, or expert user. You can also provide some examples of how and when you used the technology. If you are unfamiliar with the technology in question, be honest but explain that you would be willing, able, and excited to learn new technological skills associated with the position.

Not all general information questions are appropriate for an interviewer to ask. For example, federal and state laws prohibit employers from asking questions related to a candidate's

- age;
- disability;
- ethnicity or national origin;
- gender;
- marital or family status; or
- religion.

If an interviewer asks you a question that does not relate to your ability to perform a job, it is acceptable to politely decline to answer the question. For example, "I apologize, but I am not comfortable discussing this matter."

Behavioral Questions

Interviewers may ask questions that relate to your behavior or how you might typically conduct yourself. A **behavioral question** is a question that draws on an individual's previous experiences and decisions. An interview that focuses on behavior-based questions is known as a *behavioral interview*. Your answers to these types of questions indicate past behavior, which can be used to predict future behavioral patterns. These questions are typically more focused than general information questions. They require job seekers to provide a specific example of when they used a skill to successfully complete a task. When answering these questions, include what the task was, the action that was taken, and the results of the action. While you cannot prepare specific answers to these questions, remain poised, answer honestly, and keep your answers focused on the question. Some examples of behavioral questions include the following:

- Tell me about a situation in which you needed to persuade your supervisor to make a change in a process or procedure.
- Tell me about a time when you needed to assume a leadership position in a group. What were the challenges, and how did you help the group meet its goals?
- Describe a time when you missed the opportunity to provide the best possible service to a customer. How would you have changed your approach for a more successful outcome?
- Describe a situation in which you needed to be creative in order to help a customer with a problem. What was the problem and how did you solve it?
- Describe a situation when you made a mistake. Tell me how you corrected the mistake and what measures you put in place to ensure it did not happen again.

Stress Questions

Stress questions are posed to candidates to see how they react to pressure. This type of question might shake a candidate's confidence and can indicate whether candidates can "think on their feet." Stress questions are often subjective, and it is difficult to predict the interviewer's preferred response. Most times, employers ask these in order to see how well a candidate can use reason and logic to come to an answer. Some people become defensive when they do not have an answer. Others become embarrassed or tongue-tied. It is critical to remain positive and professional. These questions may be uncomfortable or difficult to answer, but answers can be generated through careful thought.

When presented with a stress question, take time to process it and formulate a coherent answer to respond articulately. To gain more time to answer a challenging question, consider using reflective techniques that

acknowledge the question while giving you time to think of an answer. Some reflective technique responses are:
- "That is a great question."
- "I had not considered that angle."
- "Exactly. That happens sometimes."

When presented with stress questions, it is your responsibility to transform an awkward moment into a positive one. Answer such questions in a positive manner, and do not panic or lose your composure. Some examples of stress questions and answering strategies include the following:

| What is your biggest weakness?

Suggested strategy: Choose something you are honestly challenged by but will not jeopardize being considered for the position. For example, someone interviewing for a bank teller job would not offer counting money as their biggest weakness. After you have provided a response, explain what you are doing to improve your weakness.

| Why are you looking to leave your current job?

Suggested strategy: Avoid saying anything negative about your current employer. This seems unprofessional and can persuade an employer not to hire you. Instead, direct your responses toward your own growth and career goals you have set and how leaving your current job can help you achieve those goals.

| Can you explain why there is a gap in your employment?

Suggested strategy: Provide an honest answer, focusing on the positive aspects of your employment gap. For example, you could discuss classes you have been able to take as a result of your employment gap or any traveling you have done that exposed you to new cultures. If your employment gap is due to a negative reason, such as involuntary termination, be honest and explain what measures you have put in place to better yourself as an employee.

It is important to anticipate difficult questions. Focus on your professional weaknesses and expect them to be exposed throughout the course of the interview. This will allow you to have an answer prepared in case you are asked. For example, if your college major and your work experience are not consistent, recognize these inconsistencies and organize a sound explanation for any disconnect between your education and profession. If you have gaps in your employment, prepare an explanation as to why those gaps exist.

One type of stress question is a hypothetical question. A **hypothetical question** is one based on an imagined situation used to assess how one might react. Frequent topics of hypothetical questions relate to working and getting along with coworkers. For example, "What would you do if you were waiting on a customer and a coworker was constantly interrupting you?"

Specific answers to this type of question cannot be prepared in advance, so you need to rely on your ability to think on your feet. Bear in mind the interviewer is aware that you are being put on the spot. In addition to what you say, the interviewer will likely consider other aspects of your answer, as well. Body language is first and foremost. Avoid fidgeting and looking at the ceiling while thinking of an answer. Instead, make eye contact with the interviewer and calmly take a moment to compose your thoughts. Responses to these questions should be brief. If your answer runs too long, you risk losing your train of thought. Try to relate the question to something that is familiar to you and answer honestly. Maintain a professional and calm demeanor. Showing poise and projecting confidence carries a lot of weight, even if the answer is not ideal.

Another type of stress question is a blue-sky question. A **blue-sky question** is one where the interviewer describes a scenario that may or may not be related to the job duties and requires a response from the candidate. This is posed to test the candidate's life values and priorities. For example, "If you had $10 million, what would you do with it?" Answers to these types of questions reveal personal character. Since these are designed to learn about you, it is best to answer them with honesty and brevity.

CONNECT TO YOUR CAREER

Complete 10-4 Interview Questions, pg. 177

10.5 Questions to Ask

During the interview, the hiring manager will most likely provide you with an opportunity to ask questions. Be prepared with a list of intelligent questions. Study the job description and the company to formulate your list. Understand that this portion of the interview is a moment to demonstrate leadership potential. It is important to remember the interviewer is in charge. Do not be aggressive or overbearing. Avoid redundant inquiries, such as previously addressed topics, and keep in mind that questions you ask reveal your personality.

Career Persona

Plumber

Responsibilities

Plumbers are professionals who ensure that water, gas, and drainage systems are functioning properly and providing safe, efficient service to customers. They are responsible for installing, maintaining, and repairing a variety of plumbing systems, including pipes, fixtures, and appliances. Some of the specific responsibilities of a plumber may include the following:

- Diagnose issues within malfunctioning plumbing systems and make repairs
- Read or develop blueprints to show placement of pipes and fixtures
- Ensure that installations and repairs comply with building codes and safety regulations
- Test pressure to ensure a pipe system is airtight and watertight
- Provide information and answer questions from customers about plumbing systems

davooda/Shutterstock.com

Qualities and Skills

- *Technical knowledge:* Good plumbers should have a solid understanding of plumbing systems, including knowledge of pipes, fittings, valves, and fixtures. They should also be familiar with different types of materials, such as copper, PVC, and cast iron.
- *Attention to detail:* A plumber needs to be meticulous and detail-oriented, as even a small mistake can lead to leaks or other problems.
- *Physical stamina:* Plumbing work can be physically demanding, so a plumber should be in good physical shape and able to handle the demands of the job.
- *Communication skills:* A plumber should be able to communicate effectively with clients, suppliers, and other professionals in the construction industry.
- *Safety awareness:* Plumbers must be aware of safety procedures and take precautions to prevent accidents and injuries on the job.

Education

- High school diploma or GED
- Apprenticeship or vocational training
- Licenses as required by states, including journeyman, master plumber, or general contractor license
- Continuing education and certification, such as Certified Plumbing Design Technician (CPDT) and Certified Plumbing Inspector (CPI) credentials

Next Steps

There are several steps you can take to pursue a plumbing career. Start by researching plumbing apprentice programs and vocational-technical training options. These programs provide classroom instruction and on-the-job training that help prepare you to pass an exam to earn a license. Helpful courses to prepare you for this field include math, applied physics, and chemistry. A knowledge of welding is also useful.

The following are some questions you may want to ask if the interviewer has not already addressed the topic:
- To whom does this position report?
- What are the working hours?
- Can you describe the company culture and how it fosters collaboration and teamwork among employees?
- How does the company support professional development and career growth for its employees?
- How does the company measure success and what metrics are used to evaluate employee performance?

Preface your questions with a signal phrase. A **signal phrase** is a preplanned beginning phrase that enhances a question. These phrases add professional polish to the question and show that you have been listening closely to the information the interviewer has shared. Some examples of signal phrases include:
- You mentioned that...
- You referred to...
- I noted that you said...
- I appreciate the way you addressed...
- You were clear in the expectations, but I have one additional question...

Questions about salary should *not* be asked during the first interview. It is inappropriate to ask about money as doing so can give the impression that you are more concerned about compensation than the position. Attend the first interview on good faith that the salary offer will be acceptable. In addition to questions about salary, the following questions should be *avoided* in an interview:
- How many other candidates will you interview?
- May I come back so that we can talk about this position again?
- What did you think about your interview with me?
- Are you going to hire me?

If the interview was exhaustive, all potential questions were answered, and there are no further questions about the position or the company, a candidate may ask a question about the hiring process. An example might be, "What is the next step in this process?" Another closing question could be, "When might I expect to hear from you regarding your decision?" If all questions have been addressed, offer a phrase such as, "I have no additional questions to ask at this time. Thank you."

The offer from an interviewer to the candidate to ask questions becomes the best time for the candidate to thank the interviewer as well. This demonstrates professionalism, leadership potential, and recognition of the interviewer's time.

CONNECT TO YOUR CAREER

Complete 10-5 Questions to Ask, pg. 178

10.6 Interview Preparation

All successful interviews begin with preparation. You are more likely to have a successful interview if you take time to rehearse prior to the appointment. In addition, getting organized the night before an interview will boost your confidence and decrease any stress and anxiety you may have about the event.

Preparing answers to expected questions is only half of the suggested interview preparation. The other half involves rehearsing your delivery of those answers. Answering practice questions in front of a mirror can be beneficial. This activity allows you to see what the interviewer will see. Dress professionally while practicing so that you will become comfortable with the selected clothing. As you rehearse responses, pay special attention to facial expressions and posture. Decide how you will introduce yourself to the interviewer. If possible, record your voice so that you can monitor tone and inflection. It is natural to be nervous during an interview, but learn to sound as relaxed as possible.

Mock Interview

Conducting a mock interview is another preparation method for a formal interview. A *mock interview* is a practice interview conducted with another person in which one person role-plays as the interviewer and the other as the job candidate. Participating in a mock interview provides an opportunity to uncover potential mistakes and to determine how prepared you are for the interview process.

When conducting a mock interview, it is best to select a quiet place in which to work. Prepare a table or desk and chairs to simulate an office environment. If possible, record a video of the mock interview. If available, a camera on a tripod works well for this purpose. You will gain insight into how others perceive you when reviewing the video.

After conducting one mock interview as the interviewee, switch roles. This experience will allow you to see the job candidate from the interviewer's position. Observe how another person responds to your questions. Try to gain an understanding of what to do and what not to do during your interview. Regardless of the role you are assuming, be sure to stay in character for the entire mock interview. Mock interviews should be taken seriously. This practice strategy provides training necessary to polish your performance in front of another person, such as a friend, family member, or career-services representative. **Figure 10-1** provides a list of things to practice during a mock interview.

CONNECT TO YOUR CAREER

Complete 10-6 Mock Interview, pg. 179

Night Before the Interview

A sound preparation strategy is to plan the day before the interview. Waiting until the day of the interview to determine what clothes to wear, what route to take to the interview, and what materials to have with you can result in frustration, confusion, and anxiety. Therefore, prepare as much as possible the night *before* the interview. Tasks you can do the night before include the following:

- Select the outfit you intend to wear, iron it if needed, and lay it out before going to bed. Include the shoes you intend to wear.
- Determine what materials you will need. For in-person interviews, collect the materials, pack them in a professional-looking bag or briefcase, and consider placing them by the door or next to your outfit so you do not forget them. For virtual interviews, collect the materials and place them in the room where you will sit for the interview.
- Determine your route to an in-person interview. If you are driving, make sure you have directions and gas the night before. If you are using public transportation, review the schedules to ensure you will arrive to the interview on time. Plan to arrive 15 minutes early, regardless of transportation.
- For virtual interviews, do another check of your equipment to make sure everything is operational.
- Take another look at any notes you have recorded, such as talking points about the company, questions you want to ask, or skills you want to highlight.
- Get plenty of sleep the night before. Consider going to bed earlier than normal so you will be refreshed and relaxed for the interview.

FIGURE 10-1

Recording a mock interview can help prepare you for the interview process.

Mock Interview Tips
When conducting mock interviews: • Use an appropriate greeting • Smile and show enthusiasm • Keep eye contact; if interviewing virtually, practice looking at the camera lens, not at yourself on the screen • Display good posture • Avoid fidgeting in your seat • Restrain from displaying nervous habits • Answer questions naturally instead of giving memorized responses • Eliminate filler words such as "um" and "uh" • Thank the interviewer • Practice multiple times

Alena Nv/Shutterstock.com

Summary

10.1 Identify three types of job interviews to which a candidate may be invited.
Three types of interviews include a screening interview, a structured interview, and an unstructured interview.

10.2 Identify sources of information for conducting research about a potential employer.
A good place to find information about a potential employer, its products, services, size, and potential for growth and expansion is the *About Us* section of the company's website. It is also a good idea to search the Internet for news articles, press releases, and comments from customers. This research will provide you with talking points for the interview.

10.3 Contrast in-person interviews with virtual interviews.
In-person interviews require candidates to research travel time to the location and company visitation policies. Virtual interviews differ from in-person interviews because job candidates have to consider elements of their home, such as noise, Internet connection, and lighting. However, both in-person and virtual interviews require careful planning and preparation, as well as professional dress.

10.4 List types of questions that an interviewer might ask.
Three types of interview questions commonly used are general information questions, which are designed to gather facts about the candidate; behavioral questions, which draw on an individual's previous experiences and decisions; and stress questions, which are asked to see how candidates react to pressure.

10.5 List examples of questions that a candidate might ask.
Examples of questions that a candidate might ask include those about specific job duties, whom the position reports to, company policies or criteria regarding promotions, policies regarding on-the-job training, the hours of work, when a decision will be made, and the anticipated start date for the position.

10.6 Identify ways to prepare for an interview.
The best way to prepare for an interview is to practice interviewing. Answering practice questions in front of a mirror can be beneficial because it allows a person to see what the interviewer will see. Conducting mock interviews can also help a job candidate prepare. The night before the interview, ensure you get enough sleep, have your interview materials ready to go, and have your clothes ready so you do not need to rush.

Glossary Terms

behavioral question
blue-sky question
hypothetical question
panel interview
screening interview
signal phrase
structured interview
unstructured interview

Review

1. Describe the purpose of a screening interview. (10.1)

_____

_____

_____

Chapter 10   Preparing for the Interview

2. Differentiate between a structured interview and an unstructured interview. (10.1)

3. Identify sources of information for conducting research about a potential employer. (10.2)

4. Compare and contrast in-person and virtual interviews. (10.3)

5. What is a *panel interview*? (10.3)

6. Explain how an interview is an opportunity for both the interviewer and the candidate. (10.3)

7. What types of questions are commonly asked during a job interview? Describe the purpose of each. (10.4)

8. Explain how a person can prepare responses to potential questions that may be asked during an interview. (10.4)

9. List examples of appropriate questions for an applicant to ask during an interview. (10.5)

10. Describe two ways to practice for an interview. (10.6)

Application

1. What can you do during a screening interview to increase your chances of being offered a structured interview? (10.1)

2. Imagine you are invited to interview for a position in the corporate office of a restaurant chain. What type of information would be important for you to have before the interview? (10.2)

3. A panel interview is an interview in which a candidate talks with multiple interviewers in a room. Describe how you would prepare for a panel interview. (10.3)

Chapter 10 Preparing for the Interview

4. How would your preparation for an interview for a sales position at a local sporting goods store differ from an interview for an administrative assistant position at a local law firm? (10.3)

___

5. There are different types of questions that a hiring manager might ask. One type of question is general information. Select one general information question that was presented in this chapter and read its suggested strategy. How would you answer this question? (10.4)

___

6. Provide an answer to the following stress question: How can you make this company better? (10.4)

___

7. Imagine you are being interviewed for a job in your desired line of work. How would you respond to the following blue-sky question: If you had $10 million, what would you do with it? (10.4)

___

8. What questions are most important for you to ask during an interview based on your career goals and your chosen career field? (10.5)

___

9. Provide an example of an inappropriate question you asked during a job interview you wish you could take back. In what ways was the question inappropriate, and what did you learn from the experience? (10.5)

___

10. Consider a time when you went on a job interview without rehearsing or practicing first. How could your interviewing experience have been improved by practicing your answers ahead of time? (10.6)

___

CONNECT TO YOUR CAREER
Workplace Connection

10-1 Informal Interviews

An informal interview can be a great way for job seekers to learn more about a company and for employers to get to know job candidates. A company may use a screening interview to determine whether a job candidate has the necessary qualifications for the job opening. It helps employers narrow down the list of qualified candidates.

Working in small groups, conduct research about screening interviews. Then, create a list of seven tips to follow during a screening interview that will help improve a job candidate's chances of advancing to the next round of formal interviews.

1. ___
2. ___
3. ___
4. ___
5. ___
6. ___
7. ___

10-2 Company Research

1. Conduct an Internet search for a job that interests you. List the position and company name.

   Position Title:
   _____

   Company Name:
   _____

2. Visit the company's official website. Read the *About Us* or equivalent section carefully. Continue reviewing the site to learn about the products and services the company offers. List any important information that you find.

   _____
   _____
   _____
   _____
   _____
   _____

3. Type the name of the company in a search engine. Avoid returning to the company's official website. Look for press releases, articles, comments from customers, and social media posts in your search results. Record the URLs of three sites and any important information you found at each site that you could use to prepare for an interview.

   URL #1:
   _____
   _____

   URL #2:
   _____
   _____

   URL #3:
   _____
   _____

10-3 Virtual Interviews

Virtual interviews often are conducted using video conferencing. Work with a small group to conduct an Internet search using the phrase *how to interview virtually*. List several tips for participating in a virtual video interview. For each tip, provide an example that demonstrates how to properly implement it.

1. _____

2. _____

3. _____

4. _____

5. _____

6. _____

7. _____

8. _____

10-4 Interview Questions

Write a response to each of the following general information questions often asked during job interviews.

1. What can you tell me about yourself?

2. What other jobs have you held?

3. Why do you want to work for this company?

Write a response to each of the following behavioral questions often asked during job interviews.

1. Describe a situation in which you made a mistake. How did you correct it, and what measures did you put in place to avoid making the same mistake in the future?

2. Tell me about a time in which you were faced with adversity. How did you overcome it, and what did you learn as a result?

_____
_____
_____

3. Describe a time when you had to work with an upset customer. What was the customer's complaint, and how did you solve the problem? What was the level of satisfaction with your solution?

_____
_____
_____

Write a response to each of the following stress questions often asked during job interviews.
1. What is your biggest weakness?

_____
_____

2. Why are you looking to leave your current job?

_____
_____

3. How do you handle criticism?

_____
_____

10-5 Questions to Ask

1. There are standard questions you will ask about any job for which you are interviewing. Those questions will be about items such as on-the-job training and hours worked. Make a list of five common questions that you would ask about working for an employer.

   1. _____
   2. _____
   3. _____
   4. _____
   5. _____

Chapter 10 Preparing for the Interview

2. Conduct an Internet search for questions to ask during a job interview. List five questions that resources suggest you ask specific to the job.

   1. _____

   2. _____

   3. _____

   4. _____

   5. _____

3. Conduct an Internet search for questions *not* to ask. List five questions that resources recommend you avoid asking.

   1. _____

   2. _____

   3. _____

   4. _____

   5. _____

10-6 Mock Interview

Conducting a mock interview is a great way for job seekers to prepare for the actual interview process. In small groups, practice conducting mock interviews. First, collectively decide on the type of job for which the interview will be conducted. Then, research a job posting for it. Pay attention to the job description and requirements for the position. Take turns being the interviewer and interviewee, while the rest of the group observes.

After the interview, group members should provide feedback on the questions asked by the interviewer, the answers to those questions given by the interviewee, and the performance of the interview participants. Describe what you learned from the overall experience of the mock interview in the space provided.

_____

_____

_____

_____

_____

_____

CHAPTER 11

The Interview

Learning Outcomes

11.1 **Discuss** how to make a positive first impression at an interview.

11.2 **Describe** a typical job interview.

11.3 **Explain** the purpose of a second interview.

CONNECT TO YOUR CAREER

Workplace Connection

11-1   Interview Checklists
11-2   Pre-Employment Tests

OVERVIEW

There are many factors at play on the day of a job interview. While many of these factors are out of your control, such as traffic and weather, you are in complete control of your own actions. Understanding how to present yourself on a first interview can mean success or failure. Being on time and making a good first impression are basic behaviors that can influence the employer's ultimate decision.

At the interview, be prepared for introductions, questions, and the closing segment. Dress appropriately and come with the necessary documents. Have your questions prepared for the interviewer and allow time, if needed, for pre-employment tests. If you are successful, the opportunity for a second interview might be extended at a later date.

chrisdorney/Shutterstock.com

11.1 First Impressions

During an interview, subjective elements can influence a hiring manager's perception. A **subjective element** is a factor that contains bias and is more emotional than logical. Subjective elements are psychological nuances that occur when people meet for the first time.

Often unintentionally, an interviewer will make split-second judgments about an interviewee. While subjective elements may not be a fair assessment of a candidate's skills and qualities for the job, the first visual impression makes a powerful impact on potential employers.

From within the first few seconds of meeting an interviewer, that person will decide a great deal about you based on the way you look. This judgment is a first impression of you, which usually comes from outward appearances, such as eye contact; the way you dress, smile, and walk; and even your posture. It is important to make these first moments count in your favor.

The way in which a candidate dresses will make an immediate impression with the interviewer. While each company will likely have different expectations for employee attire, there are interview clothing choices that are acceptable across many types of professional environments. An appropriate way to dress for an interview is to wear conservative, neutral clothes. If the interview is in person, plan for outer garments when the weather is inclement. A single outer garment that you can easily remove, such as an overcoat or raincoat, is an asset to a professional wardrobe.

Clothing should be neat, clean, and in good condition. Shoes should be clean and free of scuff marks or obvious wear. For all jewelry choices, choose conservative items over flashy accessories. Do not wear anything to the interview that will disrupt or distract a potential interviewer from focusing on your skills. The goal is to help the interviewer focus on your strengths as an employee, not on your clothes.

Pay close attention to personal grooming, hygiene, and cleanliness. Refrain from wearing cologne or perfume. Your hands are important aspects of the impression you make at an interview as well. Make certain that your fingernails are clean and not broken or uneven. Style your hair in a conservative manner for both virtual and in-person interviews. Your smile should be inviting. One of the single, most-effective personal details is a genuine, warm smile.

In addition to proper attire, you can make a positive first impression by showing the interviewer how much time and effort you put into preparing for the interview. Have all the documents you need on hand. This will demonstrate your professionalism and initiative. If you will be going to the company's office to interview, carry your documents in a bag that complements your professional attire, such as a briefcase or satchel. If interviewing virtually, have the documents nearby or the files easily accessible. Items you may need include:

- appointment calendar
- copies of your résumé
- list of references
- multiple pens with which to write
- notes from your company research
- pad of paper for taking notes
- prepared questions for the interviewer
- list of job requirements compared to your experience, qualifications, and skills
- business cards (optional for in-person interviews)

Having your notes about the company and job requirements handy can be useful. If you have time before the interview, you can review these documents to remind you of the points you want to discuss. Employment documents that you want to leave with the interviewer can be secured with a paper clip but should not be stapled or folded. Consider keeping those documents in a separate envelope, folder, or binder with organizational dividers to give to the employer. If you have created a print portfolio, bring a copy to leave with the interviewer. For electronic portfolios, include the URL on your business card. For virtual interviews, you can send or post these documents or files as directed by the interviewer.

There are some things you should avoid during an interview. Do not bring your cell phone into the interview. If you do, place it out of sight and silence it.

Workplace Skills

Punctuality means being on time. Punctual employees are at their workstations at the starting time agreed to by them and the employer. Demonstrating punctuality in the workplace may require arriving five to ten minutes early so that an individual is settled and prepared to work. Simply being in the parking lot or building does not count as "being on time."

Career Persona

Nutritionist

Responsibilities

Nutritionists play an essential role in promoting and maintaining the health and well-being of their clients through education of proper nutrition. As a nutritionist, daily tasks may include meeting with clients to discuss their dietary needs and goals and providing nutritional counseling. Additional responsibilities of a nutritionist may include the following:

OurWork/Shutterstock.com

- Assess the nutritional needs of clients through interviews, questionnaires, and medical records
- Develop personalized meal plans based on clients' diet restrictions, food preferences, and budgets
- Educate clients on the importance of proper nutrition to a healthy lifestyle
- Advise clients on food selection and preparation
- Monitor clients' progress and make adjustments to meal plans as needed
- Develop programs and counsel the public on topics related to food, health, diet, and nutrition

Qualities and Skills

- *Strong knowledge of nutrition science:* A nutritionist must have a deep understanding of the human body's nutritional needs, including macro and micronutrients, food groups, and dietary guidelines.
- *Excellent communication skills:* A nutritionist must be able to communicate complex nutritional information to clients in a clear and understandable manner, as well as work collaboratively with other healthcare professionals.
- *Analytical thinking:* A nutritionist must be able to critically evaluate scientific research, analyze dietary patterns, and identify nutrition-related problems in individuals and communities.
- *Creativity and problem-solving skills:* A nutritionist must be able to develop personalized and practical dietary plans for clients, taking into consideration their lifestyle, preferences, and health conditions.

Education

- Bachelor's degree in food and nutrition or a related field, such as dietetics, public health, or food science
- Dietetic internship or supervised training program
- Registered Dietitian Nutritionist (RDN) or Certified Nutrition Specialist (CNS) credentials
- Continuing education to stay current in the field

Next Steps

To become a nutritionist, it is helpful to conduct research to learn about the various career paths and settings in which nutritionists can work. Nutritionists may be employed in hospitals and other care facilities or be self-employed. There are several areas of focus, including sports, holistic, oncology, and pediatric nutrition. Taking general courses in biology, chemistry, and anatomy is recommended. You can obtain practical experience by looking for volunteer or part-time job opportunities in the field of nutrition.

You also should not chew gum during an interview because you want to be able to speak clearly.

CONNECT TO YOUR CAREER

Complete 11-1 Interview Checklists, pg. 190

11.2 The Interview

After all your preparation, you will be ready to participate in the actual interview. As previously discussed, this may happen in person or virtually. Regardless of the type of interview, you will want to handle yourself with confidence and make a good impression. Display a positive attitude and act relaxed. Show your enthusiasm about the job and the company throughout the interview.

In-Person Interviews

Upon arrival at the interview location, you will likely have to check in at a reception desk. The front-desk attendant will need to know your name, reason for visit, and whom you have come to see. Then, the interviewer will be alerted of your arrival. A company representative will greet you and escort you to the room where the interview will take place.

Introduction

The initial introduction is your opportunity to make a positive first impression with the interviewer. If socially acceptable, extend your hand to deliver a firm handshake when the interviewer approaches you. Make eye contact and offer a pleasant greeting.

Introductions often begin with preliminary comments and a greeting that might include brief questions such as, "Did you have any difficulty finding our offices?" These preliminary questions are meant to break the ice and allow the interviewer to gain an impression of how the candidate handles new challenges. Avoid complaining about traffic, commute time, unclear directions, or other obstacles that you negotiated in order to arrive successfully. A good example of a response is, "I made a trial run yesterday based on the directions from your assistant, which made the drive today very easy." This shows that you listen, follow directions well, and take initiative.

After introductions have been made, wait to be seated. The interviewer might say, "Please, have a seat," or something similar. Most interviewers use a hand gesture to indicate the appropriate seat for the interview candidate. At that time, it is advisable to sit in a formal seated position. A **formal seated position** entails sitting upright, with both feet on the floor and both hands comfortably resting either on chair armrests or in the lap. This is the opposite of slouching and projects professionalism. Your body positioning may change slightly during the interview process as the conversation begins to unfold; however, try not to fidget during the conversation.

It is likely your interviewer will not remember your credentials from your application. Before the interviewer begins asking questions, offer a hard copy of your résumé. If applicable, also offer a copy of your portfolio. This will help refresh the interviewer's memory as to who you are and why you are qualified for the position.

Interview Questions

Your interview preparation will pay off as you answer questions posed by the interviewer and ask questions that you might have. In all interview situations, be aware of your body language. **Body language** is communication sent through gestures, facial expressions, and posture. These nonverbal cues should reinforce your professionalism, qualifications, and enthusiasm for the job opening.

Employer Questions

Focus on the keywords of the available position when articulating personal qualifications. Language choices should be respectful and formal as well. For example, if the interviewer elicits a response where a "yes" is expected, do not offer "yeah" as a substitute. Your primary focus as an employment candidate is to answer interview questions to the best of your ability and sell yourself as the best candidate for the job.

Candidate Questions

After the interviewer has finished asking questions, you will likely be asked if you have any questions of your own. This is the time to ask questions you have prepared. Be respectful of the interviewer's time. If you believe the interview is complete, do not extend time by asking additional, unnecessary questions. However, make certain that you have asked for any important information that was not already covered.

Interview Closing

When the interview concludes, wait for a signal from the interviewer to offer your closing remarks. Take the opportunity to reiterate your personal brand statement or elevator pitch while briefly summarizing your skills. If during the interview you did not highlight a skill or some experience that fits the position, use this time to highlight these positive qualities.

Time Management

Monitor Your Well-Being

When you are in the thick of career planning, it is easy to forget about your overall health and well-being. Wellness can have an impact on every aspect of your life, including your career. It is important to devote time to your health and wellness. Setting and tracking wellness goals can be difficult, but time-management strategies can help. You can start by creating a weekly or monthly planner with sections for goal-setting, habit tracking, mental and physical health, and a gratitude list.

- *Goal-setting.* Write down your top fitness and health goals for the week and break them down into smaller, actionable steps. This can help you stay focused on what matters most and make progress toward your long-term aspirations.

- *Habit tracking.* Tracking your fitness or eating habits keeps you accountable. It can help you develop daily routines and positive habits that support your goals. By tracking these habits, you are more likely to stick to them consistently.

- *Mental and physical health.* Allot time for activities that promote your mental and physical well-being, such as taking breaks throughout the day, going for a walk, socializing with friends, or practicing mindfulness exercises.

- *Gratitude list.* Cultivate a positive mindset and focus on the things that bring you joy and fulfillment. Take a few minutes each day to write down things for which you are grateful, no matter how big or small. This can help you stay motivated and appreciate the good things in your life.

Stay mindful of your well-being throughout your career search and beyond. Having good physical and mental health will make you a better job candidate and employee.

Reinforce your interest in the position to the interviewer and express the belief that you would make many positive contributions in the organization. Ask for any follow-up activities that must be completed. It is also appropriate to ask when a decision will be made to fill the position.

Thank the interviewer for their time. A firm handshake, if socially acceptable, is as appropriate to conclude a meeting as it is to begin one. If convenient, extend your hand to initiate this interaction. Remember, your closing remarks and thank-you should be brief but positive. Ask for a business card from each interviewer and offer one of your own.

Virtual Interviews

Virtual interviews, which are conducted remotely using a phone or video conferencing technology, have become increasingly popular in recent years. Many of the same interviewing techniques used for in-person interviews can also be applied to virtual interviews. For example, be sure to "arrive" for the interview early by logging in at least five minutes beforehand. Whether the interview is in-person or virtual, you still want to make a good impression with your appearance by dressing appropriately. You will also want to introduce yourself and use a friendly greeting at the start of the interview. Sitting up straight and not slouching is also important.

Before your virtual interview, test your equipment and download and open the meeting app from the link that your interviewer provided to make sure it is working properly. During the interview, have all the necessary documents and materials on hand. This includes your résumé, list of questions you have prepared to ask the interviewer, and a notepad and pen. Other tips to help ensure a successful virtual interview are shown in **Figure 11-1**.

Pre-Employment Tests

Often, employers screen potential job candidates by giving them pre-employment tests. These tests consist of questions to measure basic skills necessary for employment. Employers that give pre-employment tests do not always share the results with job candidates.

Some employers give simple mathematical or grammatical tests, while others administer personality tests. Governmental agencies use their own tests to measure a variety of skills, such as writing ability and reading comprehension. Businesses such as retailers, banks, utility companies, and staffing agencies are likely to

FIGURE 11-1

Be aware of the dos and don'ts for virtual interviews.

Virtual Interview Tips	
Dos	**Don'ts**
Make eye contact by looking directly into the camera.	Do not stare into space or look at yourself on the screen.
Conduct the interview in a clean, quiet room.	Do not sit in a messy room or in a location with background noise.
Stay engaged and focus on the conversation, referring to your notes only when necessary.	Do not read from a script or consistently refer to your notes, which can cause you to lose focus.
If you need to share examples of your work, keep the files open on a tab so they are easily accessible.	If sharing your screen, do not leave inappropriate tabs or apps open.
Avoid interruptions and distractions from family members, roommates, or pets.	Do not use an unprofessional background screen, such as beach scenery, that can be distracting.
Position yourself in front of the camera so that your face and shoulders can be fully seen.	Do not sit too close to or too far from the screen.
Take handwritten notes.	Do not type notes to avoid the clicking noise of the keyboard.

Goodheart-Willcox Publisher

administer a test that measures the integrity of a candidate when interviewing for a position related to money, public safety, or merchandise.

If you know you will be taking a test, conduct a search on the Internet for practice tests common to your industry and complete multiple examples. This will help make you comfortable with the test-taking process.

CONNECT TO YOUR CAREER

Complete 11-2 Pre-Employment Tests, pg. 191

Lying in an Interview

Lying is making an untrue statement. Lying is unacceptable in any situation, and lying in an interview can cost you a potential job or career. It can be tempting to tell an interviewer you have worked in a role that you never have or have experience with software or systems with which you have no familiarity. However, if you accept the position, you will likely be found out. Stretching the truth or exaggerating your abilities is also unacceptable. Be forthright, sincere, and honest in your interview. Your interviewer will respect your honesty in regard to what you can and cannot do.

11.3 Second Interview

Occasionally, some employers request a second interview. A *second interview* is a second formal interview that occurs after it has been determined that the candidate is qualified and more information is needed before making a hiring decision.

If you are contacted for a second interview, prepare for the event as diligently as you did for the first one. The same protocol is in order. Maintain a clear mindset that you are a top candidate. Being unprepared could leave the employer with a poor impression. Again, pay attention to your wardrobe and which documents to have on hand. If possible, do not wear the identical outfit worn at the first interview. Vary your attire, even if you only wear something slightly different, such as a different color or type of shirt.

During a second interview, you will have the chance to ask additional questions and to discuss specific working expectations and benefits that were not asked in the first interview. Additional questions might relate to travel expectations, telecommuting, flextime, job sharing, overtime expectations, and work attire. Make a list of questions prior to the interview and rank them according to priority. Time may be limited, so asking the most important questions first is a must.

Summary

11.1 Discuss how to make a positive first impression at an interview.
First impressions usually come from outward appearances, such as eye contact and the way a person dresses, smiles, and walks. To facilitate a good first impression, professional attire that matches the working environment should always be worn to an interview. Additionally, for in-person interviews, it is helpful to carry a professional bag, briefcase, or satchel to hold documents you may need, such as your résumé and list of references. For virtual interviews, be sure to have any necessary documents or files accessible. Having the necessary materials on hand for your interview demonstrates your professionalism.

11.2 Describe a typical job interview.
A job interview may take place in person or virtually. Many of the same interviewing techniques are used for both types of interviews. Introductions and friendly greetings will be made at the start of the interview, and then the interviewer will begin asking questions. Once the interviewer's questions have been exhausted, the interviewee can take some time to ask questions. The interview should close with pleasantries, and the candidate should follow up by taking any necessary pre-employment tests.

11.3 Explain the purpose of a second interview.
A second interview is another formal interview that occurs after it has been determined that the candidate is qualified and more information is needed. If called for a second interview, preparation for the event should be as diligent as the first one.

Glossary Terms

body language
formal seated position
lying
subjective element

Review

1. Discuss how to make a positive first impression at an interview. (11.1)

   _____

   _____

   _____

   _____

2. Define *subjective element*. List examples. (11.1)

   _____

   _____

   _____

   _____

Chapter 11   The Interview

3. Describe how your attire can make a difference in an interview. (11.1)

4. List necessary materials to have on hand for the interview. (11.1)

5. What is the purpose of preliminary questions asked by an interviewer? (11.2)

6. What is a formal seated position? Why is it important during an interview? (11.2)

7. What should your body language reinforce about you? (11.2)

8. What are some things to avoid when participating in a virtual interview? (11.2)

9. How can you prepare for a pre-employment test? (11.2)

10. Explain the purpose of a second interview. (11.3)

_____
_____
_____

Application

1. Recall a situation in which a person with whom you spoke did not create a positive first impression with you. How can this experience help you in your interview preparation? (11.1)

_____
_____
_____
_____

2. Describe the type of attire you would wear to a first interview at a company to which you have applied. Why is this attire appropriate for that employer? (11.1)

_____
_____
_____
_____

3. Explain why a person might wear something other than a business-professional or business-casual outfit to an interview. (11.1)

_____
_____
_____
_____

4. Aside from the materials list in this chapter on pg. 181, what additional materials would you have on hand for an interview and why? (11.1)

_____
_____
_____
_____

Chapter 11 The Interview

5. Recall a situation in which you had a conversation with someone whose body language did not reflect their interest in the discussion. How successful was that conversation? (11.2)

6. In Chapter 10, you created a standard list of questions to ask during interviews. How would you reorder these questions to ensure you get the most important information first? (11.2)

7. Write a closing statement that you will present at the conclusion of an interview. (11.2)

8. What kinds of pre-employment tests would you expect to see in your desired line of work or industry? (11.2)

9. How would you prepare for a pre-employment test? (11.2)

10. Describe the differences in your preparation for a first interview compared to that of a second interview. (11.3)

CONNECT TO YOUR CAREER
Workplace Connection

11-1 Interview Checklists

There are many tasks involved in the interviewing process. Having a checklist to ensure you do not forget any of these tasks can be useful. A checklist can help you be prepared and stay organized, which can reduce the stress often associated with interviewing.

1. In the space below, or in a separate file, create a checklist of 10 items related to the interviewing process. List important points about preparing for the interview, participating in the interview, and closing the interview.

___

2. After you have compiled your list, share it with the class. Write down any additional items that you want to add to your checklist based on your classmates' lists.

___

Chapter 11 The Interview

11-2 Pre-Employment Tests

Some employers give pre-employment tests to help predict on-the-job performance. These tests measure skills and aptitudes as well as psychological qualities, such as personality, character, and interests.

1. Conduct an Internet search using the phrase *pre-employment tests*. Complete the table by listing five of the most common pre-employment tests used to evaluate job candidates and describing what each test assesses. If you prefer, search for pre-employment tests that may be used in your desired industry.

Pre-Employment Tests	
Name of Test	**Qualities It Evaluates**

2. Conduct an Internet search using the phrase *pre-employment test preparation*. Select three of the most helpful tips and techniques suggested for preparing for these tests.

   Test Preparation Tip #1:
   _____
   _____

   Test Preparation Tip #2:
   _____
   _____

   Test Preparation Tip #3:
   _____
   _____

3. Summarize what you learned about pre-employment testing.
   _____
   _____
   _____

Copyright Goodheart-Willcox Co., Inc.

CHAPTER 12: Evaluating the Interview

Learning Outcomes

12.1 **Identify** post-interview techniques.

12.2 **Describe** the employment process after a job offer has been extended.

CONNECT TO YOUR CAREER

Workplace Connection

12-1 Interview Evaluation
12-2 Thank-You Message
12-3 Job Offer Evaluation
12-4 Salary Negotiation
12-5 Job Offer Responses

OVERVIEW

An important part of the interviewing process is to evaluate the interview once it has occurred. If you are successful and get the job, take time to reflect on the experience. If you do not get the job, do not feel defeated. You will not get every position for which you apply. Look at each interview opportunity as an experience to prepare you for the next one. Utilizing post-interview techniques at the conclusion of each interview will help put things in perspective.

nelzajamal/Shutterstock.com

If you are offered a position, take time to evaluate all aspects of the job and compensation package before you accept or reject the offer. Negotiation may be necessary to get the salary that you desire. If you do accept the offer, be prepared for the employment processes that follow.

12.1 Post-Interview Techniques

Post-interview techniques consist of a series of steps you will need to complete after an interview. Immediately after an interview has ended, evaluate your experience. This will enable you to learn from the interview and move forward with confidence. Next, follow up in a professional way with a formal thank-you message. Finally, you should think positively and continue your job search. Common post-interview techniques are illustrated in **Figure 12-1.**

Evaluate the Interview

An effective evaluation technique is to identify how you felt immediately after the interview. It is common to feel doubt and anxiety, but it is important to accept that the interview has ended, and you cannot go back to alter your performance. Instead of dwelling on what is out of your control, evaluate your experience. Make notes about your overall impression of the company, interviewers, and process. Measure your desire to work for that company based on what you learned and develop a plan to move forward.

Even if you think the interview was successful, assess your performance and design a plan addressing how you can improve for your next interview. Look at each interview as an opportunity to learn and grow as a professional. You can assess your performance by asking yourself the following questions:

- Did I prepare as thoroughly as I should have for the interviewer's questions?
- Did I have all the documents requested?
- Did I dress appropriately?
- Did I greet the interviewer properly?
- Did I smile pleasantly and naturally?
- Did my voice project confidence but not arrogance?
- Did I articulate my prepared responses as planned?
- Did I answer the questions with thoughtful intelligence?
- Did I talk too much or not enough?
- Did I thank the interviewer in real-time when the interview concluded?

Expand this list with your own set of questions to evaluate your interview skills. Each job interview is an opportunity to practice, learn, and improve.

CONNECT TO YOUR CAREER

Complete 12-1 Interview Evaluation, pg. 205

Send a Thank-You Message

After an interview, follow up with the interviewer in the form of a written thank-you message. A *thank-you message* is unsolicited communication demonstrating professional courtesy from you to the interviewer. This communication reaffirms your interest in the position and exhibits your professionalism. Etiquette dictates a thank-you message be sent within 24–48 hours of the interview to each person with whom you met. For example, if you met with the head of the department and the head of human resources, then each person should receive a separate thank-you message. Thank-you messages can be sent as a letter, card, or an e-mail. If you discussed any follow-up actions on your part during the interview, such as providing references or work samples, include these materials with your thank-you message.

If you are sending your thank-you message as a letter, write it using a standard letter format similar to a cover letter. Thank the interviewer for meeting with you, express your continued interest in the position, and close with the desire to hear back concerning the hiring decision. If any follow-up material was promised, add an enclosure notation to your message and enclose the material with the letter in the envelope. Insert one of your business cards into the envelope before mailing. **Figure 12-2** shows an example of a thank-you letter.

FIGURE 12-1

Post-interview techniques consist of a series of steps you will need to complete after an interview.

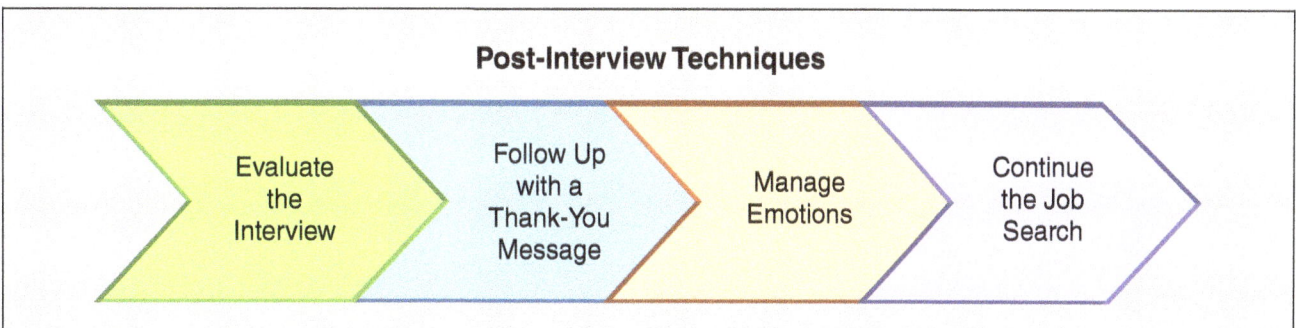

Goodheart-Willcox Publisher

FIGURE 12-2

A thank-you message is unsolicited communication demonstrating professional courtesy from you to the interviewer.

Jalia Cortez
111 First Street, Redwood City, CA 94061
(619) 555–1235 • jcortez@e-mail.com • www.linkedin.com/in/jalia-cortez

December 3, 20--

Mr. Joshua Mitchell
Great Corporation
12344 Main Street
Redwood City, CA 94061

Dear Mr. Mitchell:

Thank you for the opportunity to interview for the technical support assistant position with Great Corporation on Wednesday, December 2. The interview process provided me with a clear synopsis of the role and responsibilities for the position.

My enthusiasm for the position has grown after talking with you and members of your team. Working in the information technology industry and providing companywide technical support is my career goal. I would enjoy being a part of the company and having the opportunity to contribute to its success.

Thank you, again, for your time and consideration. As requested, I am enclosing a copy of professional references. I look forward to hearing from you soon.

Best regards,

Jalia Cortez

Jalia Cortez

Enclosure

Goodheart-Willcox Publisher

Thank-you letters can also be handwritten. Some candidates purchase thank-you cards to handwrite and send in the mail. Interviewers often appreciate handwritten cards, as they are more personal and take more time. If you decide to handwrite a thank-you note, select a high-quality card or stationery, and be sure your handwriting is legible. Again, include one of your business cards in the card or letter before mailing it.

A thank-you message sent via e-mail is also acceptable, as shown in **Figure 12-3**. Just like a letter, an e-mail should be polite and respectful and convey the job candidate's appreciation for the interviewer's time and consideration. If you decide to e-mail your thank-you message, attach any follow-up material to the e-mail.

CONNECT TO YOUR CAREER

Complete 12-2 Thank-You Message, pg. 205

FIGURE 12-3

A thank-you message can be sent as an e-mail for a timelier response.

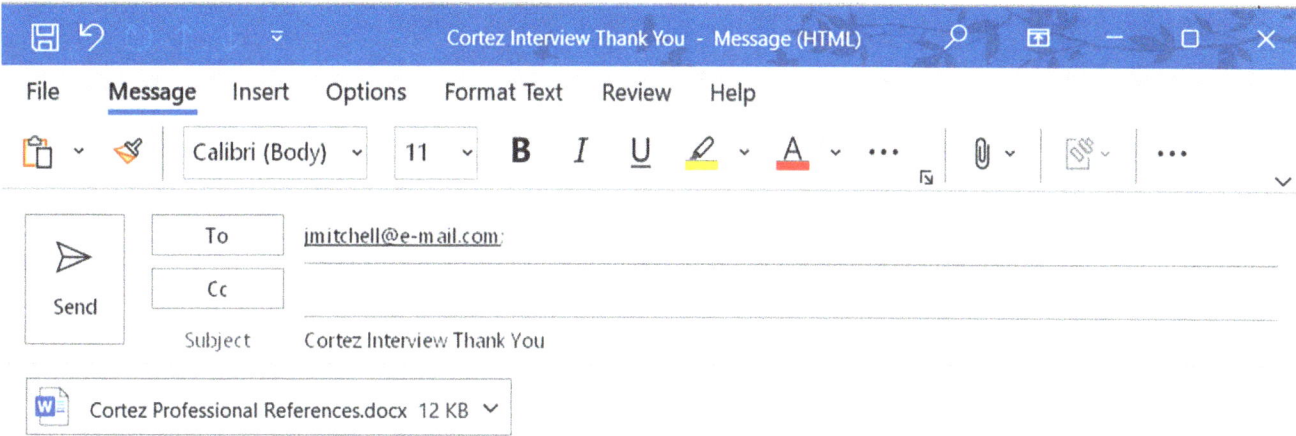

Goodheart-Willcox Publisher

Career Persona

IT Professional

Responsibilities

Art studio G/Shutterstock.com

The work performed by IT (Information Technology) professionals can vary widely depending on their specialization and the nature of the organization for which they work. Some may focus primarily on software development, while others may be responsible for managing large-scale IT infrastructure. Regardless of their specific role, IT professionals are responsible for ensuring that the technology used by their organization is reliable, secure, and effective. Additional responsibilities for an IT professional can include the following:

- Write and test software code to develop new programs or applications
- Configure and manage computer networks, including firewalls, routers, and switches
- Monitor and maintain computer systems and servers, including backup and recovery processes
- Provide technical support to end-users or customers, answering questions and resolving problems
- Troubleshoot and resolve technical issues that may arise

Qualities and Skills

- *Analytical skills:* Analyzing data to resolve problems and increase a system's efficiency is part of an IT professional's job.
- *Technology skills:* IT professionals must be familiar with programming languages such as Java, Python, or C++, as well as be proficient with software development tools and platforms such as GitHub or Microsoft Visual Studio.
- *Attention to detail:* IT professionals need to be able to focus on details and ensure that their work is accurate and precise. This is particularly important when writing code, debugging programs, or working with complex systems.
- *Communication skills:* IT professionals need to be able to explain complex technical concepts to nontechnical stakeholders, such as managers or clients. This requires strong verbal and written communication skills.
- *Adaptability:* IT professionals need to be able to adapt to new technologies, tools, and software as they emerge. This requires a willingness to learn and stay up to date with the latest trends in the field.

Education

- Bachelor's degree in computer science, computer and information technology, or a related field
- Industry-specific certifications, such as CompTIA A+, Cisco Certified Network Associate (CCNA), or Certified Information Systems Security Professional (CISSP)
- Continuing education courses to stay up to date on new technologies

Next Steps

Many IT jobs require candidates to have practical experience working with technology. You can gain experience through internships, part-time jobs, or volunteer work. Focus on developing technical skills by studying programming languages, operating systems, databases, and other technologies commonly used in the IT industry. You can do this by taking relevant courses, participating in coding challenges, and networking with IT professionals.

Manage Emotions

Finding a job is far from a relaxing experience. Similar to waiting to hear whether your job application will be selected for an interview, waiting for the results after an interview can be stressful. Not knowing how an interviewer perceived your performance might be unnerving. It is important to recognize there are parts of the job-search process that you *can* control, such as positive or negative thoughts, what you include on your résumé, and how you perform at a job interview. One of the things you *cannot* control is who the company chooses to select for a position. Focus on the items you can control and try not to concern yourself with what you cannot. This will help you control your stress. Keep in mind that interviewing multiple times for various companies helps you gain confidence and much-needed experience in the job-search process.

Some companies communicate to candidates that they were not chosen for the position. However, many companies do not contact candidates at all if they are not selected. If you do not hear from a representative of the company after a period of time, it often means another person was selected for the position. Nearly every person has had the experience of interviewing for a job and not being selected for the position. Not every job for which you interview is the best match for you. In fact, you may find that you are not offered a position for a majority of the jobs for which you apply.

Continue the Job Search

Some job seekers become confident after one interview, ending their search while waiting to hear from the interviewer. However, the best course of action is to continue to look for a position until you have a job. While you wait to hear the results from an interview, continue to seek additional employment opportunities. You can always decline an offer of employment if need be. Be persistent in searching for the job that you want.

12.2 The Employment Process

There is excitement and personal gratification that comes from being selected for a position for which you interviewed. However, the process is not complete once you receive a job offer. First, you will evaluate the offer. Next, if necessary, you will negotiate the compensation. Then, you must respond to the job offer. If you accept the position, employment verification will conclude the process.

Evaluate the Job Offer

At some point during this process, you will be offered a position. If the interview process was successful, an employer will contact you by telephone or e-mail with a job offer. A **job offer** is a formal invitation to work under mutually agreed terms and conditions.

The job offer typically includes the title of the position, description of duties, expected hours, location of work, and the compensation package you will receive. The **compensation package** is everything an employee receives in return for their work. Part of the compensation is *salary*, which is the amount of money an employer agrees to pay an employee. A compensation package may include paid time off, such as vacation days and sick days, and retirement benefits, such as a 401(k) plan. Other types of compensation include the following:

- annual bonuses tied to personal or company performance
- employer-paid medical, dental, and life insurance
- overtime pay
- reimbursement for job-related travel
- salary increases based on performance reviews
- tuition reimbursement for continuing education

When you are offered a job, it is your responsibility to evaluate the offer. Consider whether it is the job you want. While it is flattering to be offered a position, you must make sure the job, benefits, responsibilities, and compensation fit your expectations. Examine the position and the expectations of the job. Remember, the decision to accept or reject a job offer is entirely yours.

Determine if the company and job meet your career expectations. To evaluate a job offer, first carefully read all of the details. Then ask yourself important questions, such as the following:

- Does the job offer meet the expectations I had at the interview?
- How does this position fit within my career plan?
- Is the job interesting?
- Does the salary offered represent a fair value for the skills I offer?
- Do I want to work for this company?
- Am I comfortable with the required duties?
- Will I need training or additional education right away?
- Does the growth potential for this position fit within my career plan?

Weigh the financial benefits offered with what it costs you to work each day. Calculate the amount of money you will take home after commuting expenses and taxes are paid. To determine this, consider the following questions:

- Will I be entitled to, or expected to, work overtime?
- If overtime work is expected, what is the rate of any hourly overtime pay?
- Does the employer offer health insurance?

- If the employer offers health insurance, how much will be deducted from my pay to cover the premium?
- If the employer does *not* offer health insurance, how much will I have to pay to get health insurance?
- Will there be costs for clothing or uniforms?
- What will it cost to commute to the job location?
- What is the cost of gas and parking?

Discuss the details of the compensation package with the employer, and make sure you understand what is being offered. Carefully consider the job offer, and do not rush through your decision. It is important that you are comfortable with the offer and all details before you accept a position. Once you accept the offer, you agree to all the terms of employment.

CONNECT TO YOUR CAREER

Complete 12-3 Job Offer Evaluation, pg. 206

Negotiate

If the job meets your expectations, but the salary or compensation is not sufficient, consider negotiating. If you have been offered a salary and benefits package that does not meet your expectations, inquire about the opportunity to discuss a more appropriate package with the employer. Some items are negotiable, while others are not. Generally, the salary for minimum-wage jobs and entry-level jobs is not negotiable.

The Best App for That

Snagajob

Snagajob is an online job search platform that connects hourly workers with part-time, full-time, and seasonal jobs in a variety of industries. The Snagajob app allows job seekers to create a profile, search for jobs by location, industry, or job title, and apply for jobs directly through the app. Users can also set up job alerts to be notified when new jobs are posted that match their search criteria. The app is designed to help people who are looking for flexible work schedules, such as students, retirees, and those who work multiple jobs.

When you negotiate for salary, you are taking a risk. If your negotiation is baseless, the employer can withdraw the offer of employment. Remember that the employer may have multiple candidates willing to take the position at the salary offered.

If you decide to negotiate, establish a strong position by compiling the research to support your stance. For example, if you believe the job warrants a higher salary, research trends in your field for the same job title at various companies. Conduct research on the Internet using phrases such as "salary comparisons" or "median annual pay" to locate comparative information about the salaries of people with similar job titles and responsibilities. Free online salary calculators can also help you project what salary you can expect based on the job title and your location, years of experience, and education.

Next, prepare a brief presentation with a script so that you can create a logical argument. Your presentation should include an introduction, the research you found noting the discrepancy in salary offerings, and a closing with a request for a moderate increase in your compensation package. Have a firm number in mind and suggest it. Rehearse your presentation or ask someone to role-play it with you. Solicit feedback before you present it to an employer.

Finally, contact the employer. Always begin with gratitude and acknowledgement of the position offered. Explain how you feel about the prospect of the new position and that you want to be compensated fairly. Ask if the salary is negotiable. If the response is a flat "no," thank the individual and say that you will consider the matter further. If the response indicates the salary or benefits package is negotiable, present your information. Close with your counteroffer. Wait for the response and proceed from there. Do not ask the employer to come up with a better number.

Avoid giving the company an ultimatum. An *ultimatum* is a proposition in which one party issues a final demand or set of conditions that, if unmet, can result in severance of the relationship. Sometimes, especially in highly competitive fields, ultimatums can be effective. However, most times issuing one will backfire on the candidate, and the job offer will be rescinded.

CONNECT TO YOUR CAREER

Complete 12-4 Salary Negotiation, pg. 207

Respond to the Job Offer

Regardless of whether you will be accepting or rejecting the offer, a timely response is required. Notifying the

Connect to Your Community

Supporting local businesses is crucial to the growth and development of a community, and it can benefit all involved. Local businesses provide a unique character to a community, creating a sense of place and identity. They can also offer products and services that are tailored to the specific needs and interests of the community. When people shop at local businesses, they are investing in their community and helping to support the local economy. This, in turn, can create more job opportunities and increase the overall wealth and prosperity of the community. In addition, local businesses are often more sustainable and environmentally friendly than large corporations, which can have a positive impact on the environment. Moreover, local business owners are often more invested in the community and more likely to give back by supporting local events and organizations. Consider working for local businesses to do your part in supporting the local economy and building a sustainable and prosperous future for all community residents.

giggsy25/Shutterstock.com

employer of your decision is an important professional courtesy. Failure to do so will reflect poorly on you.

Accept a Job Offer

Once you are offered a job and you have agreed to the terms of employment and salary, formally acknowledge that you accept the position. The individual who contacts you with the job offer is the person with whom you will communicate regarding the acceptance of your position. A personal phone call is preferable. However, an e-mail may be necessary in order to submit a timely response. An example of an acceptance message is shown in **Figure 12-4**.

If you accept the position, you will receive a *formal offer letter*. This document will include the salary and compensation package that was agreed upon after the job offer was made. It is important that you take your time to read the documents carefully. If there are any passages that you do not understand, ask for clarification. You will be required to sign the document, which affirms that you understand, agree, and accept the terms and conditions of employment.

Decline a Job Offer

If you must decline an offer of employment, contact the person who extended the job offer as soon as possible.

FIGURE 12-4

Acceptance of a job offer should be sent to the employer as soon as possible.

Dear Ms. Boswell:

I am delighted to accept the position of Quality Control Lab Technician for Becker Labs. I am excited about the opportunity of working with you and your team.

As soon as I receive the formal offer letter and additional forms you mentioned, I will complete and return them immediately. As we discussed, I will wait to hear from Mark Evans for further instructions about the medical exam and background check. I understand that there are required forms and processes that must be completed before I can start work.

Thank you again for the opportunity.

Sincerely,

Goodheart-Willcox Publisher

Communicate that you are appreciative of the opportunity, but it is necessary for you to decline the position. It is not necessary to state a reason for declining the offer, but be sure your communication is respectful and professional. If the potential employer telephones you, express your decision on the phone, but follow up the conversation with a written notice. You may use e-mail for this message. An example of a rejection message is shown in **Figure 12-5.**

Handling the rejection of a job offer in a professional manner is important. You never know when, during the course of your career, you will cross paths with the company or its representatives in the future. Therefore, leave a positive, professional impression if you must decline a job offer from a company.

CONNECT TO YOUR CAREER

Complete 12-5 Job Offer Responses, pg. 208

Employment Verification Process

There are processes that must be completed before you are officially hired. The employer will complete employment verification using the information on your application or résumé. **Employment verification** is a process in which a job candidate's employment history is checked to confirm the accuracy of the information submitted. Employers typically verify only the dates of employment, position title, and other objective data. Most past employers will not provide subjective information about their employees, such as whether you were considered a good worker.

Another important aspect of the employment process is a background check. A **background check** is an evaluation of personal data that is publicly available. This information is generated from governmental records and other sources, including public information on the Internet. An employer must ask for written permission before obtaining a background check. While you are not legally obligated to give permission, a company can reject you as a candidate based on unknown or unverified background information.

For positions that require interaction with company finances, employers often will request a candidate's credit history. They must demonstrate a viable business need in order to access this information. Similarly to a background check, employers are legally required to obtain your permission before conducting a credit check. If you believe your credit score might impact a job offer, obtain a copy of your credit report first and try to resolve any negative entries.

If an employer decides not to offer employment to a job candidate based on a credit report, the employer should provide a copy of the report to the individual. In addition, a summary of rights should be provided.

Some employers require drug screenings for new employees. The employer pays for the test as part of the hiring process. You are required to use the lab facility designated by the employer. Most times, an offer of employment is contingent on your ability to pass this screening. If you pass it, the hiring process will continue. If not, you will no longer be eligible for employment with the company.

FIGURE 12-5

It is important to be timely, professional, and respectful when declining a job offer.

Dear Ms. Boswell:

Thank you for offering me the position as Quality Control Lab Technician for Becker Labs. I considered your offer, but I have decided that I must decline.

I am grateful for the opportunity you extended. I appreciate your confidence in my abilities to perform the tasks required for the position.

Thank you again for the opportunity.

Sincerely,

Goodheart-Willcox Publisher

Chapter 12 Evaluating the Interview

Summary

12.1 Identify post-interview techniques.
Post-interview techniques consist of a series of tasks to complete after the interview. These steps include evaluating the interview, following up with a thank-you message, managing emotions, and continuing the job search.

12.2 Describe the employment process after a job offer has been extended.
After a job offer has been extended, a candidate must complete several steps before the employment process is complete. The job offer must be evaluated and negotiated, if desired. Then, the applicant must respond to the job offer and complete employment verification. Employment verification might include a background check and a drug test.

Glossary Terms

background check
compensation package
employment verification
job offer

Review

1. Identify post-interview techniques. (12.1)

   _____
   _____
   _____

2. What are some ways you can evaluate an interview? (12.1)

   _____
   _____
   _____

3. Why is it important to send a thank-you message to the person or persons who interviewed you? (12.1)

   _____
   _____
   _____

4. How can you manage the emotions that come with not being offered a job for which you interviewed? (12.1)

   _____
   _____
   _____

5. List the steps of the employment process that occur after a job offer has been made. (12.2)

6. Explain what typically is included in a compensation package. (12.2)

7. When should you consider negotiating a job offer? What risks are associated with negotiating with a potential employer? (12.2)

8. Describe how to accept or reject a job offer. (12.2)

9. What is a *background check*? How do employers access information when conducting one? (12.2)

10. Why might some employers conduct credit checks on potential employees? (12.2)

Chapter 12 Evaluating the Interview

Application

1. What can you expect to learn by evaluating your performance in an interview? (12.1)

2. Thank-you messages can be a formal letter, a handwritten note, or an e-mail message. Give your opinion as to when each of these formats is appropriate for your desired career field. (12.1)

3. Managing emotions during the job-search process can be a challenge. How will you put the interviewing process in perspective and manage the emotions and stress of the experience? (12.1)

4. Not every employer will let you know if a final hiring decision has been made. How will you determine whether you have been eliminated as a candidate or if you are still in consideration? (12.1)

5. Describe how you plan to continue your job search even after you begin interviewing. (12.1)

6. Salary is often only part of employee compensation. What other forms of compensation are you hoping to acquire? Are any of them "must-haves"? (12.2)

7. List criteria you will use to evaluate a job offer. (12.2)

8. Recall a time when you participated in a negotiation, such as when buying a car. What did you learn from this experience? What can you apply from this experience to negotiating compensation with a potential employer? (12.2)

9. List reasons why you might reject a job offer. (12.2)

10. An important part of the employment process is a background check. What steps should you take prior to your interview to ensure your background check will be well received by an employer? (12.2)

Chapter 12   Evaluating the Interview

CONNECT TO YOUR CAREER

Workplace Connection

12-1 Interview Evaluation

Post-interview techniques help prepare you for the next opportunity to interview for a position. The first step is to evaluate the interview. Use the Internet to research questions that can help evaluate interview experiences in an objective manner. In addition, consider questions you think are important to ask yourself based on your actual interview experiences. Compile a list of five questions.

1. _____

2. _____

3. _____

4. _____

5. _____

12-2 Thank-You Message

Writing a thank-you message after an interview is expected, and it demonstrates professionalism. Consider each part of the thank-you message. Your introduction should thank the interviewer for the opportunity to discuss a position; your body should reiterate the interview experience; and your closing should thank the interviewer for their time and confirm any necessary follow-up actions.

1. In the space that follows, write the first draft of a thank-you message by composing each message element individually. Keep your message succinct and to the point. Remember to use keywords as you describe your qualifications. Follow the example for writing a thank-you message as shown in Figure 12-2 of this chapter.

    Introduction:

    _____

    _____

    _____

Copyright Goodheart-Willcox Co., Inc.

Body:

_____
_____
_____
_____
_____
_____

Closing:

_____
_____
_____
_____

2. After you have finished your thank-you message, share it with a partner. Have your partner evaluate your message. Then, incorporate any feedback and prepare a final thank-you message in a separate file.

12-3 Job Offer Evaluation

Although receiving a job offer is exciting, you must take the time to carefully evaluate it. Financial factors, such as salary and job-related expenses, are two of the most important components to evaluate.

1. Conduct Internet research for salary calculators, salary-comparison calculators, cost-of-living calculators, and other resources that will help you evaluate the salary offered to you. These calculators will help you determine if the salary meets your requirements. Record the URLs of the resources that are most helpful to you.

   URL #1:
   _____

   URL #2:
   _____

   URL #3:
   _____

   URL #4:
   _____

2. The compensation package is obviously an important part of a job offer. However, there are personal factors that you must also consider. One subject of importance is that of expenses involved in working for the employer. Make a list of questions you might ask yourself or the employer to help determine if the job is a good financial fit for you.

Question #1:
_____
_____

Question #2:
_____
_____

Question #3:
_____
_____

Question #4:
_____
_____

12-4 Salary Negotiation

There will be job offers in which the salary is lower than you would like to accept. You may have to consider negotiating a more appropriate salary. It is important to be prepared for the negotiation process.

1. Conduct Internet research on *how to negotiate a salary*. Compile a list of facts and data that you will use as negotiation points with a hiring manager.

Negotiation Point #1:
_____
_____

Negotiation Point #2:
_____
_____

Negotiation Point #3:
_____
_____

2. After you have compiled your list of negotiation points, work in small groups to practice delivering them. As you listen to the negation points presented by others, pay attention to the techniques they use. Describe what you learned from this process.

12-5 Job Offer Responses

Suppose you have received a job offer for a position. However, the person who made the offer is in meetings all day and can only be reached via e-mail.

1. Write a response you would include in an e-mail *accepting* the job offer for the position.

2. Consider a situation in which, after careful consideration, you have decided the job offer presented does not fit your career plans. Write a response you would include in an e-mail *declining* the job offer for the position.

UNIT 5
Your Career

Chapter 13 Your First Day on the Job
Chapter 14 Starting Your Career

Dzmitry Abrazhevich/Shutterstock.com

Why It Matters

Congratulations—you have a job! Your diligence and preparation in the job-search process has paid off. Out of all the candidates considered, you were selected for a position you worked hard to earn. You have put in a lot of time, effort, and energy to make this a reality. Embrace the fact that you were the best candidate for the position and be proud of your accomplishment. This event ushers in a new chapter of your life.

The first days in a new place of employment can be overwhelming. There will be forms to complete, people to meet, and processes to learn. Professionalism will be a key to your future success. Demonstrate the ability to act responsibly, learn from others, and work hard. Be positive, punctual, and respectful. Stay current in your profession, continue networking, and plan for your financial future. Your career begins now.

CHAPTER 13
Your First Day on the Job

Learning Outcomes

13.1 **Describe** a typical first day of a new job.

13.2 **Describe** performance evaluations in the workplace.

13.3 **Identify** ways to be safe in the workplace.

13.4 **Update** your professional network.

CONNECT TO YOUR CAREER

Workplace Connection

13-1 Employment Forms
13-2 Employee Performance Self-Evaluation
13-3 Workplace Safety
13-4 Update Your Professional Network

OVERVIEW

Your first day on the job is an important step in beginning your career and should be taken seriously. Arrive on time, with a positive attitude, and ready to work. Be confident in yourself and your abilities. This first impression can have great influence on your success with this company.

As you begin your new position, your employer will require that you complete a variety of employment forms and processes. Once you officially start your job, be the best employee you can be. Performance evaluations will be conducted to make sure you are performing your job well. Knowing how to stay safe at your place of work is one of the key things you will learn when you begin your new position.

A new job is a great way to continue to expand your professional network. Most likely you will meet many new people as you start your job. Once you get to know them, it is a good idea to ask them to join your network.

adtapon duangnim/Shutterstock.com

13.1 Day One

The first day on the job will be both overwhelming and exciting. You will probably spend the first day meeting coworkers and getting to know the facility. It is important to your career to make a positive first impression with those you meet.

Learn all you can about the company *before* your first day of work. During the interview process, you should have acquired information about the company's culture, mission, customers, and other valuable details. Use this information to aid your transition as a new employee. Contact the human resources department to inquire as to whether you need a badge or a security code to enter the premises. Ask which building entrance you should use and whom you should call when you arrive. If you are driving, find out where employees are expected to park and whether you need a parking pass.

If You Are Hired as an On-Site Worker

Before reporting to work your first day, confirm the expected attire so you dress appropriately. The company will likely have a dress code that must be followed. A *dress code* is a set of rules or guidelines that defines acceptable attire in a certain place. In the workplace, dress codes can be used for safety reasons or to ensure a professional atmosphere. Even if there is no official dress code, dress professionally to match the culture of the workplace.

Be on time for your first day of work. Your first impression sets the stage for your working career. Greet each new coworker with an enthusiastic smile and pleasant conversation. Exhibit a positive attitude and your excitement to be part of the team. When you meet with your new supervisor, convey your enthusiasm to be an asset to the company. Ask for guidance on your activities, people you should meet, and other information to make your first few days productive.

If You Are Hired as a Remote Worker

In recent years, remote work has become increasingly popular, with more companies offering the option to work from home. With the rise of remote work, the job market has expanded beyond geographical boundaries, offering more opportunities for workers. Landing a remote job can be a great way to achieve work-life balance, avoid long commutes, and provide more flexibility in your schedule. It is important to understand the key differences between traditional and remote jobs and have a strategic approach that will increase your chances of working successfully.

Tips and strategies for working remotely include:
- *Create a dedicated workspace.* Having a designated workspace in your home can help you stay focused and productive. Try to find a quiet spot where you can work without distractions.
- *Attend onboarding sessions.* **Onboarding** is a new employee's introduction to a company's brand, mission statement, values, and practices. As a remote worker, you may have to participate in training courses virtually. Your manager will provide guidance on the procedures to follow. Complete your training sessions as soon as possible.
- *Establish a routine.* Develop a routine that includes regular work hours. You may be expected to work the same schedule as your on-site coworkers. Having a routine will help you stay organized.
- *Communicate effectively.* When working remotely, communication is key. Make sure to use technology such as video conferencing, e-mail, and instant messaging to stay in touch with your team and manager.
- *Take care of your physical and mental health.* Working remotely can be isolating and can lead to feelings of loneliness and stress. Make sure to take breaks, exercise, and stay connected with friends and family to avoid burnout.

Employment Forms

Whether you are working on-site or remotely, you likely will have several employment forms to complete on your first day. Be prepared with the personal information or documentation that will be required for a multitude of forms. You will need your Social Security number, emergency contact information, and other personal information. Examples of employment forms you will need to complete include Form I-9, Form W-4, and benefits forms.

Form I-9

You must complete a *Form I-9 Employment Eligibility Verification*. Form I-9 is a US government form used to verify an employee's identity and authorization to work in the United States. Both the employer and the employee are responsible for completing parts of the form. **Figure 13-1** illustrates the portion of the form that shows citizenship status. Both citizens and noncitizens must complete this form.

FIGURE 13-1

The Form I-9 is used to verify an employee's identity and authorization to work in the United States.

Employment Eligibility Verification
Department of Homeland Security
U.S. Citizenship and Immigration Services

USCIS
Form I-9
OMB No. 1615-0047
Expires 10/31/20--

▶ **START HERE:** Read instructions carefully before completing this form. The instructions must be available, either in paper or electronically, during completion of this form. Employers are liable for errors in the completion of this form.

ANTI-DISCRIMINATION NOTICE: It is illegal to discriminate against work-authorized individuals. Employers **CANNOT** specify which document(s) an employee may present to establish employment authorization and identity. The refusal to hire or continue to employ an individual because the documentation presented has a future expiration date may also constitute illegal discrimination.

Section 1. Employee Information and Attestation *(Employees must complete and sign Section 1 of Form I-9 no later than the **first day of employment**, but not before accepting a job offer.)*

| Last Name *(Family Name)* | First Name *(Given Name)* | Middle Initial | Other Last Names Used *(if any)* |

| Address *(Street Number and Name)* | Apt. Number | City or Town | State | ZIP Code |

| Date of Birth *(mm/dd/yyyy)* | U.S. Social Security Number | Employee's E-mail Address | Employee's Telephone Number |

I am aware that federal law provides for imprisonment and/or fines for false statements or use of false documents in connection with the completion of this form.

I attest, under penalty of perjury, that I am (check one of the following boxes):

☐ 1. A citizen of the United States
☐ 2. A noncitizen national of the United States *(See instructions)*
☐ 3. A lawful permanent resident   (Alien Registration Number/USCIS Number): _____
☐ 4. An alien authorized to work   until (expiration date, if applicable, mm/dd/yyyy): _____
    Some aliens may write "N/A" in the expiration date field. *(See instructions)*

Aliens authorized to work must provide only one of the following document numbers to complete Form I-9:
An Alien Registration Number/USCIS Number OR Form I-94 Admission Number OR Foreign Passport Number.

1. Alien Registration Number/USCIS Number: _____
   OR
2. Form I-94 Admission Number: _____
   OR
3. Foreign Passport Number: _____
   Country of Issuance: _____

QR Code - Section 1
Do Not Write In This Space

| Signature of Employee | Today's Date *(mm/dd/yyyy)* |

Preparer and/or Translator Certification (check one):
☐ I did not use a preparer or translator.   ☐ A preparer(s) and/or translator(s) assisted the employee in completing Section 1.
(Fields below must be completed and signed when preparers and/or translators assist an employee in completing Section 1.)

I attest, under penalty of perjury, that I have assisted in the completion of Section 1 of this form and that to the best of my knowledge the information is true and correct.

| Signature of Preparer or Translator | Today's Date *(mm/dd/yyyy)* |

| Last Name *(Family Name)* | First Name *(Given Name)* |

| Address *(Street Number and Name)* | City or Town | State | ZIP Code |

🛑 *Employer Completes Next Page* 🛑

Form I-9 10/21/20--   Page 1 of 3

US Citizenship and Immigration Services; Goodheart-Willcox Publisher

In addition to completing Form I-9, you must provide certain documents to establish your identity and employment eligibility. Examples of acceptable documents include a US passport or a Permanent Resident Card. If presenting a driver's license, Social Security card, or birth certificate, other documents will also be required. A complete list of acceptable documents can be found in the instructions for Form I-9 and on the US Department of Homeland Security's website. Make sure you check ahead of time so you will have all the documentation you need. If you work remotely and are unable to produce these documents in person, the employer may direct you to an authorized agent acting on its behalf, such as a Notary Public. The agent will review the documents, verify their authenticity, complete the appropriate parts of the form, and return it to the employer.

If you want to check your employment eligibility before you are asked to complete Form I-9, you can use myE-Verify, a US Department of Homeland Security website. You will be asked to enter identifying information that will be compared to government records. Your employment eligibility will either be confirmed or denied. If denied, there are steps to take to resolve any errors. This process will help you be certain that your employment eligibility will be confirmed when the time comes for you to complete Form I-9.

Form W-4

You will also need to complete a *Form W-4 Employee's Withholding Certificate*. A Form W-4 is used by the employer to determine the appropriate amount of taxes to withhold from your paycheck. Withholdings are based on your marital status and the number of dependents you claim. A *dependent* is a child or other person for whom a taxpayer is financially responsible. Based on your elections, the amounts withheld from your paycheck are forwarded to the appropriate government taxing agencies. **Figure 13-2** shows a Form W-4.

By the end of January of each year, an employer must send every employee a *Form W-2 Wage and Tax Statement* to use when filing income tax returns. This form summarizes an employee's wages and withholdings for the previous year.

Benefits Forms

The human resources department will provide you with a variety of forms that are specific to the compensation package offered by the employer. You will complete forms to confirm whether you elect to participate or decline participation in the various programs. A number of these forms will need to be completed on your first day.

One benefit of working full time is that many employers offer insurance coverage for employees. The insurance coverage might include medical, dental, vision, or life insurance. Conditions and terms apply for employees who accept insurance from an employer. For example, premium payments for insurance might be deducted from each paycheck.

Compensation packages are different for every employer, so plan to spend time learning what benefits your new company offers. Inquire about 401(k) plans, tuition assistance, retirement benefits, and day care assistance for dependents. Additionally, ask about your eligibility for these benefits. Some companies require employees to work for 90 days before they are eligible for benefits.

CONNECT TO YOUR CAREER

Complete 13-1 Employment Forms, pg. 224

New-Hire Training

As a new employee, you will be a part of an orientation for new hires. If you are one of several people hired at the same time, you may participate in group training. If you are the only individual hired at that time, your training may be one-on-one, or even conducted remotely.

As previously discussed, *onboarding* is a new employee's introduction to a company's brand, mission statement, values, and practices. Many companies conduct onboarding via PowerPoint presentations conducted by a human resources representative or posted to a remote site for viewing by new hires. These presentations will likely include information such as organizational charts, company history, emergency evacuation procedures for on-site workers, and other details that will help you fit in and be successful with your new employer. Most companies have an employee handbook that will be part of the training materials. Topics such as the history of the company, its mission, and company policies will likely be introduced. Certain topics, such as education about harassment in the workplace, will be addressed as mandated by the government. Other topics, such as employee safety and security, compensation, and benefits, will also be covered.

Take notes during the onboarding presentation. Although you may not need all of the information presented on the first day of your new job, you will likely need to refer to your onboarding information throughout the course of your employment.

After the company policies have been presented, your supervisor or someone on your team will train you on the processes and procedures for your specific job. Each team generally has specific guidelines for accomplishing tasks that you will need to learn. This is an opportunity to start learning the expectations for your new position.

FIGURE 13-2

A Form W-4 is used by the employer for the information necessary to withhold the appropriate amount of taxes from your paycheck.

Form **W-4**
Department of the Treasury
Internal Revenue Service

Employee's Withholding Certificate
Complete Form W-4 so that your employer can withhold the correct federal income tax from your pay.
Give Form W-4 to your employer.
Your withholding is subject to review by the IRS.

OMB No. 1545-0074

20--

Step 1: Enter Personal Information

(a) First name and middle initial | Last name

(b) Social security number

Address

City or town, state, and ZIP code

Does your name match the name on your social security card? If not, to ensure you get credit for your earnings, contact SSA at 800-772-1213 or go to *www.ssa.gov*.

(c) ☐ Single or Married filing separately
☐ Married filing jointly or Qualifying surviving spouse
☐ Head of household (Check only if you're unmarried and pay more than half the costs of keeping up a home for yourself and a qualifying individual.)

Complete Steps 2–4 ONLY if they apply to you; otherwise, skip to Step 5. See page 2 for more information on each step, who can claim exemption from withholding, other details, and privacy.

Step 2: Multiple Jobs or Spouse Works

Complete this step if you (1) hold more than one job at a time, or (2) are married filing jointly and your spouse also works. The correct amount of withholding depends on income earned from all of these jobs.

Do **only one** of the following.

(a) Reserved for future use.

(b) Use the Multiple Jobs Worksheet on page 3 and enter the result in Step 4(c) below; **or**

(c) If there are only two jobs total, you may check this box. Do the same on Form W-4 for the other job. This option is generally more accurate than (b) if pay at the lower paying job is more than half of the pay at the higher paying job. Otherwise, (b) is more accurate . . . . ☐

TIP: If you have self-employment income, see page 2.

Complete Steps 3–4(b) on Form W-4 for only ONE of these jobs. Leave those steps blank for the other jobs. (Your withholding will be most accurate if you complete Steps 3–4(b) on the Form W-4 for the highest paying job.)

Step 3: Claim Dependent and Other Credits

If your total income will be $200,000 or less ($400,000 or less if married filing jointly):

Multiply the number of qualifying children under age 17 by $2,000 $ _____

Multiply the number of other dependents by $500 . . . . . $ _____

Add the amounts above for qualifying children and other dependents. You may add to this the amount of any other credits. Enter the total here . . . . **3** $

Step 4 (optional): Other Adjustments

(a) **Other income (not from jobs).** If you want tax withheld for other income you expect this year that won't have withholding, enter the amount of other income here. This may include interest, dividends, and retirement income . . . . **4(a)** $

(b) **Deductions.** If you expect to claim deductions other than the standard deduction and want to reduce your withholding, use the Deductions Worksheet on page 3 and enter the result here . . . . **4(b)** $

(c) **Extra withholding.** Enter any additional tax you want withheld each **pay period** . . **4(c)** $

Step 5: Sign Here

Under penalties of perjury, I declare that this certificate, to the best of my knowledge and belief, is true, correct, and complete.

_____   _____
Employee's signature (This form is not valid unless you sign it.)   **Date**

Employers Only

Employer's name and address | First date of employment | Employer identification number (EIN)

For Privacy Act and Paperwork Reduction Act Notice, see page 3.   Cat. No. 10220Q   Form **W-4** (20--)

United States Department of the Treasury, Internal Revenue Service; Goodheart-Willcox Publisher

Career Persona

Interior Designer

Responsibilities

An interior designer is responsible for creating functional and aesthetically pleasing interior spaces for clients. An interior designer may also attend industry events, research new products and materials, and learn about design trends and best practices. An interior designer's work is a mix of creativity, project management, and client communication. Daily responsibilities can include the following:

- Meet with clients
- Develop design concepts and create design plans
- Select materials and finishes
- Conduct site visits
- Collaborate with contractors and vendors
- Manage project timelines and budgets

DEEMKA STUDIO/Shutterstock.com

Qualities and Skills

- *Creativity:* Interior designers must have a creative eye and be able to visualize how different elements of a space will work together to create a cohesive look.
- *Attention to detail:* An eye for detail is crucial in interior design as small details can make a significant impact on the overall look and feel of a space.
- *Communication skills:* Interior designers must have excellent communication skills to effectively communicate with clients, contractors, and other professionals involved in the design process.
- *Project Management:* Interior designers must have strong project management skills to ensure that projects are completed on time, within budget, and to the client's satisfaction.
- *Business skills:* Interior designers must have a good understanding of business principles, including budgeting, marketing, and client management.

Education

- Associate or bachelor's degree in interior design, fine arts, or a related field
- National Council for Interior Design Qualification (NCIDQ) certification
- Voluntary certification in an interior design specialty through professional and trade associations

Next Steps

If you are interested in pursuing a job as an interior designer, you can start by researching accredited interior design programs and work toward getting a degree. When applying to these programs, you may need to submit a portfolio of sketches or other examples of your artistic and creative ability. Taking courses in drawing and computer-aided design (CAD) will be helpful. Network by attending industry events and joining professional organizations such as the American Society of Interior Designers (ASID) to increase your number of contacts in the industry.

Workplace Skills

Cultural competency is the acknowledgment of cultural differences and the ability to adapt one's communication style to successfully send and receive messages despite those differences. The first step in becoming culturally competent involves recognizing cultural barriers. Being aware of potential disruptions is the best way to prevent or avoid them. The second step of cultural competency involves the willingness to adapt to those barriers.

If you are an on-site employee, you may be taken on a tour of the facilities to become familiar with the layout of the building in which you work. During this tour, you will probably be introduced to the people with whom you will work or have contact during your first few days on the job. You may also be invited to sit in on meetings from other departments to learn more about the company and its values, culture, and workflow. Remote employees may be introduced to their new coworkers or attend department meetings through video conferencing.

Figure 13-3 provides a list of topics to ask about during the onboarding process. In addition, there are other common workplace topics of which you should be aware, such as flextime, overtime, personal cell phone use, and workspace etiquette.

Flextime

Flextime is a concept in which an employee can choose the start and end times for the workday, provided the employee has worked the required number of hours for the day. However, there are likely limitations. For example, employees may not be permitted to start at 5 a.m. and end at 1 p.m. There may be certain core hours that employees are required to work, such as between 10 a.m. and 4 p.m. Ask if the company allows flextime and what the limitations are.

Overtime

Make sure you understand your employer's overtime policy. Never assume you will receive overtime pay for time worked beyond 40 hours per week. For example, those eligible for overtime may first require preapproval from management in order to qualify for overtime pay. An overtime policy will likely be printed in the employee handbook, but asking about it during onboarding ensures you will receive all pertinent information.

Personal Cell Phone Use

Generally, employees are not permitted to use cell phones for personal use during work hours. However, every employer may approach this issue differently. It is worth your time to inquire about your employer's policy during onboarding. This ensures you understand all aspects of the policy and avoid unintentionally breaking the rules.

Workspace Etiquette

As an on-site employee, you will be assigned a workspace on your first day of employment. A *workspace* is the specific area within a company's location where an employee works. It is an individual's personal space while at work. It is important to be aware of proper workspace etiquette. *Workspace etiquette* is applying the rules of good manners while you are in your own space and the space of others. Proper respect helps to maintain positive relationships with your coworkers.

In some businesses, all employees are assigned a cubicle regardless of title or position. Cubicles offer some privacy, but they are not protected from noises or distractions. If this is your assigned area, remember to respect those in the cubicles around you. When in conversations on the phone or with those who are visiting you, remember to keep your voice low so as not to disturb others. If listening to music as you work, use headphones. Digital devices should be turned off or silenced.

Depending on your career and position, you may have your own office as a workspace. Having an office provides a quiet, private space to complete tasks. If you have an office, treat it as a privilege. Close the door when you are in conversations with visitors or on the phone.

Respect should be shown to your employer by keeping your workspace clean, organized, and free from clutter. Overdecorating with photographs and personal items can be distracting in a business situation, so discretion should be used. Personal items, such as briefcases and lunch containers, should be placed in a drawer or closet to maintain discretion and safety, as well as to keep the space presentable and orderly.

Some businesses permit employees to drink coffee and water and eat snacks or lunch at their desks. If you choose to do so, avoid bringing foods to your workspace that have strong odors that might offend coworkers. Remember to maintain a clean work environment and dispose of leftovers and packaging in the employee

FIGURE 13-3

Asking questions during the onboarding process can provide helpful information.

Onboarding Topics	
Type of Employee	**Questions to Ask**
All Employees	• What hours am I expected to work?
	• Who do I call in an emergency?
	• Who do I call for computer or technical assistance?
	• How do I log into the company's computer system?
	• Who is the human resources contact and how do I reach them?
	• How do I call in sick or request time off?
	• How do I obtain office supplies?
On-site Employees	• During what hours is the building open?
	• How do I use the company's telephone system?
	• What are the policies for lunch and breaks?
	• Is there a break room?
	• Where is the photocopier located?
	• How do I clock in and out, if required?
Remote Employees	• Will I have regular check-ins with someone in the office?
	• What is the preferred method of communication with coworkers—telephone, e-mail, or video conferencing?
	• Am I expected to follow the same work schedule as on-site employees?
	• How do I record my hours worked?
	• What expenses are covered?

Goodheart-Willcox Publisher

break room or cafeteria rather than in the garbage can at your desk.

13.2 Performance Evaluations

During your career, your performance on the job will be evaluated. A **performance evaluation** is a formal process designed to evaluate an employee's work and offer productive feedback. The evaluation will take into account not only your actual job performance and how you execute your duties, but also how well you interact with your coworkers as a team player.

Performance evaluations are generally formal meetings with a manager or supervisor. They will review the evaluation with you and discuss the results. These meetings are an opportunity for you to conduct self-evaluations about what you want from your job and how you may advance in the future.

A *performance evaluation form* will be used in an evaluation. Ask for a copy of the form early in your employment. Review the criteria often and execute each category to the best of your ability. If at any time you feel that you are not meeting the minimum criteria as detailed on the performance evaluation form, ask your immediate supervisor for guidance. Your supervisor should be able to provide feedback that you can use to help overcome obstacles that stand in the way of your success.

Remember, you created a career plan. During a performance evaluation, it is up to you to decide if the outcome of your meeting is what you want for your career. Use each evaluation as a chance to revisit your plan.

CONNECT TO YOUR CAREER

Complete 13-2 Employee Performance Self-Evaluation, pg. 225

13.3 Workplace Safety

As a new employee, it is necessary to become acquainted with workplace safety guidelines for the organization. Workplace safety in the United States has continuously improved since the beginning of the 20th century. Injury, death, and illness related to working conditions have gradually declined. This is due to a change in the type of work done today and in the safety precautions that have been put in place. For example, some professions now require the use of personal protective equipment (PPE), such as hard hats, safety glasses, and gloves.

Accident Prevention

Falling hazards, lifting hazards, and material-storage hazards account for most of the workplace accidents that occur in offices. Falls are the most common workplace accidents in an office setting. To prevent falling injuries, take the following precautions:
- Close drawers completely.
- Do not stand on a chair or box to reach an object.
- Secure cords, rugs, and mats.
- Keep the work area clean and free of hazards, such as spills and exposed wires.

Lifting hazards are sources of potential injury from improperly lifting or carrying items. Most back injuries are caused by improper lifting. To prevent lifting injuries, take the following precautions:
- Make several small trips with items rather than one trip with an overly heavy load.
- Use dollies or handcarts whenever possible.
- Lift with the legs, not the back.
- Never carry an item that blocks vision.

Material-storage hazards are sources of potential injury that come from the improper storage of files, books, office equipment, or other items, such as hazardous chemicals or flammable materials. A cluttered workplace is an unsafe workplace. Material stacked too high can fall on employees. Paper and files stored on the floor or improper storage of chemicals is a fire risk. To prevent material-storage accidents and injuries, take the following precautions:
- Do not stack boxes or papers on top of tall cabinets.
- Store heavier objects on lower shelves.
- Keep aisles and hallways clear.
- Keep fire extinguishers on hand.

Maintaining a safe workplace is the joint responsibility of the employer and employee. The employer makes sure the facility and working conditions are such that accidents are unlikely to occur, and the employee uses common sense and care while on the job. Keys to maintaining a safe working environment include reading and understanding equipment safety manuals, following safety instructions, and staying informed about safety laws and best practices. When an accident does occur, report it immediately to your supervisor or manager.

CONNECT TO YOUR CAREER

Complete 13-3 Workplace Safety, pg. 227

Ergonomics

Ergonomics is the science concerned with designing and arranging things a person uses so they can be used efficiently and safely. In the workplace, it can include designing workstations to fit the unique needs of the worker and the equipment used. Effective application of ergonomic principles results in a comfortable, efficient, and safe working environment.

There are many types of ergonomic accessories that may improve a workstation, including wrist rests for keyboards, specially designed chairs, and back supports. In addition, **Figure 13-4** identifies actions and accessories that can be taken to create a comfortable

---

The Best App for That

Trello

Once you have landed a job, you may need help managing your work. Trello is a productivity tool that helps users organize tasks and projects using digital boards, lists, and cards. With Trello, users can create boards for different projects, create to-do lists, add tasks (cards) to those lists, and assign due dates and labels to those tasks. Trello also allows users to collaborate with team members, share files, and track progress. It is a simple, user-friendly interface that makes it easy for employees to stay on top of their work as they transition into their new job.

FIGURE 13-4

An ergonomic workstation can help improve health and reduce injuries.

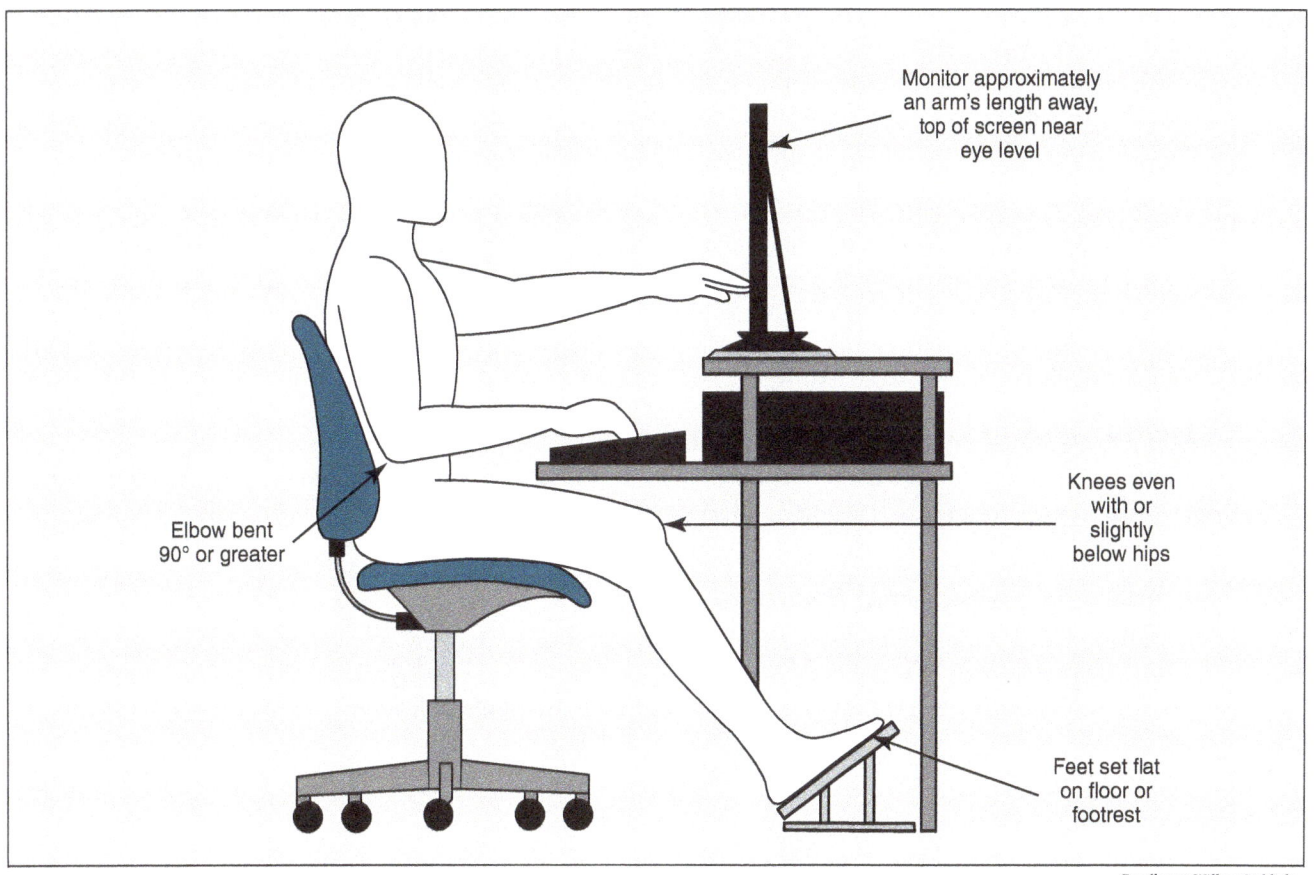

Goodheart-Willcox Publisher

environment and help prevent injury or strain to the worker's body.

13.4 Update Your Professional Network

When you begin your new job, update your LinkedIn, Twitter, Instagram, and other professional networking accounts to reflect your employment status. Enter your new title, the month and year that you begin your job, and the name of the company at which you are employed. After you add your new company to your profile, search for and join the company's groups or social networking pages, if applicable.

Visit the employment websites and job boards where your résumé is posted. Change your job-seeking status from "searching" to "not searching." Otherwise, you will continue to get new job postings in your e-mail. Refer to your tracking documents if you do not remember all of the places where your résumé is posted.

It is important to stay up to date with those in your network who agreed to be personal references for you during the employment process. Reach out to those who helped you during your job search to let them know that you got the job and thank them for their help. This will help you maintain valuable relationships. Keep in touch with your network, even when you do not have an immediate need for help. Stay in touch by sending them an occasional message, calling them, or meeting them for coffee or lunch. This way you are keeping your network strong and active.

In addition to staying in touch with your current network, it is also important to network in your new role. Introduce yourself to your new colleagues and build connections within your new organization. This will help you learn about opportunities for growth and development and also position you as a valuable asset to the company.

CONNECT TO YOUR CAREER

Complete 13-4 Update your Professional Network, pg. 228

Summary

13.1 Describe a typical first day of a new job.
On the first day with a company, human resources will require certain forms be completed by new hires. This includes a Form I-9, Form W-4, and other documents related to the compensation package. New-hire training and onboarding will also be conducted on the first day.

13.2 Describe performance evaluations in the workplace.
Performance evaluations are generally formal meetings with a manager or supervisor. These evaluations take into account job performance and how well a person interacts with coworkers. In addition, they are an opportunity for employees to conduct self-evaluations about what they want from the job. A copy of the performance evaluation form should be requested when starting a new job and reviewed often.

13.3 Identify ways to be safe in the workplace.
Follow simple safety guidelines to avoid workplace accidents and keep everyone safe. Avoid falling, lifting, and material-storage hazards, and use ergonomics to ensure comfort and functionality in a workstation.

13.4 Update your professional network.
An individual's professional network should be updated to reflect new employment. Follow up with professional references to thank them for serving as references. Employment status on job-search websites should also be updated to avoid having advertisements delivered to a professional e-mail account.

Glossary Terms

ergonomics

onboarding

performance evaluation

Review

1. How can a person prepare for the first day on the job? (13.1)

2. What is the purpose of the Form I-9? (13.1)

Chapter 13   Your First Day on the Job

3. What is the purpose of the Form W-4? (13.1)

___

4. What information is included in a Form W-2? (13.1)

___

5. Provide an example of an onboarding experience. (13.1)

___

6. Describe the performance evaluation process. (13.2)

___

7. Identify how to be safe in the workplace. (13.3)

___

8. List three keys to maintaining a safe working environment. (13.3)

___

9. List examples of ergonomic accessories. (13.3)

___

10. Why is it important to update your professional networks after getting a job? (13.4)

_____
_____
_____

Application

1. What information will you inquire about before the first day on the job? (13.1)

_____
_____
_____

2. What types of benefits do you hope to be offered by your future employer? (13.1)

_____
_____
_____

3. What benefits are typically offered in your field or chosen industry? (13.1)

_____
_____
_____

4. Describe typical new-hire training in your industry. (13.1)

_____
_____
_____

5. What types of onboarding would you expect to experience in your chosen career field? (13.1)

_____
_____
_____

Chapter 13   Your First Day on the Job

6. How have onboarding experiences helped you in your past work experience? (13.1)

_____

_____

_____

_____

7. By what criteria do you expect to be evaluated in your desired career? (13.2)

_____

_____

_____

_____

8. Describe what you think is the most common cause for workplace injury in your chosen career field. (13.3)

_____

_____

_____

_____

9. What type of safety training have you completed in your industry? (13.3)

_____

_____

_____

_____

10. Why is it beneficial to stay in touch with your network even while employed on a full-time basis? (13.4)

_____

_____

_____

_____

CONNECT TO YOUR CAREER
Workplace Connection

13-1 Employment Forms

1. Download the Form I-9 Employment Eligibility Verification from the US Citizen and Immigration Services website at www.uscis.gov. Print a copy of this form and complete it as a practice exercise. Use blue or black ink and your best handwriting. The form must be neat, clean, and error-free. However, *do not* fill in your Social Security number. This should only be completed when you are ready to submit the form to an employer. Were there any parts of the form that were unclear to you? List these items.

   _____
   _____
   _____
   _____
   _____

2. Review the acceptable forms of identification for the Form I-9. Record which documents you have in your possession that you will provide to your new employer. Does your eligibility come from List A, List B, List C, or a combination of the lists?

   _____
   _____
   _____
   _____
   _____

3. Download the Form W-4 Employee's Withholding Certificate from the US Internal Revenue Service website at www.irs.gov. Print and complete the form, excluding your Social Security number, as a practice exercise. Were there any parts of the form that were unclear to you? List these items.

   _____
   _____
   _____
   _____
   _____

13-2 Employee Performance Self-Evaluation

Self-evaluation is an important part of the performance evaluation process. Often, an employer will request that an employee complete a self-evaluation prior to being evaluated by a supervisor. This provides the supervisor with an opportunity to learn more about the employee's professional goals and help guide the employee toward continuous improvement throughout a career. The evaluation form that follows is typical of one that you might receive as an employee. Study the form and review each section. Then complete the questions that follow.

Employee Self-Evaluation				
Name:		Title:		
Department:		Date:		
Time in Position:		Supervisor:		
Goals or achievements completed over the past year				
1.					
2.					
3.					
Goals that were not completed				
1.					
2.					
3.					
New skills acquired and important experience gained:				
Professional development I completed:				
New tasks for which I'd like to be responsible and assignment preferences:				

(continued)

Professional development I'd like to pursue:
Where I see myself in the next 12–24 months:
What I ultimately aspire to be doing:
Additional comments:

1. What did you learn from reviewing this self-evaluation form?

   _____
   _____
   _____

2. What type of information or questions would you add to the self-evaluation form and why?

   _____
   _____
   _____

3. Why would a supervisor want to know an employee's aspirations?

   _____
   _____
   _____

4. How important do you think a self-evaluation is in terms of an employee's overall performance evaluation?

_____
_____
_____

5. How can a self-evaluation help prepare an employee for a formal evaluation that a supervisor will conduct?

_____
_____
_____

6. What does "be the best employee you can be" mean to you? Explain how you plan to carry this out in your career.

_____
_____
_____

13-3 Workplace Safety

Workplace safety is different in every industry. When safety practices are not followed, accidents and injuries are more likely to occur. Poor ergonomics can be the cause of some workplace injuries. It is important to be aware of safety and ergonomics hazards in the workplace and know how to prevent them.

1. Working with a partner, select a career field. Conduct an Internet search for safety concerns in your selected career field. List one safety concern and explain preventive measures that can be taken to avoid it. Share your findings with the class.

Career field:

_____

Safety concern:

_____
_____

How to prevent it:

_____
_____

2. What are the ergonomic concerns for the equipment commonly used in the field you researched? Examples of equipment include computers, desks and chairs, machinery, and automobiles. Describe one ergonomic concern related to equipment used in your selected field. Then, explain how the design of the equipment can be more ergonomically friendly to prevent injuries. Share your findings with the class.

Ergonomics concern:

_____

_____

How to prevent it:

_____

_____

13-4 Update Your Professional Network

Describe the steps you will take to update your professional networking profiles on social media, follow up with your professional references, and update your job-seeking status on employment websites and job boards.

Step #1:

_____

_____

Step #2:

_____

_____

Step #3:

_____

_____

Step #4:

_____

_____

Step #5:

_____

_____

Step #6:

_____

_____

CHAPTER 14 Starting Your Career

Learning Outcomes

14.1 **Define** professionalism.

14.2 **Explain** how to work in a multigenerational and multicultural workplace.

14.3 **Cite** actions that ensure a successful career.

CONNECT TO YOUR CAREER

Workplace Connection

14-1 Multigenerational Workplace
14-2 Take Charge of Your Career

OVERVIEW

Landing the job you want is just the beginning. You should do all you can to succeed and advance in your chosen field. Exhibiting professionalism means taking responsibility for your behavior and your work. Certain work habits and traits demonstrate professionalism in almost any job in business and industry, from stock clerk to top executive. These habits and traits include promptness, reliable attendance, dependability, positivity, and eagerness to do the work as best you can.

As your career progresses, remember to put your best foot forward. Make an effort to treat coworkers with respect and as valuable contributors to the workplace, despite differences. This will result in a pleasant working experience and ensure you are able to continually connect to your career.

Naypong Studio/Shutterstock.com

14.1 Professionalism

As a new employee, your primary responsibility is to help the business operate and make a profit. You will be expected to perform assigned job duties to the best of your ability. While performing those duties, your employer will insist that you behave in a professional manner. **Professionalism** is a soft skill that includes the judgment, character, and behavior expected of a person who is trained for a given job. You will be required to exhibit professionalism while at work or when representing the company.

In addition to the workplace skills introduced in Chapter 2, professionalism includes self-management skills. **Self-management skills** are the skills that enable an individual to control personal habits and make the best use of one's time and abilities. Examples are punctuality, dependability, time management, and emotional regulation.

Punctuality

Punctuality means being on time. It is important to show up ready for work on time every day. This is true for both on-site and remote employees. Being late or unexpectedly absent is inconsiderate and not tolerated in the working world. If you are late or are unexpectedly absent, your coworkers may have to take on your work. In addition to being rude and unprofessional, these actions can lead to resentment or animosity in the workplace. If you know you will be late or have to miss work entirely, it is expected that you will notify your employer with enough time for alternative plans to be established.

Dependability

Punctuality is a sign of dependability. **Dependability** is a person's ability to be reliable and trustworthy. Being dependable means others can count on you to do what needs to be done, keep your word, be honest, and carry your share of the workload. Dependable employees tend to be given the important jobs in a company.

Time Management

Professionals understand how to manage their time and priorities. "Work smarter, not harder" is a phrase often quoted in business and industry. **Time management** is the practice of organizing time and work assignments to increase personal efficiency. It is an important soft skill in the workplace because work assignments may include a variety of tasks. Often, you will need to work on several tasks at the same time. You will be expected to prioritize those tasks by determining which ones should be completed before others. When uncertain as to which tasks are the most important, always ask your direct supervisor. The difference between average and excellent workers is often not how hard they work, but how well they prioritize assignments.

Emotional Regulation

Learning how to control your emotions is a skill that, if you lack, can cost you your job. Your emotional state of being is complicated, and it takes work and determination to keep it under control. Coworkers who annoy you, situations that do not go your way, and other daily work incidents can cause you to be irritable and show how you are feeling. As a professional, this is behavior that can make or break your career. By exhibiting self-control, you can manage your feelings and emotions in a manner that is socially acceptable. If you think this may be an issue for you, be proactive and get professional help before a situation gets out of hand.

14.2 Multigenerational and Multicultural Workplace

A **generation** is a group of people who were born during the same time period. The period of history in which a group of people grew up has a major effect on their values and attitudes. Occurring events will impact each generation differently.

You will probably be most comfortable interacting with those from your own generation. However, to be an effective employee, it will be necessary to learn to work with individuals from all generations. As you begin your career, you will find yourself a part of a **multigenerational workplace,** which is a work environment where employees from different age groups, typically spanning over several decades, collaborate and interact with each other.

Understanding how to communicate with members of a different generation than your own begins with understanding the traits common to each generation. While individuals in a given generation will not share the exact traits, some characteristics are common for people within each group. The four generations most common in the workforce today are the Baby Boomers, Generation X, Millennials, and Generation Z.

- *Baby Boomers:* Born between 1946 and 1964, baby boomers are known for being ambitious, competitive, and goal-oriented. They are also known for their strong work ethic and their desire to make a difference. They tend to value relationships, making them valuable team members. Baby Boomers are often characterized as being hard-working, disciplined, and independent.

Connect to Your Community

In today's diverse workforce, it is essential for college students to learn about other cultures and build cultural competency. Attending local cultural events, such as festivals, music events, or art exhibits, is an excellent way to learn about different cultures and traditions. Similarly, trying new foods and dining at restaurants offering ethnic foods can provide an opportunity to experience different flavors and learn about the customs and traditions surrounding the food. Visiting museums, especially those with cultural exhibits, can also provide an opportunity to learn about different cultures and their history. Moreover, volunteering with refugees or other marginalized groups can provide a first-hand experience to learn about their unique cultures and backgrounds. In addition, students can also seek out opportunities to study or travel abroad, which can provide an immersive experience to learn about other cultures and ways of life. Ultimately, learning about other cultures is essential for building empathy and understanding, which is crucial for success in today's diverse workforce.

BABAROGA/Shutterstock.com

- *Generation X:* Born between the mid-1960s and the early 1980s, Generation X is sandwiched between the larger baby boomer and millennial generations. Members of Generation X grew up during a time of significant social, economic, and technological change, which has shaped their attitudes and values in unique ways. They are often practical, resourceful, and independent. They place a strong emphasis on work-life balance. Generation Xers are often characterized as being self-sufficient, adaptable, and pragmatic.
- *Millennials (Generation Y):* Born between 1981 and 1996, millennials are known for being tech-savvy, ambitious, and collaborative. Millennials are innovative and look for ways to be more efficient. They also value flexibility, personal growth, and social responsibility. Many millennials are socially conscious and passionate about social and environmental issues.
- *Generation Z:* Born after 1996, members of Generation Z are known for being digital natives and independent learners. They prioritize technology and accessibility in their work lives. They tend to be highly adaptable to new technologies, open to diversity, and have entrepreneurial attitudes. They also tend to value social justice, environmentalism, and equality. Gen Zers are often characterized as being creative and socially conscious.

It's important to note that these characteristics are generalizations and not all individuals within a generation will fit into these categories. Additionally, individuals may have traits that span multiple generations, as generational characteristics can overlap.

Not only will you work with people from different generations, but you will also work with others in multicultural settings. A **multicultural workplace** is an organization or work environment that comprises individuals from diverse backgrounds, cultures, and identities. Working in a multicultural environment requires cultural competence. **Cultural competence** is the ability to understand, communicate, interact, and collaborate with people from different cultures. When employees come from different cultures, they may offer unique ideas and perspectives. Embracing and respecting others' viewpoints can lead to creative problem solving. By being open-minded, respectful, and communicative, and by embracing diversity and building relationships, you can contribute to a positive and inclusive work environment.

CONNECT TO YOUR CAREER

Complete 14-1 Multigenerational Workplace, pg. 239

Time Management

Pomodoro Method

The Pomodoro method is a time-management system that was developed in the late 1980s by Francesco Cirillo. It is named after the Pomodoro kitchen timer, which Cirillo used to time his work sessions. The method involves breaking work down into intervals, typically 25 minutes in length, separated by short breaks. These intervals are known as "pomodoros."

To use the Pomodoro method, you will start by selecting a single task to complete. Then, you must set a timer for 25 minutes and work on the task until the timer goes off. Once the pomodoro interval is complete, you should take a short break, typically 5 to 10 minutes. After four pomodoros, take a longer break, typically 15 to 30 minutes.

The Pomodoro method is designed to help individuals stay focused and avoid distractions. By breaking work down into shorter intervals, individuals can concentrate on the task at hand without becoming overwhelmed or burned out. The short breaks between pomodoros provide an opportunity to rest and recharge, which can help improve overall productivity.

14.3 Your Career

You will spend many hours of your life at work, so you must take charge of your career. Start planning for your future as soon as possible. Take actions that will help ensure a long, productive, and happy career.

Become a Good Employee

The easiest way to ensure a long, successful career is to become a good employee. Take your work seriously and maintain your professionalism in the workplace. Nurture relationships with your supervisor as well as your coworkers. Being a good employee generally involves the following:
- consistently meeting or exceeding job performance expectations
- having a positive attitude and strong work ethic
- effectively communicating and collaborating with others
- being dependable and reliable
- being open to feedback and willing to learn and improve
- taking initiative to contribute to the success of the company or organization

Respect Money

Be wise with your money and start saving for your retirement as soon as possible. Saving money early can make your retirement years more comfortable and easier to attain. Research the retirement benefits your new employer offers, and take full advantage of them. Some companies will make contributions to an employee's retirement account, which can make savings grow even more.

Grow a Professional Network

Grow and maintain your professional network as you progress in your career. The individuals you meet and work with along the way can help you throughout your career in many different ways. Additionally, being in touch with other professionals in your field will make you aware of new developments and opportunities in your career field.

Stay Current

Continue your professional development by staying up to date in your field. Successful employees continually seek opportunities to improve their career skills. **Professional development** is training that builds on skills and knowledge that contribute to personal growth and career development. There are many options for professional development. Many businesses are willing to pay to provide professional development training or continuing education for their employees. By keeping abreast of the most current expectations in your field, you can achieve success in the workplace and exhibit leadership qualities.

Have Realistic Expectations

Establishing realistic career expectations is essential for maintaining your career. It is easy to be overconfident and expect instant success, power, and respect, but this is simply unrealistic. No one is *entitled* to career success; it must be earned. A successful career can be defined in different ways depending on one's personal goals and values.

Career Persona

CAD Professional

Responsibilities

A CAD (computer-aided design) professional is responsible for creating technical drawings and designs using specialized software, often working closely with engineers and other professionals. Most CAD professionals specialize in architectural, civil, electrical, or mechanical drafting. Designs can be for something as small as a microchip or as large as a skyscraper. Some of their daily responsibilities may include the following:

- Create 2D or 3D digital models using CAD software
- Specify dimensions, materials, and procedures for new products
- Ensure that designs are accurate, meet project specifications, and adhere to industry standards
- Collaborate with engineers, architects, and other professionals to interpret design specifications and troubleshoot design issues
- Communicate design ideas and recommendations to team members and clients

Bert Flint/Shutterstock.com

Qualities and Skills

- *Creativity:* A CAD professional must be able to turn ideas into technical drawings and digital blueprints.
- *Technical skills:* CAD professionals must be proficient in CAD software and various programming languages.
- *Knowledge of engineering and architectural principles:* Knowledge of industry standards and engineering principles, such as structural planning and visualization, is required.
- *Math skills:* Strong math skills are needed to calculate dimensions, angles, weights, and other values.
- *Analytical skills:* CAD professionals must be able to analyze and evaluate information in order to make decisions and identify solutions that will result in a viable design.
- *Communication skills:* CAD professionals are often working on projects with other team members and clients and must be able to clearly communicate design ideas and recommendations.

Education

- CAD program at community college or technical school
- Associate degree in applied science in drafting or a related field
- Autodesk Certified Professional certification
- Bachelor's degree in manufacturing, architecture, or engineering

Next Steps

If you want to become a CAD professional, you can start by taking higher-level courses in math, science, computer technology, design, and computer graphics. You should also research the field to determine a specialty, such as mechanical or architectural drafting. By completing an apprenticeship or internship, or getting an entry-level job in the field, you can learn more about the industry and begin to build a portfolio to showcase your work.

Although success can be measured in different ways, some common elements of a successful career are shown in **Figure 14-1** and described below.

- *A sense of fulfillment and satisfaction:* This comes from feeling that your work is meaningful and contributes to your overall sense of well-being. This can be achieved when you believe the work you are doing makes a positive impact and that you are good at your job.
- *Professional development:* Continuously learning new skills, taking on new challenges, and growing in your field will help ensure success. This could involve taking classes, attending workshops, networking, or taking on new roles in your current job.
- *Good relationships:* Building strong relationships with colleagues, mentors, and clients is an important part of a successful career. These people can provide support, guidance, and opportunities for growth.
- *Sense of purpose:* A successful career often includes a sense of purpose, whether it be in the form of meaningful work or an overarching goal that the individual is striving to achieve.
- *Flexibility:* A successful career allows for some degree of flexibility, meaning the individual is able to adapt to changes in the workplace and pivot when needed to pursue new opportunities and achieve a work-life balance.
- *Personal growth:* A successful career includes opportunities for personal growth, whether it be in the form of new skills, experiences, or opportunities for self-improvement.

No one can achieve workplace success on their own. It takes a team of workers. Make an effort to be an effective team player by openly communicating, cooperating, and showing positivity. As you gain more work experience, you will also gain a better understanding of how to grow, learn, and adapt in order to move forward in your career. What makes a successful career is a personal decision and can change over time. It is important to set goals and reevaluate them regularly.

CONNECT TO YOUR CAREER

Complete 14-2 Take Charge of Your Career, pg. 240

FIGURE 14-1

The definition of a successful career will not be the same for everyone, but there are some common elements.

CeltStudio/Shutterstock.com

Summary

14.1 Define professionalism.
Professionalism is a soft skill that includes the judgment, character, and behavior expected of a person who is trained for a given job. In addition to basic skills, thinking skills, people skills, and personal qualities, professionalism also includes self-management skills. Self-management skills include punctuality, dependability, time management, and emotional regulation.

14.2 Explain how to work in a multigenerational and multicultural workplace.
Four generations most common in the workforce today are the Baby Boomers, Generation X, Millennials (Generation Y), and Generation Z. Learning about generational traits and characteristics can improve your interactions at work. In addition, being culturally competent can help you embrace and respect the viewpoints of coworkers from different backgrounds.

14.3 Cite actions that ensure a successful career.
The easiest way to ensure a successful career is by being a good employee. This may involve having a sense of satisfaction, participating in professional development, building good relationships with coworkers, having a sense of purpose, being flexible, and achieving personal growth. Other factors include respecting money, growing a professional network, and having realistic expectations.

Glossary Terms

cultural competence
dependability
generation
multicultural workplace
multigenerational workplace
professional development
professionalism
punctuality
self-management skills
time management

Review

1. How would you define professionalism in the workplace? (14.1)

   _____
   _____
   _____
   _____

2. List examples of self-management skills. (14.1)

   _____
   _____
   _____
   _____

3. Aside from it being rude and unprofessional, being late or unexpectedly absent can lead to what? (14.1)

4. What does it mean to be dependable? (14.1)

5. What is the difference between average and excellent workers? (14.1)

6. What generations are likely to be encountered in the workplace? (14.2)

7. Describe the differences among the generations you may encounter in the workplace. (14.2)

8. Describe actions that ensure a successful career. (14.3)

9. Why is it important to start saving for retirement early? (14.3)

Chapter 14   Starting Your Career

10. How can professional development help you achieve success in a career? (14.3)

Application

1. How would you describe your personal level of professionalism? Provide examples of situations in which you presented yourself in a way that reinforced your professionalism. (14.1)

2. How do you maintain a professional demeanor in high-stress or difficult situations? (14.1)

3. What does "work smarter, not harder" mean to you? (14.1)

4. Do you think you can be a dependable employee? Cite examples to support your answer. (14.1)

5. On a scale of one to ten, with one being the weakest and ten being the strongest, rate your top five time-management or prioritizing skills. Describe how this information can help you improve your time-management skills. (14.1)

6. Explain how you will successfully regulate your emotions in the workplace. (14.1)

7. How does cultural competence impact the workplace? (14.2)

8. How can a multicultural workforce improve problem solving? (14.2)

9. List types of professional development that are important to your career and explain their necessity. (14.3)

10. How do you stay current with developments in your industry and maintain professional credibility? (14.3)

Chapter 14 Starting Your Career

CONNECT TO YOUR CAREER
Workplace Connection

14-1 Multigenerational Workplace

Each generation you encounter in the workplace has developed and adheres to expected behavior while at work. Generational traits can result in vastly different work styles.

1. List your generation in the space provided. Conduct an Internet search for workplace characteristics common to your generation and list examples in the left column of the table. Then, in the right column, list your personal workplace characteristics. Note any similarities.

   List your generation: _____

My Generation	
My Generation's Workplace Characteristics	**My Workplace Characteristics**

2. To what extent would you agree or disagree that your workplace characteristics are similar to those of your generation?

   Agree: _____

   _____

   Disagree: _____

   _____

Copyright Goodheart-Willcox Co., Inc.

14-2 Take Charge of Your Career

Taking charge of your career includes accepting responsibility for your role in the company, taking necessary steps to improve and grow professionally, and planning for your future. It also includes personal financial management. Once you start earning a regular paycheck, it is important to create a budget so you can manage your money wisely. Your budget should include paying your living expenses as well as paying off school loans and saving for retirement.

1. Conduct a search on the Internet using the phrase *personal budget* to learn about various methods and formats for the creation of a budget. Select a method that will work for you and use the following space to help organize your budget items.

   Expenses (monthly):

   _____

   _____

   _____

   Savings (how much you can afford to save):

   _____

   _____

   _____

   Discretionary Spending (surplus money for wants, *not* needs):

   _____

   _____

   _____

2. Professional development is an important aspect in one's career, as it can affect a career path. In Chapter 1, you learned how to write SMART goals that are specific, measurable, attainable, realistic, and timely. Use the SMART goals model to write one short-term professional development goal for your career and one long-term goal.

   Short-term goal:

   _____

   _____

   _____

   Long-term goal:

   _____

   _____

   _____

Chapter 14 Starting Your Career

3. Now that you have a job, it is time to update your personal career plan. Revisit the career plan you created in Workplace Connection activity 1-2. Throughout this chapter, you learned how to use job-search strategies to connect to your career. Based on what you have learned, update your career plan.

Career Plan		
Career Item	**Specific Action to Take**	**Target Completion Date**

APPENDIX A: Punctuation

Terminal Punctuation

In writing, **punctuation** consists of marks used to show the structure of sentences. Punctuation marks used at the end of a sentence are called *terminal punctuation*. Terminal punctuation marks include periods, question marks, and exclamation points.

Periods

A **period** is a punctuation mark used at the end of a declarative sentence. A *declarative sentence* is one that makes a statement. A period signals to the reader that the expressed thought has ended.

> The final exam will be on May 26.
>
> Alma traveled to Lexington to visit her friend.

A period can be used within a quotation. A period should be placed inside a quotation that completes a statement. If a sentence contains a quotation that does not complete the thought, the period should be placed at the end of the sentence, not the end of the quote.

> Jacobi said, "The project is on schedule."
>
> She told me, "Do not let anyone through this door," and she meant it.

Bullet points are a great way to organize information on a résumé because they make it easier to scan and read information quickly. Bullet points are often used for each job duty or accomplishment and start with a strong action verb. If your bulleted points are complete sentences, use a period for ending punctuation.

> Schedule appointments for school faculty.
>
> Answer telephones and direct calls.
>
> Prepare e-mails, reports, and letters.

In some cases, no terminal punctuation is required. Generally, if your bulleted points are all sentence fragments, do not use ending punctuation. The important thing is to be consistent and use the same punctuation style at the end of bullet points throughout your résumé.

> Microsoft Word, PowerPoint, and Excel
>
> Project management
>
> Customer service

Exclamation Points

An **exclamation point** is a punctuation mark used to express strong emotion. Exclamation points are used at the end of a sentence or after an interjection that stands alone. An exclamation point can be used at the end of a question rather than a question mark, if the writer wishes to show strong emotion. Do not overuse exclamation points; otherwise, they may lose their impact.

> Ouch! Stop hurting me!
>
> Will you ever grow up!

As with other terminal punctuation, an exclamation point can be part of a sentence that contains a quotation. Place the exclamation point inside the quotation marks when the quote expresses the strong emotion. Place the exclamation point outside the quotation marks if the entire sentence expresses the strong emotion.

> All of the students shouted, "Hooray!"
>
> She said, "You are disqualified"!

Internal Punctuation

Punctuation marks used within a sentence are called **internal punctuation**. These marks include commas, dashes, parentheses, semicolons, colons, apostrophes, hyphens, and quotation marks.

Commas

A **comma** is a punctuation mark used to separate elements in a sentence. Commas are used to separate items in a series.

> Apple, pears, or grapes will be on the menu.

A comma is used before a coordinating conjunction that joins two independent clauses.

> The sun rose, and the birds began to sing.

Commas are used to separate a nonrestrictive explanatory word or phrase from the rest of the sentence.

> Gloria's husband, Jorge, drove the car.
>
> Yes, I will attend the meeting.

A comma is placed before and after an adverb, such as *however* or *indeed*, when it comes in the middle of a sentence.

> Preparing a delicious meal, however, requires using fresh ingredients.

When an adjective phrase contains coordinate adjectives, use commas to separate the coordinate adjectives. The comma takes the place of the word *and*.

> The *long, hot* summer was finally over.

Commas are used to separate words used in direct address. The words can be proper nouns, the pronoun *you*, or common nouns.

> Quon, please answer the next question.
>
> Everyone, please sit down.

Commas are used to separate elements in dates and addresses. When a date is expressed in the month-day-year format, commas are used to separate the year.

> On December 7, 1941, Japan attacked Pearl Harbor.

When only the month and year or a holiday and year are used, a comma is not needed.

> In January 2010 she retired from her job.

A comma is used after the street address and after the city when an address or location appears in general text.

> Mail the item to 123 Maple Drive, Columbus, OH 43085.

A comma is used to introduce a quotation.

> The speaker attempted to energize the workers by saying, "The only limits are those we put on ourselves."

Dashes and Parentheses

A **dash** is a punctuation mark that separates elements in a sentence or signals an abrupt change in thought. There are two types of dashes: *em dash* and *en dash*. The em dash can be used to replace commas or parentheses to emphasize or set off text. To give emphasis to a break in thought, use an em dash.

> My history teacher—an avid reader—visits the library every week.

The en dash is used as a span or range of numbers, dates, or time.

> We won the baseball game 6–3.
>
> Barack Obama served as President of the United States from 2009–2017.

Parentheses are punctuation marks used to enclose words or phrases that clarify meaning or give added information. Place a period that comes at the end of a sentence inside the parentheses only when the entire sentence is enclosed in parentheses.

> Deliver the materials to the meeting site (the Polluck Building).

Use parentheses to enclose numbers or letters in a list that is part of a sentence.

> Revise the sentences to correct errors in (1) spelling, (2) punctuation, and (3) capitalization.

Semicolons, Colons, and Apostrophes

A **semicolon** is an internal punctuation mark used to separate independent clauses that are similar in thought. A semicolon can also be used to separate items in a series. Typically, items in a series are separated with commas, but if the serial items include commas, a semicolon should be used to avoid confusion.

> Twelve students took the test; two students passed.
>
> We mailed packages to Anchorage, AK; Houston, TX; and Bangor, ME.

A **colon** is an internal punctuation mark that introduces an element in a sentence or paragraph.

> The bag contains three items: a book, a pencil, and an apple.

A colon is also used after a phrase, clause, or sentence that introduces a vertical list.

> Follow these steps:

An **apostrophe** is a punctuation mark used to form possessive words. It is most commonly used in conjunction with the letter *s* to show possession. Position of the apostrophe depends on whether the noun is singular or plural. If singular, place the apostrophe between the noun and the *s*. If plural, place the apostrophe after the *s*.

> Akeno's dress was red.
>
> The students' books were to be put away before the exam.

A **contraction** is a shortened form of a word or term. It is formed by omitting letters from one or more words and replacing them with an apostrophe to create one word—the contraction. An example of a contraction is *it's* for *it is*.

Apostrophes can also be used to indicate that numbers or letters are omitted from words for brevity or writing style.

> Leisure suits were in style in the '60s. (1960s)
>
> The candidates will meet to discuss activities of the gov't. (government)

Hyphens

A **hyphen** is a punctuation mark used to separate parts of compound words, numbers, or ranges. Compound words that always have a hyphen are called **permanent compounds**.

Some adverbs, such as *on-the-job*, always have hyphens.

> The close-up was blurry.
>
> My mother-in-law made dinner.
>
> Their orientation includes on-the-job training.

Compound adjectives have hyphens when they come before the words they modify, but not when they come after them.

> The well-done pot roast was delicious.
>
> The delicious pot roast was well done.
>
> These out-of-date books should be thrown away.
>
> Throw away the books that are out of date.

In some words that have prefixes, a hyphen is used between the prefix and the rest of the word.

> The car wash is self-serve.

When a word is divided at the end of a line of text, a hyphen is used between parts of the word.

> Carter ran down the hall-
> way to answer the door.

Quotation Marks

Quotation marks are used to enclose short, direct quotations and titles of some artistic or written works.

> "Which color do you want," he asked.
>
> "The Raven" is a poem written by Edgar Allan Poe.

A quotation need not be a complete sentence; it can be a word or a phrase as spoken or written by someone.

> When the mayor refers to "charitable giving," does that include gifts to all nonprofit organizations?

When writing dialogue, the words of each speaker are enclosed in quotation marks with the appropriate punctuation mark.

> Anna arrived at the office and greeted her coworker, Joan. "Good morning. You're getting an early start today."

Chapter or section titles within complete books, movies, or other artistic works are typically shown in quotation marks. The full title of the work is typically italicized.

> "Books and Journals" is the first chapter in *The Chicago Manual of Style*.

Quotation marks are used to enclose words that are meant to show irony.

> Although Connie had the afternoon off, she was too "busy" to help me.
>
> In a survey of small businesses, one in five managers said their companies are "sinking ships."

APPENDIX B: Capitalization

Capitalization

Capitalization is writing a letter in uppercase (B) rather than lowercase (b). Capital letters signal the beginning of a new sentence and identify important words in titles and headings. Capital letters are also used for proper nouns, for some abbreviations, in personal and professional titles, and for parts of business letters.

Capitalization for Résumés and Cover Letters

When creating a résumé or cover letter, ensure that you use the appropriate capitalization by following these tips.

- *Follow the company's branding guidelines:* Many companies have specific branding guidelines that dictate how their name and other branded elements should be capitalized. You can usually find these guidelines on the company's website or by reaching out to its HR department. For example, *Coca-Cola* has initial capitalization with a hyphen in between the words. *LOUIS VUITTON* uses all uppercase letters, while *eBay* starts with a lowercase letter.
- *Capitalize job titles:* When listing your job titles, capitalize the first letter of each word (except for articles and prepositions), such as "Production Manager" or "Software Engineer."
- *Consider the industry and job function:* Generally, proper nouns (like company names and job titles) should be capitalized, while common nouns (like industry terms or job functions) should be lowercase. However, there may be specific capitalization conventions that you should follow. For example, if you are applying for a job in finance, you may need to capitalize certain financial terms or acronyms, such as "AP department" for accounts payable department.
- *Use consistent capitalization throughout:* Ensure that use of capitalization on your résumé is consistent, both within individual sections and across the entire document. For example, if using bulleted points on your résumé, use the same capitalization style for the first word in all bullets (i.e., all initial cap or all lowercase).

General Capitalization Rules

A sentence begins with a capital letter. Numbers that begin a sentence should be spelled as words, and the first word should be capitalized.

> Thirty-three students took part in the graduation ceremony.

Capitalize the first, last, and all important words in a heading or title.

> *The Little Prince*
>
> *The Adventure of the Hansom Cabs*

For numbers with hyphens in a heading or title, capitalize both words.

> *Twenty-One Candles*

Do not capitalize articles or prepositions within a heading or title unless it is the first word in the title.

> *The Finest Story in the World*

When a title and subtitle are written together, only the first word of the subtitle is capitalized regardless of the part of speech.

> *Presidential Priorities: College's 10th president outlines three campus goals*

Do not capitalize coordinating conjunctions (*yet*, *and*, *but*, *for*, *or*, and *nor*) in a heading or title.

> *Pride and Prejudice*
>
> *Never Marry but for Love*

Do not capitalize parts of names that normally appear in lowercase (Ludwig van Beethoven).

> His favorite composer is Ludwig van Beethoven.

Capitalize the first word in the salutation for a letter.

> Dear Ms. Lisa Stockton:

Capitalize the first word in the complimentary close for a letter.

> Sincerely yours,

Proper nouns begin with a capital letter. A proper noun is a word that identifies a specific person, place, or thing.

> Joe Wong is the principal of George Rogers Clark High School.

Capitalize initials used in place of names.

> UCLA won the football game.

Capitalize abbreviations that are made up of the first letters of words.

> HTML stands for hypertext markup language.

Months and days, as well as their abbreviations, should be capitalized.

> Mon. is the abbreviation for Monday.

Abbreviations for names of states and countries should be capitalized.

> The price is given in US dollars.

Capitalize abbreviations for directional terms and location terms in street addresses.

> She lives at 123 NW Cedar Ave.

Capitalize call letters of a broadcasting company.

> My favorite television show is on CBS.

Abbreviations that note an era in time should be in capital letters.

> The article included a map of Europe for the year 1200 CE.

Capitalize titles that come before personal names and seniority titles after names.

> Sen. Carl Rogers called Mr. Juarez and Dr. Wang.
>
> Mr. Thomas O'Malley, Jr., spoke at the ceremony.

Capitalize abbreviations for academic degrees and other professional designations that follow names.

> Jane Patel, LPN, was on duty at the hospital.

APPENDIX C

Number Usage

Number Expression

Numbers can be expressed as figures or as words. In some cases, as in legal documents and on bank checks, numbers are written in both figures and words. When the two expressions of a number do not agree, readers are alerted to ask for clarification.

On a résumé, numbers are used for dates indicating years of experience, date of graduation, or other time-related items.

Formats for dates listed on résumés may include month/year or month/day/year.

> Graduated: May 20--
>
> Graduated: June 5, 20--

For work experience, include start and end dates of employment. Additionally, the duration of your employment can be specified.

> Administrative Assistant, 20-- to present
>
> Carpenter, March 20-- to November 20--
>
> Computer Programmer, January 20-- to October 20-- (3 years, 9 months)

Follow the guidelines below for general writing. Since number expression guidelines are not as widely agreed upon as rules for punctuation and capitalization, ask whether there are specific guidelines you should follow when writing a report, article, or other item for a particular group or organization.

Use words for numbers one through nine.

> One dog and three cats sat on the porch.

Use figures for numbers 10 and greater. (See other style guides for exceptions to this guideline.)

> She placed an order for 125 blue ink pens.

When some numbers in a sentence are 9 or less and some are 10 or greater, write all the numbers as figures.

> The box contains 5 books, 10 folders, and 15 pads of paper.

Use words for numbers that are indefinite or approximate amounts.

> About fifty people signed the petition.

Use words for numbers one through nine followed by *million*, *billion*, and so forth. For numbers 10 or greater followed by *million*, *billion,* and so forth, use a figure and the word.

> Two million people live in this region.
>
> By 2016, the population of the United States had grown to over 300 million.

When a number begins a sentence, use words instead of figures. If the number is long when written as words, consider revising the sentence so it does not begin with a number.

- Twenty copies of the report were prepared.

When two numbers come together in a sentence, use words for one of the numbers.

- On the bus, there were 15 ten-year-olds.

Use words for numbers with *o'clock* to express time.

- Come to my house for lunch at eleven o'clock.

Use figures with *a.m.* and *p.m.* to express time.

- The assembly will begin at 9:30 a.m.

To express amounts of money, use figures with a currency sign.

- The total amount is $18,395.40.

Do not use a decimal and two zeros when all dollar amounts in a sentence are whole amounts.

- The charges were $5, $312, and $89.

For an isolated amount less than $1, use figures and the word *cents*.

- Buy a cup of lemonade for 75 cents.

When an amount less than $1 appears with other amounts greater than $1, use figures and dollar signs for all of the numbers.

- The prices were $12.50, $0.89, and $12.45.

For a large, whole dollar amount, use the dollar sign, a figure, and a word, such as *million* or *billion*.

- The profits for last year were $5 million.

Days and years in dates should be identified with figures.

- On February 19, 2015, the court was not in session.

Use words for fractions. Note that a hyphen is placed between the words.

- Place one-half of the mixture in the pan.

Use figures for mixed numbers (a whole number and a fraction).

- I bought 3 1/2 yards of red fabric.

When writing a number with decimals, use figures.

- The measurements are 1.358 and 0.878.

Use figures in measurements, such as distance, weight, and percentages.

- We drove 258 miles today.
- The winning pumpkin weighs 50 pounds.
- Sales have increased 20 percent in the last year.

Pages, chapters, figures, or parts in a book should be referenced with figures.

- Open your book to chapter 3, page 125.
- Refer to figure 6 on page 72 for an example.

Glossary

A

ability. Mastery of a skill or the capacity to do something. (1)

adware. Form of software that displays or downloads advertisement material automatically without the user's knowledge. (6)

aggregate job board. Job-search website that collects data from multiple online sources and combines the results. (9)

applicant tracking system software. Tool that allows employers and recruiters to keep track of job postings, applications, and résumés on job boards. (7)

application cover letter. Letter used to apply for and provide personal qualifications for a position that has been posted by an employer. (8)

aptitude. Characteristic that an individual has developed naturally. (1)

B

background check. Evaluation of personal data that is publicly available. (12)

basic skills. Fundamental skills necessary to function effectively in society. (2)

behavioral question. Question that draws on an individual's previous experiences and decisions. (10)

blue-sky question. Question where the interviewer describes a scenario that may or may not be related to the job duties and requires a response from the candidate. (10)

body language. Communication sent through gestures, facial expressions, and posture. (11)

C

career. Long-term progression in one particular field with opportunities for growth and advancement. (1)

career ladder. Sequence of jobs in one career field, from entry to advanced levels. (1)

career lattice. Series of lateral and vertical moves in one career field. (1)

career persona. Unique blend of characteristics that defines who an individual is as a professional. (1)

career plan. Documentation of where a person is today in the job-search process and would like to be over the course of a career. (1)

certification. Professional status earned by an individual after passing an exam focused on a specific body of knowledge. (2)

cloud computing. Type of Internet-based computing that allows users to access and use shared computing resources, such as servers, storage, and software applications. (2)

collaboration. Act of working together with another person to accomplish a goal. (2)

compensation package. Everything an employee receives in return for their work. (12)

complimentary close. Sign-off for a letter. (8)

compromise. To come to a mutually agreed-upon decision. (2)

connection. Person in an individual's network on LinkedIn who is added only by invitation. (4)

cookies. Bits of data stored on a computer that record information about the websites a user has visited. (6)

copyright. Acknowledges ownership of a work and specifies that only the owner has the right to sell the work, use it, or give permission for someone else to sell or use it. (2)

cover letter. Formal written communication that accompanies a résumé or a job application to introduce an applicant and express interest in a position. (8)

cultural competence. Ability to understand, communicate, interact, and collaborate with people from different cultures. (14)

D

dependability. Person's ability to be reliable and trustworthy. (14)

digital citizenship. Responsible use of technology and the Internet. (2)

digital footprint. Data record of an individual's online activities. (2)

Note: The number in parentheses following each definition indicates the chapter in which the term can be found.

discrimination. Unfair treatment of an individual based on race, gender, religion, national origin, disability, or age. (2)

diversity. Representation of different backgrounds, cultures, or demographics in a group. (2)

E

emerging occupations. New occupations that have developed or changed due to technological or other advancements. (1)

employment verification. Process in which a job candidate's employment history is checked to confirm the accuracy of the information submitted. (12)

ergonomics. Science concerned with designing and arranging things a person uses so they can be used efficiently and safely. (13)

ethics. Moral principles or beliefs that direct a person's behavior. (2)

etiquette. Art of using good manners in any situation. (5)

F

firewall. Program that monitors information coming into a computer and helps ensure only safe information gets through. (6)

follower. Twitter member who views another user's tweets in their own Twitter feed. (4)

formal seated position. Entails sitting upright, with both feet on the floor and both hands comfortably resting either on chair armrests or in the lap. (11)

G

generation. Group of people who were born during the same time period. (14)

H

harassment. Any unsolicited conduct toward another person based on race, gender, national origin, age, or disability. (2)

hard skills. Measurable, observable, and critical skills necessary to perform the required, work-related tasks of a given position. (1)

hashtag. Searchable keyword that links users to all tweets marked with the same keyword. (4)

heading. Person's full name, phone number, e-mail address, and geographic location. (7)

hypothetical question. Question based on an imagined situation used to assess how one might react. (10)

I

identity theft. Illegal act that involves stealing someone's personal information and using that information to commit theft or fraud. (6)

infographic résumé. Visual résumé in which the content is displayed using a combination of words, icons, and graphics to present information clearly and quickly. (7)

informational interviewing. Strategy used to interview and ask for advice and direction from a professional, rather than asking for a job opportunity. (5)

infringement. Any use of intellectual property without permission. (2)

inquiry cover letter. Letter written to learn if any potential positions are available for which the job seeker would like to be considered. (8)

intellectual property. Something that comes from a person's mind, such as an idea, invention, or process. (2)

Internet protocol address. Number used to identify an electronic device connected to the Internet, known as an *IP address*. (6)

J

job. Short-term employment for compensation. (1)

job application. Form used by employers to gain more information about a person applying for a job. (9)

job offer. Formal invitation to work under mutually agreed terms and conditions. (12)

job-search website. Website on which multiple employers post-employment opportunities on a daily basis. (9)

job-tracking spreadsheet. Single spreadsheet with separate sheets for applications, leads, and interviews to record and track jobs for which a person applies. (9)

K

keywords. Words that specifically relate to the functions of the position for which the employer is hiring. (1)

L

lying. Making an untrue statement. (11)

M

malware. Term given to software programs that are intended to damage, destroy, or steal data on a computer, short for *malicious software*. (6)

microblog. Short communication limited to a certain number of characters per post. (4)

multicultural workplace. Organization or work environment that comprises individuals from diverse backgrounds, cultures, and identities. (14)

multifactor authentication. Process in which a website requires multiple identity verifications before granting access to an account. (6)

multigenerational workplace. Work environment where employees from different age groups, typically spanning over several decades, collaborate and interact with each other. (14)

N

networking. Talking with people and establishing relationships that can lead to career growth or potential job opportunities. (4)

networking cover letter. Letter that introduces an applicant by noting that a person in their network recommended they apply for the position. (8)

non-aggregate job board. Website on which employers post job openings directly on the board. (9)

O

Occupational Information Network (O*NET). Occupational resource that provides descriptions of in-demand industry areas in emerging occupations. (1)

onboarding. New employee's introduction to a company's brand, mission statement, values, and practices. (13)

online job board. Website that hosts job postings for employers and allows applicants to apply for jobs seamlessly. (7)

online presence. What an Internet search reveals about someone. (4)

P

panel interview. Interview in which a candidate talks with multiple interviewers in one room. (10)

people skills. Skills that enable people to develop and maintain working relationships with others, also called *interpersonal skills*. (2)

performance evaluation. Formal process designed to evaluate an employee's work and offer productive feedback. (13)

personal brand. Individual's reputation. (3)

personal brand statement. One sentence that describes what a potential job candidate offers an employer. (3)

personal commercial. Rehearsed introduction that includes brief information about a person's background and a snapshot of their career goals, also known as an *elevator pitch*. (3)

personality. Unique blend of qualities that predict attitudes, values, and work habits. (1)

personal qualities. Characteristics that make up an individual's personality. (2)

phishing. Use of fraudulent e-mails and copies of valid websites to trick people into providing private and confidential personal data. (6)

plagiarism. Claiming another person's material as one's own, which is both unethical and illegal. (2)

portfolio. Compilation of materials that provide evidence of a person's qualifications, skills, and talents. (1)

professional development. Training that builds on skills and knowledge that contribute to personal growth and career development. (14)

professionalism. Soft skill that includes the judgment, character, and behavior expected of a person who is trained for a given job. (14)

professional network. Consists of people who support an individual in their career and other business endeavors. (5)

professional reference. Person who knows an individual's skills, talents, or personal traits and is willing to provide a recommendation. (5)

profile. Information that describes who a person is professionally. (4)

proprietary information. Any work created by company employees on the job that is owned by that company. (2)

punctuality. Being on time. (14)

R

ransomware. Software program that takes over a computer system and locks it until the owner pays a sum of money to regain control of the computer system. (6)

respect. Feeling or belief that someone or something is good, valuable, and important. (2)

résumé. Written document that lists an individual's qualifications for a job, including work experience and education. (7)

S

screening interview. Preliminary, informal interview designed to determine if a candidate's skills are good enough to merit a formal interview. (10)

search engine optimization (SEO). Process of indexing a website so it will rank higher on the list of returned results when a search is conducted. (4)

secure password. Code used to access a private account or other private information. (4)

self-management skills. Skills that enable an individual to control personal habits and make the best use of one's time and abilities. (14)

self-talk. Internal thoughts and feelings about oneself. (4)

signal phrase. Preplanned beginning phrase that enhances a question. (10)

signature block. Full name, phone number, and e-mail address of the owner of the e-mail account. (4)

skill. Something an individual does well. (1)

skills résumé. Résumé that lists work experience according to categories of skills or achievements rather than by employer, also known as a *functional résumé*. (7)

SMART goal. Goal that is specific, measurable, attainable, realistic, and timely. (1)

soft skills. Applicable skills used to help an individual find a job, perform in the workplace, and gain success in any job or career. (1)

software virus. Computer program designed to negatively impact a computer system. (6)

spyware. Software that spies on a computer. (6)

structured interview. Formal interview in which a predetermined list of questions is posed to each candidate interviewing for a position, also known as *directive interview*. (10)

subjective element. Factor that contains bias and is more emotional than logical. (11)

Sunday Evening Plan. Routine or schedule that job seekers set for themselves on Sunday evenings to review their job-search progress and plan their job-search activities for the upcoming week. (9)

T

thinking skills. Skills that enable a person to solve problems. (2)

timeline résumé. Résumé that emphasizes employers and work experience with each, also known as a *chronological résumé*. (7)

time management. Practice of organizing time and work assignments to increase personal efficiency. (14)

trending. Refers to keywords and phrases that have the highest number of online searches in any given day. (7)

U

unstructured interview. Interview that is less formal and may not necessarily consist of a specific list of questions. (10)

V

values. Principles and beliefs that a person considers important. (1)

visual résumé. Résumé that presents information in a graphically appealing format. (7)

Index

A

ability
  aptitudes and, 22
  defined, 7
acceptance letter, job offer, 199
accident prevention, 218
action items, 5
adware, 91
aggregate job board, 145, 147
antimalware software, 92
antivirus software, 92
applicant tracking system software, 106–107
application. *See* job application
application cover letter, 128
apps
  job search, 150
  See also Best App for That (feature)
aptitudes
  defined, 6
  example, health services worker, 7
  inventory, 21
aptitude tests, 6
architect, 137
Armed Services Vocational Aptitude Battery (ASVAB), 6
assessment. *See* performance evaluations; self-assessment; skills assessment
attainable goals, 10
attire. *See* dress, interviewing; dress code
attitude, 211
automotive service technician, 45

B

Baby Boomers, 230
background check, 200
backups, cloud-based, 93
behavioral interview, 165
behavioral questions, 165
Best App for That (feature)
  CareerShift, 32
  Glassdoor, 3
  Google Drive, 89
  Handshake, 44
  Monster, 128
  Snagajob, 198
  Trello, 218
Better Business Bureau (BBB), 89
biometric verification, 92
bio, Twitter, 63
blue-sky question, 166
body, cover letter, 132, 134, 135
body language
  defined, 183
  job interview and, 166
browser, Internet, 90

bulleted lists, cover letter, 132, 133
business cards, 75–76
businesses, supporting local, 199
business etiquette, 76

C

CAD professional, 233
calendar software, 150
candidate questions, 183. *See also* behavioral questions
career
  defined, 3
  measures of success, 232, 234
  pathways, 3, 4
  preparation, 3
CareerBuilder, 147
career development, 232, 234
career ladder, 11–12
career lattice, 12
career-level position, 11
career pathing, 10–12
career pathways, 3–4
career persona, 13
Career Persona (feature)
  architect, 137
  automotive service technician, 45
  CAD professional, 233
  carpenter, 94
  culinary professional, 78
  HVAC technician, 28
  interior designer, 215
  IT professional, 196
  journalist, 148
  nutritionist, 182
  physical therapist, 14
  plumber, 167
  stonemason, 109
  welder, 60
career plan, 3–6
  action items for, 5
  creating, 20
  template, 6
career portfolio, 12–13
career preparation, 3
CareerShift app, 32
carpenter, 94
cell phone usage
  security and, 92
  at work, 216
certification
  benefits of, 31–32
  by industry, 31
  defined, 30
  earning, 32
  résumé and, 108
  transferable skills and, 33
chronological resume, 110, 111

Cirillo, Francesco, 232
closing, cover letter, 132, 135
cloud-based backups, 93
cloud computing, 29–30
cloud storage, 93
code of conduct, 29, 39
code of ethics, 29, 39
cognitive aptitudes, 6
collaboration, 27
combination résumé, 110, 113, 114
communication
  body language as, 183
  etiquette and, 77
  multigenerational/multicultural workplace and, 230–231
  remote work and, 211
community engagement. *See* Connect to Your Community (feature)
company research, interview preparation, 161–162
compensation package, 197, 213
complimentary close, cover letter, 132
compromise, 27
computer safety
  adware, 91
  antivirus software, 92
  backups, 93
  firewall, 92
  malware and, 91
  passwords, 92–93
  ransomware and, 91
  software viruses, 91
  spyware and, 91
Connect to Your Community (feature)
  businesses, support local, 199
  clubs, 161
  cultural competence, 231
  networking events and, 77
  personal brand and, 46
  volunteering, 113
  working for local organizations, 149
continuing education, 31
continuing education units (CEUs), 31
cookie hijacking, 90
cookies, online privacy and, 90
copyright, 30
cover letter
  application, 128
  best practices for writing, 129
  body, 132, 134
  bulleted lists, 132, 133
  checklist, 135
  complimentary close, 132
  defined, 128
  example, 131
  formatting, 132
  greeting, 130
  heading and date, 130
  inquiry or prospecting, 128–129

cover letter—*Cont.*
 introduction, 130, 132
 networking, 128
 submission via e-mail, 132, 136
cover letter checklist, 135
creative thinking, 26
credibility, 80
credit reports, 200
culinary professional, 78
cultural competency, 216, 231
cursive handwriting, 132

D

date, cover letter, 130
deadlines, missing, 63
decision making, 26
Department of Homeland Security, 213
dependability, 230
dependent, 213, 214
development, professional. *See* professional development
digital business cards, 76
digital citizenship
 cloud computing, 29–30
 defined, 29
 intellectual property and, 30, 40–41
 netiquette, 30
 software and file downloads, 30
digital etiquette, 62. *See also* etiquette; networking etiquette
digital footprint, 29, 57
directive interview, 161
discrimination, 29
diversity, 27
documentation portfolio
 defined, 13
 interviewing and, 181
dress, interviewing, 169, 181
dress code, 77, 211
Dropbox, 93
drug screening, 200

E

education section, résumé, 108, 118
electronic portfolio, 13, 115
elevator pitch, 44, 53–54
e-mail
 accounts, 58–59
 cover letter submission and, 132, 136
 employment scams and, 89
 phishing and, 91
 post-interview thank-you message, 195
e-mail address
 defined, 58
 professional, 107
emerging occupations, 3, 5
emotions, managing, 197
employability skills, 8, 26
employer questions, 183
employment forms
 benefits, compensation packages, 213
 Form I-9 Employment Eligibility Verification, 211–213
 Form W-2 Wage and Tax Statement, 213
 Form W-4 Employee's Withholding Certificate, 213, 214
employment gap, 166
employment process
 accept job offer, 199
 decline job offer, 199–200
 employment verification, 200
 job offer, evaluating, 197–198
 work, first days, 211–217
employment scams, 88–89
employment verification, 200
entry-level position, career ladder, 11
ergonomics, injury prevention, 218–219
ethics
 codes of, 29, 39
 defined, 29
 intellectual property and, 30
 software and file downloads, 30
 See also workplace ethics
etiquette
 defined, 76
 digital, 62
 in-person, 77
 networking, 76–77, 79
 workspace, 216–217
evaluations, job, 217
executive-level position, 11–12
experience section, résumé, 108, 118
eye contact, 77

F

Facebook, 57
face-to-face networking, 75–76
Federal Bureau of Investigation (FBI), 89
Federal Trade Commission (FTC), 88, 89
file downloads, 30
firewall, 92
first impressions, 181, 183
flammable materials, 218
flexibility, 234
flextime, 216
followers, Twitter, 63
formal aptitude placement tests, 6
formal offer letter, 199
formal seated position, interviews, 183
Form I-9 Employment Eligibility Verification, 211–213
Form W-2 Wage and Tax Statement, 213
Form W-4 Employee's Withholding Certificate, 213, 214
foundational skills, 8, 26
freemium model, 59
functional résumé, 110

G

gaps in employment, 166
general information questions, interviewer, 164–165
generation, 230
Generation X, 231
Generation Y, 231
Generation Z, 231
Glassdoor app, 3
Glassdoor Economic Research, 152
goals, SMART, 6, 10
Google Drive, 89, 93
greeting, cover letter, 130, 135
grooming, for interview, 181

H

hackers, Wi-Fi and, 90
Handshake app, 44
harassment, 29
hard skills, 8–9, 24
hashtags, 62
hazards, workplace, 218
headings
 cover letter, 130, 135
 résumé, 107, 118
health, 211
Health Services Worker, aptitudes, 7
honesty, 185
HTML document, 115
HVAC technician, 28
hybrid portfolio, 13

I

I-9 Employment Eligibility Verification form, 211–213
identity, online. *See* online presence
identity theft, 88
image, 152
incognito mode, browsing, 90
infographic résumé, 115, 117
informal aptitude test, 6
informational interviewing, 75
infringement, 30
in-person etiquette, 77
in-person interview, 162
 closing, 183–184
 formal seated position, 183
 introduction, 183
 questions, employer/candidate, 183
in-person job applications, 145
inquiry cover letter, 128–129
Instagram, 57, 64
intellectual property, 30, 40
interior designer, 215
Internet
 digital citizenship and, 29–30
 netiquette and, 62
 online networking and, 76
 private information and, 57
Internet Crime Complaint Center (IC3), 89
Internet protocol (IP) address, 90
Internet usage, online privacy and
 computer safety and, 91
 cookies, 90
 Internet protocol (IP) address, 90
 multifactor authentication, 93
 passwords and, 92–93
 phishing and, 91
 security plan, 91–93
 session hijacking, 90
interpersonal skills, 27

interviewer questions, job interview strategies
  behavioral questions, 165
  blue-sky question, 166
  general information questions, 164–165
  stress questions, 165–166
interviewing. *See* job interview
interview preparation
  company research, 161–162
  mock interview, 168–169
  night before, 169
introduction, cover letter, 130, 132, 135
IP address, 90
IT professional, 196

J

job, 3
job advertisements, employment scams and, 89
job alerts, setting, 150
job application
  defined, 145
  example, 146
  in person, 145
  job-tracking spreadsheet, 150
  online, 149
job application process
  download apps, 150
  job alerts, setting, 150
  managing, 149–150
  network contacts, 150
  stay current, 150
  time management, 150
job fair, 162
job interview, 161
  body language, 183
  first impressions, subjective elements, 181, 183
  informational, 75
  in-person, 162, 183–184. *See also* in-person interview
  lying in, 185
  panel, 162
  post-interview techniques, 193–197
  pre-employment tests, 184–185
  preparing for, 168–169. *See also* interview preparation
  questions, employer/candidate, 161, 164–166, 168, 183. *See also* questions, job interview
  remote-location, 162
  scheduling, 151–152
  screening interview, 161
  second interview, 185
  telephone, 163
  types of, 161
  video, 163–164
  virtual, 162–163, 181, 184, 185
job leads, 151
job offer
  acceptance letter, 199
  accepting, 199
  compensation, 198
  declining, 199–200
  defined, 197
  negotiating, 198–199
  responding to, 198–199
  work, first days. *See* work, first days
job search
  application process, 149–150. *See also* job application process
  apps for, 128
  continuing, 197
  employment process, 197–200. *See also* employment process
  employment scams and, 88–89
  identity theft and, 88
  interviewing. *See* job interview
  LinkedIn and, 59, 61–62
  online, 145, 147, 149
  persistence, process, 152
  post-employment, 219
  Sunday Evening Plan, 149
  tracking applications, 150–152. *See also* job-tracking spreadsheet
  Twitter and, 62
job-search website, 145, 147
job-tracking spreadsheet
  applications tab, 150–151
  defined, 150
  example, 151
  interviews, scheduling, 151–152
  leads, 151
journalist, 148

K

keywords
  applicant tracking system software, 106–107
  employer questions, interview, 183
  job requirements and, 8
  personal brand statements and, 44
  résumés and, 105–106, 108
  trending and, 106

L

leadership skills, 27, 110
lifting hazards, 218
LinkedIn
  connections on, 61
  defined, 59
  job-search, 145
  profile creation, 59, 61
  tips, 61
LinkedIn for Students, 59
listening skills, 26
local businesses, supporting, 199
lying, interviewing and, 185

M

malicious software, 91
malware, 91
material-storage hazards, 218
math skills, 26
measurable goals, 10
meeting etiquette, 77
microblog, 62
Microsoft OneDrive, 93
Microsoft PowerPoint, 13
Microsoft Teams, 163
Microsoft Word
  cover letter format, 132
  electronic portfolio, 13
  résumé file, 113
Millennials, 231
mobile security, 92
mock interview, 168–169
money management, 232
Monster app, 128, 147
multicultural workplace skills, 230–231
multifactor authentication, 93
multigenerational workplace skills, 230–231
Myers-Briggs Type Indicator® (MBTI®), 7

N

National White Collar Crime Center (NW3C), 89
natural interests, 6
negative online presence, 57
negative self-talk, 11
negotiate, salary and compensation, 198–199
negotiation skills, 27
netiquette, 30
networking
  community events and, 77
  connections and, 61
  defined, 59, 75
  face-to-face, 75–76
  online, 76
  professional, 75. *See also* professional networking
  Twitter and, 62
  update professional, 219
networking cover letter, 128
networking etiquette
  defined, 76
  in-person, 77
  online, 79
  respect and, 77
non-aggregate job board, 147
nonexistent online presence, 57
nontraditional résumé
  visual and infographic, 115, 117
  web-based, 115
nutritionist, 182

O

Occupational Information Network (O*NET), 3, 19
occupations, emerging, 3, 5
onboarding, 211
onboarding presentation, 213
onboarding topics, 217
online etiquette, 79
online job board, 107, 136
online job search, 145, 147
online networking, 76
online presence
  defined, 57
  Instagram account, 64
  LinkedIn account, 59–61
  netiquette, 30

online presence—*Cont.*
   professional e-mail account, 58–59
   Twitter account, 62–64
   See also Internet; Internet usage, online privacy and; job-search website
on-site worker
   hired as, 211
   onboarding topics, 217
   workplace orientation, 216
optimism, 136
overtime, 216

P

panel interview, 162
passcode, 92
password manager software, 92
password security, 58
   identity protection and, 92
   strength of, 93
PayPal, 89
PDF résumé file, 113, 115
performance evaluations, 217
Permanent Resident Card, 213
personal brand
   community connections and, 46
   defined, 42, 43
   factors contributing to, 43
   personal commercial and, 44, 46–47
   references and, 80
   statements, 43–44, 47, 108
personal commercial
   defined, 44
   developing, 46
   examples, 47
   rehearsing, 47
personal e-mail account, 58–59
personal growth, 234
personal information, Internet privacy and, 90–92
personality, self-assessment and tests, 7–8
personal protective equipment (PPE), 218
phishing, 91
physical aptitudes, 6
physical therapist, 14
plagiarism, 30
plain text résumé, 115, 116
plumber, 167
Pomodoro method, time management, 232
pop-up blocker, 93
portfolio, 12. *See also* career portfolio
positive online presence, 57
positive self-talk, 11
positive thinking, 64–65
post-interview techniques
   continue job search, 197
   emotion management, 197
   evaluate interview, 193
   thank-you message, 193, 194, 195
pre-employment tests, 184–185
Prezi, 13
prioritizing, time management, 163
privacy
   identity theft and, 88–89
   Internet and, 90–91. *See also* Internet usage, online privacy and

networking etiquette and, 79
privacy settings, social media and, 57
private browsing, 90
problem solving, 26
process portfolio, 13
professional development
   defined, 232
   success and, 234
professional image, 152
professionalism, 230
professional networking
   business cards and, 75–76
   defined, 75
   face-to-face, 75–76
   grow and maintain network, 232
   online, 76
   updating, 219
professional portfolio, 13
professional references, 79–80
promotions, online networking and, 76
proprietary information, 30
prospecting cover letter, 128–129
protocol, 76
punctuality, 181, 230

Q

QR (quick response) codes, 76
qualifications
   required *v.* desired, 147
   résumé and, 108
questions, job interview
   candidate, 161, 166, 168
   interviewer, 164–166, 183

R

ransomware, 91
reading skills, 26
realistic goals, 10
reasoning, 26
references. *See* professional references
relationships, building strong, 234
relevant coursework, résumé and, 108
remote-location interviews, 162
remote worker, 211, 217
respect, 27, 77, 216
responsibility, 29
résumé
   applicant tracking software, 106–107
   cover letter and, 128–129. *See also* cover letter
   defined, 105
   experience, 108
   hard copy, 136
   headings, 107
   keywords, 105–106
   Microsoft Word Document, 113
   nontraditional, 115, 117
   online job board and, 136
   PDF, 113, 115
   personal information, Internet privacy and, 90
   plain text, 115, 116
   posting online, 147

saving file, 113, 118
special skills, 108, 110
summary, 108
Sunday Evening Plan and, 149
trending keywords, 106
résumé checklist, 118
résumé formats
   checklist, 118
   combination, 110, 113, 114
   skills or functional, 110, 112
   timeline or chronological, 110, 111
résumé template, 105
routine, remote workers and, 211

S

safety
   computer, 91–93
   workplace, 218–219
salary, evaluating and negotiating, 198
scams, employment. *See* employment scams
screening interview, 161
search engine optimization (SEO), 59
search results, online presence and, 57
second interview, 185
secure password, 58
secure URL, 90
security checklist, 92
security plan
   antivirus software, 92
   cloud-based backups, 93
   mobile security, 92
   multifactor authentication, 93
   online identity, privacy and, 91–92
   passwords, 92–93
   settings, 93
security settings, 93
self-assessment
   abilities, 7
   aptitudes, 6
   defined, 6
   personal brand and, 42
   personality, 7–8
   values, 8
self-confidence, 11
self-esteem, 29
self-management, 29
self-management skills, 230
self-talk, 11, 65
session hijacking, 90
settings menu
   cookies and, 90
   security and, 93
showcase portfolio, 13
signal phrase, candidate questions, 168
signature block, 58–59, 136
skills
   career pathways and, 5
   defined, 8
   special, résumé and, 108, 110, 118
   transferable, certification and, 33
   workplace. *See* workplace skills
   See also skills assessment
skills assessment
   hard skills, 8, 9, 23
   list and rank, 23–24

Index

soft skills, 8, 9, 23–24
technology, 9
types of, 8
skills résumé, 110, 112
Skype, 163
SMART goals, 6, 10, 13
Snagajob app, 198
social media
Instagram account, 64
LinkedIn account, 59, 61–62
online presence and, 57
Twitter account, 62–64
social media profiles, 76
social perception skills, 27
Social Security card, 213
social skills, 8
soft skills
defined, 8
inventory, 23–24
people skills, 27
personal qualities, 27, 29
professionalism, 230
thinking skills, 26
types of, 8, 9
software downloads, 30
software viruses, 91
spamming, 62
speaking skills, 26
specialist-level position, 11
specific goals, 10
spyware, 91
stonemason, 109
stress questions, 165–166
strong password, 93
structured interview, 161
submission, cover letter, 132, 136
success, realistic measures, 232, 234
summary section, résumé, 108, 118
Sunday Evening Plan, 149
supervisory-level position, 11

T

tax withholding employment form W-4, 213, 214
teamwork skills, 27
technology
digital citizenship and, 29–30
portfolio development and, 13
video interviews and, 163–164
technology skills
assessment, 9
defined, 26
telephone interview, 163
template
career plan, 6
cover letter, 128
résumé, 105

tests, pre-employment, 184
thank-you message, post-interview, 193–195
thinking skills, 26
timeline résumé, 110, 111
timely goals, 10
Time Management (feature)
job search, 130
monitor your well-being, 184
Pomodoro method, 232
poor, effects of, 63
prioritizing, 163
productivity, 88
track your time, 27
time management, 150, 230
trade secret, 30
transferable skills, 33
tweets, 62
Twitter
bio, 63
create account and profile, 62–63
discretion with posts on, 57
followers and, 63
job search and, 145
posting to, 63–64
username, 62–63

U

unstructured interview, 161
update professional network, 219
updating professional skills, 232
URL, secure, 90
US Department of Labor, 3
username, Twitter, 62–63

V

values
ranking your, 22–23
self-assessment, 8
video business cards, 76
video-conferencing software, 164
video interview, 163–164
virtual interview, 162–163, 181, 184, 185
viruses, 91
visualization, 26
visual résumé, 115
volunteering, community engagement, 113

W

W-2 Wage and Tax Statement form, 213
W-4 Employee's Withholding Certificate form, 213, 214
wages and withholding forms, 213
weak password, 93

web-based résumé, 115
welder, 60
Wi-Fi, hackers and, 90
WordPress, 13
work, first days
cell phone usage and, 216
employment forms, 211–214
flextime, 216
onboarding remote workers, 213
onboarding topics, 217
on-site, 211
on-site orientation, 216
overtime, 216
remote, 211
workspace etiquette, 216–217
workplace ethics, 29, 39
workplace readiness
basic skills, 26
certification, 30–33
defined, 25
digital citizenship and, 29–30
soft skills, 26–29
workplace ethics, 29
workplace safety
accident prevention, 218
defined, 218
ergonomics, 218–219
workplace skills
multigenerational/multicultural awareness, 230–231
professionalism, 230
soft skill, 8, 26. *See also* soft skills
See also Career Persona (feature)
Workplace Skills (feature)
cultural competency, 216
leadership, 110
netiquette, 62
optimism, 136
professional image, 152
protocol and etiquette, 76
punctuality, 181
self-confidence, 11
workspace etiquette, 216–217
workstation ergonomics, 219
writing skills, 26

Y

YouTube, 13

Z

ZipRecruiter, 145
Zoom, 163